D1738786

Contesting the Subject

The
Theory and
Practice
of Biography
and
Biographical
Criticism

William H. Epstein, general editor

Volume 1

Contesting the Subject

Essays
in the
Postmodern
Theory
and
Practice of
Biography
and
Biographical
Criticism

Edited by William H. Epstein

Purdue University Press
West Lafayette, Indiana

Printed in the United States of America

Book and jacket design by Mark McCormick

Library of Congress Cataloging-in-Publication Data

Contesting the subject : essays in the postmodern theory and practice
 of biography and biographical criticism / edited by William H.
 Epstein.
      p.   cm. — (The Theory and practice of biography and
 biographical criticism ; v. 1)
    Includes bibliographical references and index.
    ISBN 1-55753-018-1 (alk. paper) :
    1. English prose literature—History and criticism—Theory, etc.
    2. American prose literature—History and criticism—Theory, etc.
    3. Authors, American—Biography—History and criticism.
    4. Authors, English—Biography—History and criticism.
    5. Biography (as a literary form) 6. Postmodernism (Literature)
    I. Epstein, William H. II. Series
    PR756.B56C66 1991   91-17637
    828'.08—dc20   CIP

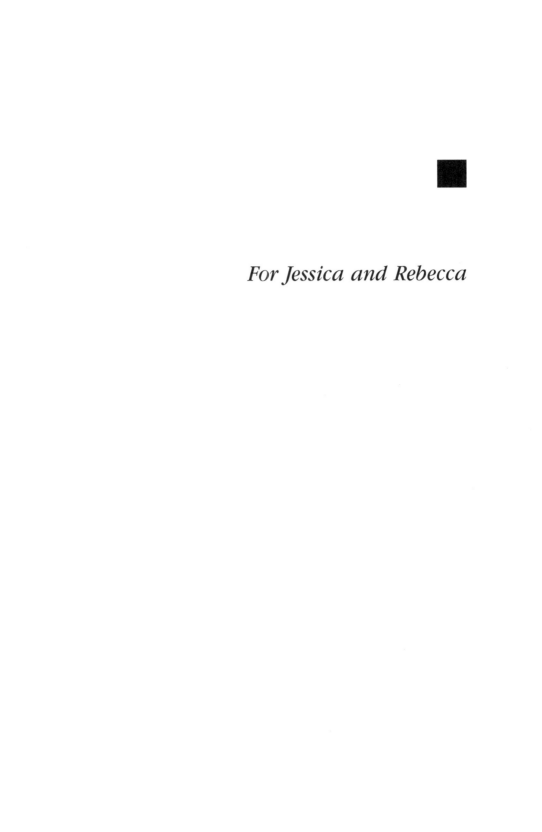

For Jessica and Rebecca

Contents

Notes on Contributors

Alison Booth, assistant professor of English at the University of Virginia, has completed a full-length study on Eliot and Woolf and their feminist revisions of history entitled *Greatness Engendered,* which is forthcoming from Cornell University Press in 1992. She is editing a collection, *Famous Last Words: Women Against Novelistic Endings,* due in 1992 from the University Press of Virginia.

Jerome Christensen, professor of English at the Johns Hopkins University, is the author of *Coleridge's Blessed Machine of Language* (Cornell, 1981), *Practicing Enlightenment: Hume and the Formation of a Literary Career* (Wisconsin, 1987), and the forthcoming *Lord Byron's Strength: Romantic Writing and Commercial Society* (Johns Hopkins, 1992).

William H. Epstein, professor of English at the University of Arizona, is the author of *John Cleland: Images of a Life* (Columbia, 1974) and *Recognizing Biography* (Pennsylvania, 1987). He is general editor of the series The Theory and Practice of Biography and Biographical Criticism.

Stanley Fish is Arts and Sciences Distinguished Professor of English and Professor of Law at Duke University. Among his many influential books on critical theory and Renaissance English literature are *Self-Consuming Artifacts: The Experience of Seventeenth-Century Literature* (California, 1972), *Is There a Text in This Class? The Authority of Interpretive Communities* (Harvard, 1980), and *Doing What Comes Naturally* (Duke, 1989).

Michael McKeon is a professor of English at Rutgers University. He is the author of *Politics and Poetry in Restoration England* (Harvard, 1975) and *The Origins of the English Novel* (Johns Hopkins, 1987), which won the Modern Language Association's annual James Russell Lowell Prize.

Sharon O'Brien, professor of English and American studies at Dickinson College, has published a biography of Willa Cather (*Willa Cather: The Emerging Voice* [Oxford, 1989]) and is working on a book on American autobiography.

Valerie Ross is an assistant professor of English at Miami University. Formerly the general editor of *Cream City Review,* she is writing a book on the social functions and institutional repressions of biography in American literary culture.

Gordon Turnbull teaches English at Yale University, where he is pursuing research in the Yale Editions of the Private Papers of James Boswell. Among his publications is "James Boswell: Biography and the Union," in *The History of Scottish Literature,* edited by Andrew Hook (Aberdeen, 1987), 2:157–73.

Cheryl Walker, Richard Armour Professor of English at Scripps College, is the author of *The Nightingale's Burden: Women Poets and American Culture Before 1900* (Indiana, 1983) and *Masks Outrageous and Austere: Culture, Psyche and Persona in Modern Women Poets* (Indiana, 1991).

Steven Weiland is a professor of education at Michigan State University. Among his books are *Intellectual Craftsmen: Ways and Works in American Scholarship, 1935–1990* (Transaction, 1991) and a forthcoming study of aging and academic careers.

Rob Wilson is an associate professor of English at the University of Hawaii. He is the author of *American Sublime: The Genealogy of a Poetic Genre* (Wisconsin, 1991) and *Waking in Seoul* (Hawaii, 1988) and general editor of the SUNY Series on the Sublime.

Preface

This is the inaugural volume in a new series of books on the theory and practice of biography and biographical criticism. Situated at the intersection of history and theory, this series will publish edited collections and individual scholarly and creative works that offer (1) critical studies of individual biographical narratives, of biographical genres and subgenres, or of themes and topics ranging across biographical discourse; (2) histories of biographical writing and reading that stress cultural context and audience reception; (3) theoretical approaches to the reading and writing of biography, especially those deploying postmodern, postcolonial, and gender theory; (4) biographical criticism, ranging from performative studies on individual subjects to theoretical studies of the critical genre of biographical criticism; or (5) experiments in biographical writing that proceed from or illustrate the assumptions and tactics of contemporary literary theory and cultural criticism.

I would like to thank Verna Emery and Margaret Hunt, the former and present managing editors of Purdue University Press, and Djelal Kadir, the former chair of its editorial board. They have all believed in this project and have given it their characteristically intelligent and sincere professional and personal attention.

This book is dedicated to my children, who have brought me to life.

William H. Epstein

Introduction
Contesting the Subject

"It makes no sense to urge a return to biography, since biography is not something from which we can swerve." This statement, from the essay by Stanley Fish that opens this volume of original articles on the postmodern theory and practice of biography and biographical criticism, articulates the assumption, if not the explicit premise, underwriting this book. Now, to some readers, who may or may not share any or all of the various postmodern perspectives discernible in these pages, Fish's assertion and the claim I have just made for it may seem antithetical. Doesn't this statement merely reiterate a conventional piece of received wisdom in literary and cultural studies, an oft-stated premise of traditional historicist scholarship? And isn't postmodernism an antihumanist, neoformalist movement that, among other things, seeks to demystify if not displace subjectivity, authorship, intentionality, facthood, totality, coherence, and other conceptual practices crucial to the recognition of the biographical? The answer to both these questions, which are constantly posed and reposed in all these essays, is no. As you will see, Fish's remark emerges from a postmodern perspective, and all the contributions to this book demonstrate that the deployment of certain postmodern tactics does not preclude or exclude the biographical or, for that matter, any "contextualizing" discourse. Of course, the use of such tactics induces us to rethink or rearticulate the theory and practice of biography and biographical criticism, but, as we hope you will come to agree, our resistance is also an affirmation. In one way or another, each of these essays evinces a *belief* in the biographical—an article of faith which is, I feel, the more sincere because so hard won, emerging from difficult and earnest struggles with a variety of familiar and unfamiliar, but persistently vexing, issues in the reading and writing of biography and biographical criticism.

Fish's statement, for example, is prompted by his desire to articulate the elusive ways in which criticism has become, and can remain, a viable cultural project, even or especially in the various contestatory environments in which this project perpetually seems to be conducted. Accordingly, he writes, "disputes about meaning are always disputes about biography" because any reading proceeds from the assumption that "it is a reading of . . . the intentional activity of a specific agent" (the author, whether or not explicitly acknowledged) or "agency" (one or another "transcendental anonymity" thus "endow[ed] . . . with an intention and a biography"). Operating from Derridean and other postmodern assumptions about the necessary but indeterminable contextuality of meaning, Fish declares that "criticism can only proceed . . . when notions of agency, personhood, cause, and effect are already assumed and are already governing the readings we produce," however various and unstable those notions and readings may be. Thus, for Fish, as for the other contributors to this volume, biography is a vital contemporary "arena of dispute" in which important issues can be, indeed, cannot avoid being, contested. This is so because, as all these essays reveal, the narratives of biography and biographical criticism are "life-texts," powerful and influential discourses precisely and strategically situated at the intersections of objectivity and subjectivity, body and mind, self and other, the natural and the cultural, fact and fiction, as well as many other conceptual dyads with which Western civilization has traditionally theorized both the practices and the representations of everyday life.

Foremost among these contestatory issues is the notion of the autonomous subject, of an individual human consciousness endowed with freedom of thought and will, of a personhood or selfhood that resists, as it submits to, political, religious, social, economic, and cultural structures of authority. As we know, in the middle passage from the Enlightenment to the modern era, biography has been an important vehicle for the transmission and transcription of these interests. Yet its discursive (re)production of individual human subjectivity has not often been interrogated, for biography has been (and in many respects, continues to be) such a deeply ingrained cultural activity that it has been taken for granted. Thus biography and biographical criticism have commonly been treated as conservative, if not reactionary, generic formations, as defenders of the cultural status quo and therefore unlikely agencies of change. The essays in this volume suggest that this situation is not inevitable and that, despite (indeed, in some cases, because of) this well-earned reputation, the theory and practice of biography and biographical criticism have been, are, and can be crucial sites of contestation.

Consider, for instance, the essays by Michael McKeon, Gordon Turnbull, and Jerome Christensen. Each is concerned with more or less the same extended moment in late eighteenth- and early nineteenth-century English cultural discourse, during which the nearly simultaneous emergence of literary biography, Romantic sensibility, and reflexive human consciousness prefigured and induced a congeries of interrelated and distinctly modern (inter)textual practices that we still associate with the notion of the autonomous subject. McKeon claims that eighteenth-century English novels and biographies mutually and reciprocally inscribe "that narrative paradigm with which the modern world has since become so familiar, the portrait of the artist," and which "came closer than any other to providing the cultural prototype for the modern autonomous subject." Thus, in the fictional and non-fictional life-writing of Defoe, Richardson, Boswell, and Sterne, McKeon finds that "the alienation of the artist converges with the alienation of the individual in commodity culture [to form] the common and paradoxical experience of social activity that feels solitary," a convergence that eventually "becomes generalized to a fundamental condition of modern experience." Indeed, this transactionality recurs throughout this volume of essays, which habitually and characteristically instance the common and paradoxical experience of modern existence in and through the lives of writers.

McKeon's post-Marxist representation of the emergence of the modern autonomous subject is situated at the nexus of economic forces and individual human creativity. Turnbull's Lacanian analysis places the modern subject at the intersection of psychodynamics and social dialectics. Reading Boswell's life-writing as "a continuing engagement with his own psychosocial points of origin" and as a "lapidary discourse" compulsively renewing Boswell's "idea of language as both permanent inscription and prior to character," Turnbull (re)presents Boswell as an Enlightenment prefiguration of "the Lacanian subject." For this subject "the unconscious is structured like a language" and, culturally and ideologically, "the acquisition of language" marks an entry into a Symbolic order "presided over by the Law of the Father" (literally, in Boswell's case, a jurist) and (re)enacted as "gender-oriented desire" through the "insistent grammar" of "maternal narrative" (for Boswell, a Calvinist catechism of damnation and conversion). Thus, through "a psychosexual repression of the Mother as agency of cultural transmission, and her incomplete erasure in favor of the authority of the Father," Boswell creates a "self-record," a textualized "I," whose "public authorial career" as Johnsonian biographer "resurrects the authority of the paternal word and represents a life-long exertion to conquer feminine narrative."

Turnbull sees the Boswellian "I" as a Lacanian deflection from the preconscious textual "I" to a consciously structured social "I"; Christensen envisions the Coleridgean "suppositional biography of the 'eye'" as "logically precedent to the integrated, insightful 'I'" of Romantic life-writing and Romantic poetry. In the wake of the French Revolution and the English counterrevolution, these two Romantic projects are virtually the same thing: "contingent codes" that "movingly demonstrate that the claim for poetic identity is incoherent except in terms of a triple analogy between poetic, personal, and national identities." Thus "Coleridge's search for a biographical paradigm purified of revolutionary and counterrevolutionary stereotyping" "'stirs' the murmurous supposition" that, beyond terror and melancholy, are "the self and all it sees." For Christensen, as for McKeon and Turnbull, this all-seeing "I" is the modern, autonomous subject prefigured by the emergence of literary biography, Romantic sensibility, and reflexive human consciousness, "a life written as the cadenced suspension of the identity we know it 'must' become."

Subjectivity is also an important and vexing site of contestation for feminist critics and biographers. As the essays by Alison Booth, Cheryl Walker, and Sharon O'Brien reveal, the recognition or misrecognition of the biographical subject has been and remains both a problem and an opportunity for women writers and readers. Traditionally, Booth maintains, "criticism of women's writings has been almost invariably biographical, whether or not the critic shares in the feminist revalorization of the personal as political." The "standard model" of this criticism, instanced here in the careers of George Eliot and Virginia Woolf, "prescribes a division between the art and the life," a dichotomized narrative in which "our subjects, the women writers, become heroines in a plot of women's education and ambition necessitating self-sacrifice and suffering because of the 'facts' of oppression." Seeking "a new, more wary kind" of feminist biographical criticism, Booth "would take into account poststructuralist assaults on textual referentiality and authorial presence," and, "with Walker, . . . would advocate the inclusion of the author's biography and of historical context(s) as contributing, unfolding *texts,* not reified entities, in an alert intertextuality."

Walker's advocacy of an alert, intertextual feminist criticism emerges here as a mode of "persona criticism, a form of analysis that focuses on patterns of ideation, voice, and sensibility" connected by a concept of "multiple authorship" "involving culture, psyche, and intertextuality, as well as biographical data about the writer." Concerned that, as a methodological consequence of recent "death-of-the-author" pronouncements, "we are in danger of seeing gender disappear or become transformed into a feature of textuality that cannot be persuasively connected to real women," yet seeking to avoid traditional patriarchal culture's exclusionary and undifferentiated invocation of "monolithic authorial presence," Walker's "persona criticism links the text to various lost mediations" that trace "the circumstances that govern relations between authors and texts, as between texts and readers." For O'Brien these lost mediations are expressed as creative "tensions and contradictions in feminist theory" that "could give rise to . . . a new and exciting era of experimentation in the writing of female biography." "Women's lives have been erased, unrecorded, or represented by patriarchal stories, and biography can be a powerful means for reinscribing women in history." Indeed, "by offering us many female voices and stories," a feminist/deconstructionist biography committed to a pluralist conception of human subjectivity can help to "deconstruct the monolithic category 'woman'" and to "imagine new forms of female biography that would neither offer a falsely unified female self nor deny the importance of gender to female experience."

As these three essays suggest, one of the most common effects of the cultural (re)constitution of subjectivity is the elision of difference by structures of authority seeking cultural reification through the imposition of unity, coherence, and totality. The last four essays in this volume pursue the dynamics of this contest in the theory and practice of (a specifically) American biography and biographical criticism. Valerie Ross explains how "the repression of biography in literary studies" since "the formation of departments of literature [in the American university] during the third quarter of the nineteenth century" has been "both generic and gendered, expressing a condensation of institutional anxieties about women, class, popular culture, affect, social and domestic existence, and other 'outside' challenges to institutional literary authority." Ross posits that the postmodern expression of the biographical in academic discourse can be remapped as "historiographies of the individual subject" marking "a path to the ways in which these 'othered' subjects [traditionally, "prodigious, monstrous, deviant, or marginalized"] negotiated, embraced, rejected, created, and transformed the rules and behaviors prescribed for them and us."

"Can the American biographer resist *Americanizing* his subject?" This contestatory question energizes Rob Wilson's study of "the latent, if not politically preconscious, mission" of American biography, which is "to represent [yet] another personality who can strikingly act out the liberal project of American culture as a consensual adventure toward achieving states of freedom and risk within a globally regenerative plot of self-invention." Indeed, what Wilson calls "this agonistic struggle to achieve representative ego-mastery in which the individual can rise above his/her time and society" as s/he simultaneously comes to represent it, is so influential a national narrative that it also becomes, as Steven Weiland shows in his essay, "the discursive form" through which Erik Erikson, a naturalized American, "could consolidate his historical, social, and developmental interests" in countertransferential psychobiographies of Luther and Gandhi that reflect Erikson's resistance to "the medical hegemony of orthodox [American] psychoanalysis" and the inquisitorial environment of American cold-war politics.

If, as Weiland asserts, Erikson's "self-consciousness of the countertransference" anticipates "postmodern theorizing" by "cross[ing] the [conventional] boundary between biographer and subject," then Wilson moves to fulfill this anticipation by "theoriz[ing] an emerging mode of biographical 'dissensus' that would better challenge this consensual rhetoric of American selfhood through the invention of postmodern forms that would critically enact 'heteroglossia' and register voices and codes from the margins, regions, or frontiers of a decentered polity." My essay, which contemplates how contemporary American biographers can "avoid burying their subjects alive in the murder file of traditional biographical narrative," also posits an "oppositional agenda" for postmodern biography, which, in order to "*make* a difference" must "constitute itself and function *as* difference. Improvising guerilla tactics that opportunistically take advantage of momentary gaps in the discursive surveillance of the proprietary powers, this emergent cultural project" must, I claim, "disruptively mimic the indifference of traditional biographical recognition—and thus *abduct* it, lead it away from its historical alliance with dominant structures of authority."

Thus the essays in this book can be said to be situated between a "swerving" and an "abducting" that inevitably return to biography, but along postmodern, contestatory paths that have not been well marked or well traveled. Although our returns to biography and our prefigurations of its future are generally expressed through rhetorics of resistance, we all believe in the biographical—not because we have the theoretical technology with which we can somehow "cure" it, but, more poignantly, because we have faith in its ancient and yet still vital therapeutic powers. Biography is a remarkable discursive formation: venerable and youthful, insensitive and empathetic, inflexible and resilient, predictable and erratic, inscrutable and articulate. Per-

haps this is so because biographical narrative is, literally and figuratively, the inscription of life. This is the inaugural volume of a series
of books devoted to the theory and practice of biography and biographical criticism. My (explicitly acknowledged if indeterminable)
intention is that they will all "contest the subject," whatever it may
be, and that, in more ways than I can possibly prefigure, they will
help to bring us back to life.

Stanley Fish

Biography and Intention

When I was an undergraduate at the University of Pennsylvania, one of my instructors told our class that no one would have ever paid any attention to *Lycidas* if it were not known in advance that Milton was its author. It was clear that by saying as much he was at once passing a judgment on *Lycidas* and making a methodological point. The judgment was negative and the methodological point was, of course, the New-Critical doctrine that the meaning and value of a work are independent of its author's biography. It may be the case that the work in question was produced by an individual with a certain history, and a set of specific intentions, but what matters finally is what the work itself says rather than the conditions of its production or what its author may have said about what he or she was trying to do. As Wimsatt and Beardsley put it in "The Intentional Fallacy," "If the poet succeeded in doing it, then the *poem itself* shows what he was trying to do. And if the poet did not succeed, then . . . the critic must go outside the poem—for evidence of an intention that did not become effective." The mistake, they continue, is to think that a work of art remains tethered to its author; but in fact they assert that the work "is detached from the author at birth and goes about the world beyond his power to intend about it or control it."[1]

These statements are regularly and correctly cited as classic instances of *formalist* thought; and yet they are strikingly similar in tone and spirit to statements made more recently by that most antiformalist of philosophers, Jacques Derrida. In his essay "Signature Event Context," Derrida declares that "for a writing to be a writing it must continue to . . . be readable even when what is called the author . . . no longer answers for what he has written . . . be it because of a temporary absence, because he is dead, or, more generally, because he has not employed his absolutely actual and present intention . . . the plenitude of his desire to say what he means."[2] Of course, there are important differences to be noted between the two American critics and the French philosopher. For Wimsatt and Beardsley, the independence of the verbal artifact from the circumstances of its production assures its ability to speak for itself, to embody a unique and stable meaning; while for Derrida, the same independence abandons the writing to its "essential drift" and thereby destabilizes a meaning that can be infinitely remade by the succession of contexts into which it is inserted. Nevertheless, it remains the case that from either the American or the continental perspective, the question of meaning is rigorously divorced from questions of biography and intention.

In what follows I would like to argue against that divorce not because it is inadvisable but because it is impossible, and I would like to make that argument by way of an argument from the philosophy of language, since it seems to me that a certain assumption often made by philosophers of language and by the lay public is largely responsible for the so-called "problem of biography." The assumption is that there are (at least) two kinds of meanings, sentence meaning or literal meaning on the one hand and speaker's meaning or contextual meaning on the other. The first kind of meaning is public and conventional and is determined by the constituent parts of a sentence, that is, by the meanings of individual words and the syntactical relationships that join them. The second kind of meaning is circumstantial or situational and is a function of, among other things, the beliefs of speakers and hearers, interpretive assumptions, special or local knowledge, and specific intentions, such as the intention to deceive or to be ironic.

The trouble with the second kind of meaning, or so the story goes, is that it is variable and unpredictable in the sense that it would have to be calculated every time if it could be calculated at all; consequently, the story continues, it cannot form the basis of a formal linguistics. It is for this reason that most linguists distinguish sharply between the two kinds of meaning and assume that the second is parasitic on the first, is a matter of "performance" rather than "competence," and is therefore philosophically uninteresting. The possibility that the situation may be the reverse—that is, that speaker or situational meaning is prior to and constitutive of sentence meaning—quite literally horrifies linguists; for, as Ruth Kempson observes, if this were the case, then the truth value of a sentence would depend not "on the relation between its constituent parts and the objects . . . to which they refer" but on what "the speaker was intending to convey," and it would follow that "sentences . . . could not be said to have a particular meaning independent of the context in which they are spoken" and that their "meaning would be dependent on what . . . was already known beforehand by the speaker and his audience." But "if this holds," she complains, "sentences become indefinitely ambiguous, the limits on a semantic theory are not definable and semantics thereby becomes an inoperable discipline."[3]

I do not think that all of these dire consequences follow, but I *do* think that meaning is a function of what a particular speaker in a specific set of circumstances was intending to say, and I think so because there is simply no such thing as sentence meaning in the sense that Kempson and others require it. That is, there is no such thing as a meaning that is specifiable *apart* from the contextual circumstances of its intentional production. If this seems counterintuitive, it is because we often hear sentences with an immediacy which suggests that there has been no need to consult contextual circumstances in order to determine what they mean. The words, we say at such moments, speak for themselves. But in fact they do not; it is just that the very act of hearing is so deeply embedded in a set of circumstances that we are not aware of them as circumstances at all, and consequently it seems that we experience the meaning directly as a function of what the words in and of themselves mean. But it is my contention that words (or sentences) in and of themselves do not mean anything and that meaning emerges only within the assumption (whether self-conscious or not) of a speaker who is in a particular situation and who is producing at the moment of utterance a piece of intentional behavior. To put the matter baldly, the act of construing meaning is ipso facto the act of assigning intention within a specific set of circumstances; you just cannot do one without the other.

Consider, for example, the perfectly ordinary sentence, "This is a fine job." It is, of course, ambiguous between praise of a particular performance and an assessment of an opportunity for employment. That, however, is merely a lexical ambiguity and could be removed by specifying the context (in this case, a statement uttered by someone to the person hired to remove leaves from a lawn). Nevertheless, ambiguity would still remain, since the speech act of praising in this hypothetical situation (not hypothetical at all, since I lived it) could be meant either straightforwardly or sarcastically. That is to say, "This is a fine job" might be intended and heard as an ironic statement of disapproval. In many standard linguistic accounts, this ironic meaning would be thought of as secondary—an effect produced by a special, out of the ordinary act of intention—and parasitic on the more ordinary meaning carried by the words themselves. The ironic meaning, the standard argument runs, could only be heard within the assumption—*added* to the words—that the speaker was a certain kind of person, difficult to satisfy and given to sarcasm. In the absence of that assumption or presupposition, the sentence would be heard quite straightforwardly. But the absence of *that* presupposition would not be the absence of presupposition; in order to hear the sentence straightforwardly, you would have to be assuming a speaker who was easy to satisfy and *not* given to sarcasm, and those assumptions would be no less contextual than any others. The difference between a straightforward or literal reading and an ironic one is not the difference between a reading that considers the words in themselves and a reading that presupposes a certain kind of speaker, but between readings that presuppose certain speakers of different kinds. The one thing you cannot do is presuppose no speaker; the one thing you cannot do is read or hear the sentence without already having received it as the expression of an intentional being with a particular, as opposed to a universal, history.

It follows, then, that neither can you read independently of biography, of some specification of what kind of person—and with what abilities, concerns, goals, purposes, and so on—is the source of the words you are reading. And if that follows, it follows too that disputes about meaning are always disputes about biography, whether or not they are explicitly so labeled. If someone were either to put forward or to reject a reading of *Lycidas* because of the relationship of that reading to Milton's Puritanism, someone else might well object that a poet's religious views were irrelevant to the meaning of his poetry. This is a perfectly reasonable position, as is its obverse; the only mistake is to think that either position involves putting biographical considerations aside. The critic who decides to ignore Milton's religious views and treat *Lycidas* as a poem has not chosen *against* biography but rather has chosen one kind of biography over another. Instead of reading within the assumption of a religious intention that critic will be reading within the assumption of a poetic intention; the meanings he or she assigns will be the meanings that could have been intended by a person who was working in a poetic tradition; so that, for example, the first three words of the poem, "Yet once more," will be heard as the author's announcement that he is in the act of continuing that tradition—and *that* will be what the words mean. Such a reading will be no less biographical than a reading that takes its cue from Milton's *Christian Doctrine* or from his opposition to the policies and programs of the Laudian Church. Any of these readings or any combination of them will be biographical, and there would be no possibility of producing a reading that was not, no possibility, that is, of producing a reading (or even a description) without already having assumed that what it is a reading *of* is the intentional activity of a specific agent.

At this point, one might object that the entire analysis depends on a debatable and naive notion of agency in which poems or other utterances are the products of a discrete individual consciousness. There has been no dearth of challenges to this notion, and once again it is interesting to note that the challenges come from both formalists and antiformalists and that they are similar. When T. S. Eliot declares that the individual mind is merely a repository for the numberless phrases and images of a tradition and is only the medium in which "the mind of Europe" changes and develops;[4] or when Wimsatt and Beardsley specify as the source of a poem's meaning grammars, dictionaries, literatures, and "all that makes a language and culture,"[5] they are hardly distinguishable from Roland Barthes when he reports that life as it happens in his head is the result of "formulae inherited from a previous style";[6] or from Lévi-Strauss when he asserts that men do not think myths, rather "myths operate in men's minds without their being aware of the fact";[7] or from Foucault when he echoes Beckett by asking, "what matter who's speaking?"[8] All of these authors or nonauthors are making the same argument, an argument that has been summarized nicely by Jonathan Culler: While in an older tradition discourse about humanity was always discourse about "the self as a conscious subject . . . which endows the world with meaning," in recent years meaning has come to be "explained in terms of conventional systems which . . . escape the grasp of the conscious subject"; consequently, the self is "'dissolved' as its functions are taken up by a variety of interpersonal systems that operate through it."[9]

Now it would seem that if the self has been thus dissolved, the notion of an intentional agent with a history and a biography must dissolve too; but in fact that is not at all the case, for, as Foucault notes in announcing the death of the self, we have "merely transposed the empirical characteristics of an author to a transcendental anonymity."[10] That is, if the originating author is dissolved into a series of functions, if the individual mind is merely the tablet on which the mind of Europe or the mind of the pastoral or the mind of myth inscribes itself, then we have not done away with intention and biography but merely relocated them. In principle it does not matter whether the originating agent is a discrete human consciousness or the spirit of an age or a literary tradition or a culture or language itself; to read something as the product of any one of these "transcendental anonymities" is to endow that anonymity with an intention and a biography. The choice, as I have said before, is not between reading biographically and reading in some other way (there is no other way) but rather between different biographical readings that have their source in different specifications of the sources of agency. The only way to read unbiographically would be to refrain from construing meaning—to refrain, that is, from regarding the marks before you as manifestations of intentional behavior; but that would be not to read at all.

That is why it makes no sense to say, as many have recently been saying, that textual meaning exceeds or escapes intention. To be sure, one can understand and even be persuaded by the line of reasoning that leads to such assertions. It is, after all, a fact of experience that you can intend to mean something by an utterance only to discover that your intention cannot control what is made of that utterance by others; the meanings that can be assigned to it are at least theoretically infinite. Indeed, the case is even worse than that, for if the thoughts you can think or the intentions you can have are constrained by the conventional and interpersonal systems that operate through you, then the knowledge you have of *your own* intentions is no less interpretive than the knowledge you can have of the intentions of others; and this means too that the knowledge you can have of yourself—of the intending entity—will also be an interpretive or mediated knowledge. In short, both the intentions you know and the "you" that is doing the knowing are always interpreted objects, and as interpreted objects they can hardly be invoked as the controlling origins of interpretation. But finally all of this is beside the point if the point is the relationship between interpretation (the specification of meaning) and intention, for the fact that intention is unstable and can only be known in representations of it does not mean that interpretation can do without or escape the notion of intention; it only means that interpretation cannot be guaranteed by, or grounded in, something outside of it. Putting intention *inside* the interpretive circle rather than positing it as the external origin of interpretation does not make interpretation any less intentional, any less a matter of specifying what some purposeful agent, itself interpretively known, meant by this or that set of marks. The slogan that "meaning is in excess of intention" should therefore be rewritten as follows: The act of intending a meaning cannot constrain the specification of intention that follows. Rewritten that way, of course, the slogan, rather than sundering meaning from intention, reaffirms their radical inseparability.

From the perspective of that reaffirmation, it is clear that the new-fashioned arguments against intention are no more coherent than the old-fashioned arguments against intention; indeed, they are the same arguments in the service of the same program, the program of reifying texts as the containers and declarers of their own meanings. It makes no difference finally whether one sets aside intention in favor of meanings that are stable or in favor of meanings that are always slipping out of one's grasp. The distinction between saying that texts read themselves and saying that texts deconstruct themselves is no more than a distinction between different conceptions of what it means for texts to be independent; but since, by the argument presented here, texts are not and could not be independent but are inextricably bound up with intentions, both conceptions, distinguishable though they may be in polemics, are equally wrong, and wrong in exactly the same way.

I should hasten to add that the fact that they are wrong, and that meaning, intention, and biography are inextricable, has no methodological consequences. That is, as a fact it does not direct us to prefer one mode of interpretation to another; it does not direct us, for example, to turn once again to biography and busy ourselves with the day-to-day details of Milton's life. Indeed, in the context of the present thesis it makes no sense to urge a return to biography, since biography is not something from which we can swerve. However, to say that biography is not something from which we can swerve is not to have forestalled dispute; it is merely to have identified the arena of dispute. All the traditional questions remain, questions about what constitutes a biography, about what is and is not biographical evidence, about what kind of entities can have biographies, and so on. My only point is that criticism can only proceed when some set of answers to these questions is firmly in place, when notions of agency, personhood, cause, and effect are already assumed and are already governing the readings we produce. Of course, there will be times when the in-place set of answers is challenged, and at those times we will explicitly debate whether Milton should be read as a Puritan or as a pastoralist or as a revolutionary or as a seventeenth-century bourgeois or as an involuntary expression of a set of cultural possibilities. But, however such debates are settled, biography will always be the winner, because we will always be reading Milton's words as the intentional product of the person or nonperson we now understand him to be. I repeat: this is not a recommendation or even a prediction, but a declaration of necessity. There remain many things we can do with texts, many ways in which we can construe them, but we cannot at the same time construe them and free ourselves from the considerations of biography. To paraphrase the words of the immortal Danny and the Juniors, I don't care what people say; biography is here to stay.

Stanley Fish

Notes

1. William K. Wimsatt (with Monroe C. Beardsley), *The Verbal Icon: Studies in the Meaning of Poetry* (Lexington: University of Kentucky Press, 1954), 4–5 (my emphasis).

2. *Glyph* 1 (1977): 181.

3. *Presupposition and the Delimitation of Semantics* (New York: Cambridge University Press, 1975), 88.

4. "Tradition and the Individual Talent," in *Selected Prose of T. S. Eliot,* ed. Frank Kermode (New York: Harcourt Brace Jovanovich, 1975), 39.

5. Wimsatt and Beardsley, 10.

6. "Style and Its Image," in *Literary Style: A Symposium,* ed. Seymour Chatman (New York: Oxford University Press, 1971), 9.

7. Claude Lévi-Strauss, *The Raw and the Cooked: Introduction to a Science of Mythology,* trans. John and Doreen Weightman (New York: Harper and Row, 1969), 1:12.

8. Michel Foucault, "What Is an Author?," in *Language, Counter-Memory, Practice: Selected Essays and Interviews,* ed. Donald F. Bouchard and trans. Donald F. Bouchard and Sherry Simon (Ithaca, N.Y.: Cornell University Press, 1977), 138.

9. *Structuralist Poetics: Structuralism, Linguistics, and the Study of Literature* (Ithaca, N.Y.: Cornell University Press, 1975), 28.

10. Foucault, 120.

Michael McKeon

Writer As Hero
Novelistic Prefigurations and the Emergence of Literary Biography

It is a commonplace of historical argument that the emergence of the novel and the transformation of biography in the seventeenth and eighteenth centuries profoundly express the modern discovery of the individual, of the autonomous subject. Although in different ways, neither genre is thinkable apart from the premise of a self-conscious subjectivity independent enough of its objective surroundings to provide, in itself, the occasion for a coherent and continuous narrative. And it is only slightly less commonplace to find, toward the *end* of this same period, the birth of the notion of the artist as professional writer or "man of letters." Not that earlier times lacked any model of the normative literary career; on the contrary, classical antiquity had bequeathed a highly influential paradigm to the Renaissance literary scene. Nevertheless, it is generally agreed that the modern status of writing as a professional occupation required the consolidation of the writer as a distinct social category, and therefore of the literary marketplace as the dominant arena of the writer's activity. Consequently, it is also only in the latter part of the eighteenth century that specifically *literary* biography—the life of one who is considered in the particular capacity of a writer—began to be composed.

In the following essay I will suggest that the connection between these two emergences—that of the biographical-novelistic subject and that of the social type of the writer—is deeper than mere chronological contiguity, that it is grounded in a matrix of common ideas and experience. Rather than analyzing this matrix in a discursive fashion, however, I will begin pursuing the connection by disclosing in the early novel what might be called "prefigurations" of the writer's life. In the plots and personages with which it is characteristically concerned, I will argue, the early novel strains to depict a social type—the writer as hero—that has as yet no social fulfillment, no actual existence. In this figurative and anticipatory sense, then, it might be said that the novel was always "about" the life of the writer. And so, when the writer's life begins to be composed around the middle of the eighteenth century, we can see in it not only that narrative paradigm with which the modern world has since become so familiar, the portrait of the artist, but also a resemblance to the sort of story that had by then already become recognizable as typically novelistic. Let me add that I have framed this argument in the language of "prefiguration" and "fulfillment" in order to make clear the nature of the relationship I am suggesting between the early novel and literary biography, a relation not of cause and effect but of tacit intimation and full articulation. And what we might expect to find articulated in the narrative fulfillment of the type of the writer late in the century is not only the full-blown writer's life but also the full-blown novel of the writer as hero.

I

The novel coalesced as a genre once it was possible to conceive of the narrative subject as fundamentally separable from the external social, historical, and metaphysical forces that were traditionally taken not simply to condition but fully to constitute human existence. In fact, early novels tend to be *about* nothing other than this experience of disengagement—as well as the obstacles that may make it problematic. Daniel Defoe's *Robinson Crusoe* and Samuel Richardson's *Pamela* provide good examples of this tendency. Repudiating the counsel of God and his father, Robinson Crusoe flees home to found a new civilization and to rule as its patriarchal monarch. A servant girl confronted by her master's efforts to corrupt her virtue, Pamela rewrites this aristocratic scenario of seduction as a progressive marriage plot and thereby catapults herself into the gentry. The following account of the early novel will concentrate on these two narratives not simply because they provide a broadly adequate representation of the form but also because they best exemplify the range and depth of the particular phenomenon I am concerned with, the novel's prefiguration of the writer's life. I then will turn to the writer's life itself.

In these familiar narratives of the successful entry of the disadvantaged into the established order, several points deserve emphasis. Most important, the protagonist initially exemplifies a paradoxical disjunction between externals and internals, worldly stature and the powers of the head and heart—a disjunction whose social expression is most concisely stated as the opposition of birth and worth. At a crucial moment in Richardson's novel, Pamela rebukes her master's privileged arrogance by opposing his aristocratic and genealogical ideal of "honor" to her own humble and singular "virtue": "I too much apprehend," she declares, "that *your* Notions of Honour and *mine* are very different from one another. . . . The Honour of the Wicked is Disgrace and Shame to the Virtuous."[1] But of course, the main work of these plots is to overcome the social injustice of worth without birth by enabling worth to win, if not birth, then its most valued emoluments. In the words of Richardson's subtitle, they are plots of "virtue rewarded" that achieve poetic justice by erasing the initial disjunction between inner virtue and external status.

This basic plot has its pattern in the Christian, and especially the Protestant, notion of an "aristocracy of grace" whose members are most likely to differ markedly from those of the worldly aristocracy. But in the novel, the pattern tends to become secularized—not only in the obvious way that internal "grace" becomes "virtue," and its external reward is found on earth rather than in heaven, but also in that ultimate responsibility for the reward of virtue subtly shifts from the goodness of God to the virtuous self. To be sure, this is a delicate process. Robinson Crusoe's astonishing success on the island ostensibly depends entirely on his religious conversion there and on the lesson it teaches him in recognizing what he calls the "secret Intimations of Providence" as they manifest themselves within his mind.[2] But once learned, the lesson also enables him to reverse the process, to validate his own subjective desires as the objective word of God, and the increasingly confident Crusoe of the latter part of the novel seems like a man who has absorbed or internalized divinity within his own self-sufficient person. In *Pamela,* the external authority is not metaphysical but social, not God but her master. And although her elevation is strictly impossible without his marriage proposal, we are left in no doubt, despite Pamela's continued social deference, that the real moving force in this drama has been her own extraordinary tenacity of will and self-reliance.

What have these qualities of the novelistic protagonist—the disengagement from traditional authorities and hierarchies, the paradoxical disjunction between internals and externals, the ambiguous but indomitable core of self-sufficiency—what have these distinguishing features of the individual subject to do with the modern notion of the artist as man of letters? The Renaissance doctrine of the artist as creator first broached the daring notion of a human spirituality imitative of the divine, but it remained for the Enlightenment to accept the challenge by propounding a doctrine of aesthetic creation that effectively replaced God's authority with that of the human author. Richardson himself recognized the danger when, years after writing of Pamela and her rewarded virtue, he ruminated on the implication of the recently formulated idea of "poetic justice": "And after all, what is the *poetical justice* . . . as the generality of writers have managed it, but another sort of dispensation than that with which God, by Revelation, teaches us, He has thought fit to exercise mankind; whom placing here only in a state of probation, he hath so intermingled good and evil, as to necessitate us to look forward to a more equal dispensation of both."[3] My point is not that Richardson and Defoe are active proponents of the doctrine of the aesthetic, which, after all, is still at this time in the process of construction. But their efforts to give narrative form to the individual subject drew crucial inspiration, I think, from the nascent and evolving social type of the artist simply because it came closer than any other to providing the cultural prototype for the modern autonomous subject. Already by the eighteenth century, social aberrancy, the disengagement from politics and its corruptions, a self-consciously singular subjectivity, a self-imposed solitude—in the all-purpose modern phrase, an "alienation from society"—already these character traits were taking form around the figure of the artist. What must be added is that the novelists deepen immeasurably their indebtedness to the prototype by giving to their protagonists the powerful and highly volatile gift of creativity.

In utter and often desperate solitude, Robinson Crusoe exercises his creative powers most memorably by the imaginative construction for himself of an elevated social status. Of the island itself he fancies "that this was all my own, that I was King and Lord of all this Country indefeasibly, and had a Right of Possession; and if I could convey it, I might have it in Inheritance, as compleatly as any Lord of a Manor in *England*" (100). Here the fantasy is one of absolute private ownership, and it helps emphasize, through the familiar model of English landed proprietorship, both the disparity between internals and externals and the power of fantasy to overcome it. This is also the effect when, at a later stage, Crusoe imaginatively populates the island and thereby turns his private into a public rule. Surrounded by his livestock, he reflects that "it would have made a Stoick smile to have seen, me and my little Family sit down to Dinner; there was my Majesty the Prince and Lord of the whole Island; I had the Lives of all my Subjects at my absolute Command. I could hang, draw, give Liberty, and take it away, and no Rebels among all my Subjects"

(148). Soon after, Crusoe's sudden fear of being truly joined by other people prompts him to rehearse for himself the real limits of human creativity: "I consider'd that this was the Station of Life the infinitely wise and good Providence of God had determin'd for me, that . . . I was not to dispute his Sovereignty, who, as I was his Creature, had an undoubted Right by Creation to govern and dispose of me absolutely as he thought fit" (157).

Yet by the time he leaves the island, these fantasies have been strictly fulfilled, a fact the reader may momentarily forget, given the way Crusoe continues to speak in the drolly metaphorical mode: "My Island was now peopled, and I thought my self very rich in Subjects; and it was a merry Reflection which I frequently made, How like a King I look'd. First of all, the whole Country was my own meer Property; so that I had an undoubted Right of Dominion. *2dly,* My People were perfectly subjected: I was absolute Lord and Law-giver; they all owed their Lives to me, and were ready to lay down their Lives, *if there had been Occasion of it,* for me" (241). In fact, these people are not livestock but people, whom Crusoe one by one allows onto the island after repeatedly undergoing the contradictory experience I have already described, the "secret intimations of providence," which seem to validate with the word of God what is in any case an irresistible desire to end his solitude. Crusoe does indeed exercise absolute command over these people, and he kills others who seemed unlikely to accept their status as his subjects. At the end of the novel, moreover, he returns to what he calls "my new Collony" (305) and shares it into parts to be farmed by its settlers while reserving to himself the property of the whole. Thus, through the merely incidental and evanescent intimations of the Creator, the creature's imaginative constructions have been decisively imposed upon reality. And this contradictory reversal is characteristic of the general movement with which I am concerned in this essay. The authority of the newly constituted subject is at first no more than that of authorial fancy. But the momentum generated by the initial detachment of subjectivity from the objective continuum that has traditionally contained it eventually empowers the subject to construct the world according to its own desires. In Crusoe's case, the connection between subjective and economic self-creation is clear enough; and we are left with a sense of him less as the new aesthetic man (for his material achievements render unnecessary our willing suspension of disbelief) than as a reminiscence of the old Faustian overreacher, whom the new age of Enlightenment reason, so far from abjuring, is content to encourage.

To see Robinson Crusoe's distinctive mode of creativity as modeled on the emergent but as-yet-unrealized prototype of the modern writer is perhaps suggestive, but in itself it is little more than that. My argument will be furthered considerably by examining *Pamela* in the same light. And in order to do this, let me briefly recall the familiar material circumstance of literary activity in early modern England that conditioned the way in which writers, in particular, experienced their relation to, and hence their disengagement from, traditional social constraints. This is the fundamental transformation of the mode of literary production from a system of aristocratic patronage to a system of capitalist publication and exchange. As in other modes of production, this changeover was widely experienced by writers as a liberation from a direct dependence on social superiors into the freedom of writing according to one's "own" unfettered sensibility and of being read in acknowledgment of one's own intrinsic literary worth. Indeed, the very notion of an internal, intrinsic core of "literary" substance and value could not be conceived apart from a system of production that seemed, in contrast with its traditional alternative, to allow the writer the freedom to be self-constituted *as* a literary figure. Sir Philip Sidney's impatient muse ("look in thy heart, and write") posits the writer as a creative subject; what is still missing in 1582 is a materially objective ground, both separable and indispensable, against which the writer's subjective autonomy might be figured.

Within this innovative economy, of course, success with the public played a complicated role. Some writers condemned the allure of sales and profit as the sign of a new and insidiously impersonal form of social constraint, entirely inconsistent with the developing image of the solitary disinterestedness of the writer. Apprehensions like these are of a piece with the image of Grub Street and its monetary corruptions. But successful publication seemed to many others the very guarantee of individual autonomy and authenticity because it insured against dependence on external forces by immediately rewarding the author's internal worth. By this means, the independence of private subjectivity was reconciled with the independence of public self-sufficiency. And the modern type of the artist as man of letters—private genius confirmed by its public reward—was born.

Central to the connection between the emergence of the autonomous subject and that of the social type of the writer is the fact that among the industries of early modern England, the book trade was one of the first to experience the full rationalization of commodity production, which both rewarded individual enterprise and celebrated it as an important by-product, individual "authorship." But the commodification of the book trade cannot be understood apart from the print technology on which it depended, for the peculiar logic of print—the logic of "multiplicity, systematization, and fixity"—was singularly compatible with that of production for the marketplace.[4] It also supported the complex process by which writing for the public constituted the man of letters as the industrious producer of a value related to but more authentic than that conferred by traditional accomplishments. The seventeenth-century bookseller-translator Francis Kirkman writes that he was transfixed by the first sight of one of his publications, for "the Name of the Translator being plac'd on the Title-page in large Characters, there was also added the honoured Word *Gent.* to import that the Translator was a Gentleman, that he was every Inch of him in his own imagination, and did believe that the so printing that word on the Title of the Book, did as much entitle him to Gentility, as if he had Letters Patents for it from the *Heralds-Office:* Nay, did suppose this to be more authentick because more publick."[5] In the end, the Renaissance contest between arms and letters was resolved by the modern ascendancy not only of the literate state servant but also of "the hero as man of letters."[6] At the same time, of course, the chronic instability of this social type is evident in the very feat of reconciliation—of private subjectivity with public self-sufficiency—it proclaims.

What does all this have to do with Richardson's narrative? *Pamela* was by no means the first epistolary novel in England, but it, more than any other, established the extraordinary vogue of a form that required of its characters that they be writers. Pamela's own status as an author (she is overwhelmingly the novel's dominant letter-writer) is a condition of her existence that Richardson insists upon with unparalleled self-consciousness. Early on, we hear the story of her attempted seduction through the letters she writes home to her parents, most of which are also secretly read by her master. By this stratagem, Mr. B. becomes her most crucial reader, the authority who cruelly constrains her but who is at the same time subject to the creative suasions of the author. Richardson's novel is therefore an allegory of the power of writing—but only because writing is itself a metaphor for the emergent power of the autonomous subject. In *Pamela* this metaphorical bond is especially close, since the most acclaimed originality of his first novel came from what Richardson later called "writing to the moment," an epistolary style so exquisitely attuned to the present instant of composition that it seemed to capture the very souls of its characters.

Now, so long as Pamela is writing single letters, Mr. B. remains relatively impervious to her powers of self-expression, angrily and traditionalistically equating her creativity with fantasy, inventions, and lies. "I tell you," he says, incensed at her letter writing, "she is a subtle, artful Gypsey," and he insists that "she will not write the Affairs of my Family purely for an Exercise to her Pen and her Invention" (39–40). But by imprisoning her in his country house so as to prevent her letters from reaching home, Mr. B. ironically enables Pamela to prevail; for as with Robinson Crusoe, solitude is the precondition for creativity. This is because, although she no longer expects a timely reading by her parents, Pamela continues writing anyway, and her sequential and disjointed letters are thereby transformed into a sustained and shapely journal. And once Mr. B. forces her to let him read it, he reads it entire, and he is obliged to relinquish his objectifying view of Pamela because he is overcome by a recognition of her authentic subjectivity. In the terms of Richardson's narration, however, this is the same as to say that he is overcome by a fully aesthetic response to Pamela's creation: "You have touch'd me sensibly," he says, "with your mournful Relation, and your sweet Reflections upon it. . . . There is such a pretty Air of Romance, as you relate them, in your Plots, and my Plots, that I shall be better directed in what manner to wind up the Catastrophe of the pretty Novel" (201, 208). As this language suggests, Mr. B. has become not only a reader of, but also a character in, Pamela's novel, and it might be said that he acquiesces in her internal virtue by willingly suspending his disbelief in it.

Richardson labors hard to connect Pamela's writing with her industrious creativity. Because the early, yet-unconverted Mr. B. is so relentless in her surveillance, Pamela is obliged to conceal her papers on her own person. And in this figurative sense, Richardson associates the creative labor of her writings with the mode of creativity to which women have been customarily limited, that of pregnancy. "How nobly my Plot succeeds!" Pamela writes at one point. "But I begin to be afraid my Writings may be discover'd; for they grow large! I stich them hitherto to my Under-coat, next my Linen" (120). And later on Mr. B. refers back to the period of her imprisonment as "the Time of her Confinement" (267). These passages also evoke the proximity that Richardson's age was establishing between creative writing and the autonomous subject, the modern "self." When Mr. B. demands to see her papers, Pamela observes that "I must all undress me in a manner to untack them" (204). That is, she must literally disclose herself, an act of apparent immodesty that really signifies—and is the means by which her master recognizes—her most inner virtue.

Like Crusoe's, Pamela's creativity is therefore in this sense most fully self-creative. And Richardson's interest in the authentic subjectivity of his protagonist is fully consistent with her objective self-sufficiency, her success as a "woman of letters." This becomes clear in the way he invites us to see her imprisonment, ostensibly a period of enforced leisure from the labors of domestic servant, as in fact a discipline in the alternative work of writing. The irony is achieved by Pamela's ingenuous plays upon the terms "employment" and "self-employment" to signify first an idle diversion entered into when real work is not to be had, but then an authentic if unprecedented species of female labor. A purposeful impersonation of idleness, an act of ostensible leisure that conceals industrious labor, Pamela's writing now becomes a self-creative "self-employment" that flourishes only because her service to her master has been formally interrupted (95, 113, 134). Of course, what she earns from this labor is not economic independence, since she remains subordinate to her husband as she had been to her master. But the enormous change entailed in a social elevation from common servant to gentlewoman was not underestimated by contemporaries and should not be by us.

So in this respect, the parallel between Pamela's social career and her metaphorical career as a writer remains plausible and serviceable. Before her elevation, her master fills the negative role of the aristocratic patron whose principal aim is simply to discourage his client's productivity, except insofar as it is for his eyes only. Once Pamela has risen, however, it is in Mr. B's interest to "publish" both her and her writings. Indeed, the latter part of the novel is taken up with these analogous modes of circulation. First, it is Pamela herself who is "read" by the local gentry in elaborate scenes of social spectacle engineered by Mr. B., whose aim is to win the accreditation of the former servant girl as an accomplished and fully formed gentlewoman. Thereafter Pamela is allowed to perform in the more detached media of language and narrative. Her papers, assuming a life of their own, circulate among the rural gentry, persuading all of her inner gentility and thereby accruing to their author the social credit and capital needed to maintain her new position. Mr. B. might be seen as playing in this process the role of interested middleman, mediating the functions of aristocratic patron and capitalist bookseller. In any case, Pamela's performance as a writer continues to dominate her characterization as much after her marriage as it had before.

My argument is that Pamela's elevation into the gentry, an ostensibly traditional means of authenticating the ostentatiously innovative value of the industrious subject, is profoundly informed and facilitated by her figurative status as woman of letters. Now, the fact that Richardson, himself an industrious printer and ambitious man of letters, impersonates a woman in *Pamela* can be fully accounted for only by reference to matters tangential to my present concern. I have argued elsewhere that the progressive ideology of internal merit or virtue, the ideal of industrious worth irrespective of patrilineal birth, has a history that precedes its gendering as female. For this reason, the progressive championing of an autonomous female virtue that culminates with Richardson may be seen as the strategic effort of a fundamentally patriarchal cultural movement to forge a limited alliance based on anti-patrilineal principles.[7] In the present context, it is nevertheless worth considering the effect of Richardson's narrative cross-dressing on the figurative evocation of writer as novelistic hero. If the novelistic allegorization of the autonomous subject as a writer works, as I have suggested, to concentrate its contradictory structure in terms of an emergent social category, the imagination of a writer who is also a woman works to redouble that effort, overdetermining the depiction of the subject as a powerfully volatile compound.

As we have seen, Richardson brilliantly exploits Pamela's sex-based capacity for literary pregnancy. Yet Sidney's famous sonnet turns upon the easy transferability of that capacity to male writers; ironically, women writers are likely to have far more trouble embracing the figure—in part because the actual experience of motherhood preoccupies them with the unwieldly ramifications of the signifier, in part because the act of going public entailed in the signified is considerably more problematic for them than for men.[8] Of course, the difficulty of publication crosses gender lines: it is crucial to the general cultural problem—the contradiction between the independence of private subjectivity and that of public self-sufficiency—that the type of the man of letters is formulated to resolve. But the figure of the writer as a woman concentrates the volatility of the compound because the figure of woman is the traditional means for articulating that contradiction as an irresolvable antagonism. In the early modern division of knowledge, "woman"'s double capacity of madonna and whore is informed and deepened by the aggravated opposition of subject and object, private and public, and the figure of the feminine becomes serviceable in expressing the "hysteria" associated not only with the private, sedentary life but also (in a secularization of the goddess Fortuna as money, credit, and exchange) with public activity and ambition.[9] Richardson's impersonation of Pamela may capitalize on the notion of a specifically female species of inner virtue currently in formation; but it also unleashes (as Fielding's *Shamela* makes clear) the complementary specter of industrious and unconstrained female corruption. For real women from Mary Carleton to Fanny Burney, the coextensive allure and menace of self-publication—of seeking to be a "woman of letters"—is by now an acknowledged and important fact of early modern literary history.[10]

II

I will now shift my attention from the early eighteenth-century novel, in which the life of the writer can be seen to be prefigured, to the later part of the century, when the writer's life itself might be said to have its fulfillment. As in the first instance, I will concentrate upon two narratives—one biographical, one autobiographical—which I take to be peculiarly reflective of the range of the writer's life at this time. Both are by James Boswell.

The Boswell of the *London Journal* is nothing if not self-creative in spirit. Here is how he describes his departure from Edinburgh in the fall of 1762: "The scene of being a son setting out from home for the wide world and the idea of being my own master, pleased me much."[11] Boswell now performs a complicated ritual of leave-taking, surveying the city and bowing ceremoniously to each of its landmarks. Then he continues: "Having thus gratified my agreeable whim and superstitious humour, I felt a warm glow of satisfaction. Indeed, I have a strong turn to what the cool part of mankind have named superstition. But this proceeds from my genius for poetry, which ascribes many fanciful propreties to everything" (42). The *London Journal* pursues into new territory the early novel's premise of the individual subject as an autonomous being, and it records a titanic struggle between the exhilarating project of creative self-generation and the vertiginous apprehension that the "self" has no substance apart from an external ground that always lies just out of reach. The struggle's resolution, such as it is, comes with the discovery of the role of the writer as man of letters.

Like Robinson Crusoe's, Boswell's disengagement from traditional authority is figured most comprehensively as a break with his father, Lord Auchinleck, Scots lawyer, judge, and country gentleman. The nine months he spent in London at the age of twenty-three represent a distinct departure from Lord Auchinleck's wish that his heir study for the Scots bar. Boswell's ambition for himself is, needless to say, considerably less bounded than this. As he remarks early in the journal, "I have discovered that we may be in some degree whatever character we choose" (47). Over the course of the journal, Boswell gives substance to pure willed choice by momentarily and experimentally taking on a series of "characters"—the man of pleasure, the character of a gentleman, the character of a soldier, and so forth. In fact, at one point, having met a dedicated Scotsman who also has "the spirited liveliness of a neat clever young fellow" (199), he even elaborates for himself a character that would permit him to combine the agreeable whim of Jamie Boswell with the solidity of a Scots lawyer. He calls this fantasy the character of the man of consequence, and for a while it enjoys a luxuriant growth in his imagination: "I considered that my notions of an advocate were false. That I connected with that character low breeding and Presbyterian stiffness, whereas many of them were very genteel people. . . . That I might show all the dull, vulgar, plodding young lawyers how easily superior parts can outstrip them." (200). By the very next day, however, the plan has lost its appeal: "The notion of being of consequence was not much, for . . . just now I knew from experience that just by strength of imagination I could strut about and think myself as great as any man" (201).

And this is the problem with all of Boswell's projects. Every public role is likely to suffer by comparison with the ideal image that the role has been embraced in order to fulfill. Indeed, his self-conscious conception of social behavior as role-playing insures that all activity will seem relatively alien to the self that preexists and provisionally selects it. This is the essence of Boswell's social aberrancy, the "alienation" of the creative mind that I have located in the early novel's preoccupation with the individual subject. And because the self can become sufficient only by generating an external ground whose very existence must challenge the self's sufficiency, the disjunction between internals and externals, between the subject and its objective domain, seems in Boswell to become an absolute condition of existence.

Yet his rejection of the character of the man of consequence is also the occasion for a remark that has a crucial, and very different, significance for the prospect of Boswell's social self-fulfillment: "I now see the sickly suggestions of inconsistent fancy with regard to the Scotch bar in their proper colours. . . . I am vexed at such a distempered suggestion's being inserted in my journal, which I wished to contain a consistent picture of a young fellow eagerly pushing through life. But . . . let me consider that the hero of a romance or novel must not go uniformly along in bliss, but the story must be chequered with bad fortune. Aeneas met with many disasters in his voyage to Italy, and must not Boswell have his rubs?" (205–6). As his self-proclaimed "love of form" would suggest, Boswell's journal has been from the outset intensely self-conscious and reflexive in its procedure; but it is rather unusual for him to acknowledge, as he does here, that he has a serious investment in it not only as a process but also as a product. This admission is deepened in a contiguous passage, where Boswell makes a striking analogy between being a lawyer and being a writer. He remarks of recent weeks "that indeed I had laboured hard, but it had been in writing my journal, letters, and essays, which were all works chiefly of the imagination. But . . . I would find it very irksome to sit for hours hearing a heavy agent explain a heavy cause, and then to be obliged to remember and repeat the dull story, probably of some very trivial affair" (202). On the one hand, the law amounts to hearing and repeating trivial stories, a description that would apply equally to Boswell's journalizing were it not for the negative cast given to it. On the other hand, writing is, like the law, hard labor: a work of the imagination but still serious work.

The latter half of this analogy is especially significant. For Boswell's pleasure in his journal has always depended on its capacity to channel pure self—on its association with internals rather than externals, with the independent subject rather than the objective domain, with the authorship of the son rather than the authority of the father. Lord Auchinleck believed that his son's journal was "a register of his follies" (338), and toward the end of his London stay he cautioned him to "be more on your guard for the future against mimicry, journals, and publications" (342). By this time, Boswell had already published a few poems and letters, but the journal was far and away his most important literary project. And like Pamela, although for different reasons, he has until this stage of the journal been unwilling or unable to think of writing as a mode of labor, as a way of making his material living. We readers, with our knowledge of his later career, are able to see that Boswell's youthful *Aeneid* has been nothing other than the checkered making of the character of the Man of Letters. But Boswell himself does not clearly recognize it in this light, nor does he ever explicitly experiment, in the *London Journal,* with the character of a professional writer. Yet the experiment is made nonetheless, and with a delicacy of suggestion that is quite remarkable. I will summarize it under two headings.

Toward the middle of his journal, one of Boswell's longest entries undertakes to describe a typical day but soon becomes preoccupied with calculating annual expenses, a subject with which he is greatly satisfied. "The desire of being esteemed a clever economist was no doubt mixed up with it," he reflects, "but I seriously think that sheer love of coin was my predominant principle" (185). Boswell continues to ruminate on these matters. "I have observed in some preceding period of this my journal that making money is one of the greatest pleasures in life. . . . It is a good deal diverting to consider my present views. A young fellow of life and spirit, with an allowance extremely moderate, in so much that most people declare it must be wonderful management that can make it support a genteel appearance, yet is this fellow gravely laying down plans for making rich and being a man of wealth" (185–86). We sense here the expansive rhythms, the pleasingly speculative prospect of a "character" under construction, and in half a page our expectations are rewarded: "The character worthy of imitation is the man of economy, who with prudent attention knows when to save and when to spend, and acts accordingly. Let me pursue this system. . . . Let me lay out my money with ease and freedom, though with judgment and caution" (186).

Boswell's man of economy is a character calculated to satisfy his desire for the independence of public self-sufficiency. But at this familiar point in the progress of a character, something unexpected happens. Boswell reflexively shifts from the substantive to the formal register while continuing to pursue the themes of the former, and the result is a treatment of *literary* economy that self-consciously exemplifies what it is about: "Upon my word my journal goes charmingly on at present. I was very apprehensive that there would be a dreary vacancy in it for some weeks, but by various happy circumstances I have been agreeably disappointed. I think, too, that I am . . . writing it in a more correct style. Style is to sentiment what dress is to the person" (186). Boswell now gracefully elaborates the analogy. And then: "How easily and cleverly do I write just now! I really am pleased with myself; words come skipping to me like lambs upon Moffat Hill; and I turn my periods smoothly and imperceptibly like a skilful wheelwright turning tops in a turning-loom. There's fancy! There's simile! In short, I am at present a genius: in that does my opulence consist, and not in base metal" (187). The form of this final metaphor, its equation of literary and financial economy, subverts the distinction between them that is made on the level of content, and it underscores the achievement of the entire passage. With an extraordinary subtlety of indirection, Boswell has reconciled the disparity between internals and externals, between the autonomy of subjectivity and that of self-sufficiency, by insinuating that the pleasures and rewards of financial and literary management are profoundly analogous. The character of the man of economy is also, by an inescapable figurative extension, the character of the man of letters.

It cannot be mere coincidence that the entry in which this reconciliation is achieved immediately precedes Boswell's final entry on his ill-fated affair with the actress "Louisa," for this affair recapitulates in other terms the effort to overcome a related contradiction. From the beginning, Boswell's desire to enjoy Louisa's company had been frustrated by her human reality, by her unwillingness to sit still for the "character" he would impose upon her. But the problem is also the contradictory expectations of which his characterization of her is composed. Torn between love and sex, the spiritual and the bodily, euphemism and billingsgate, wife and whore, Boswell suffers a series of disturbing delays and humiliating reversals until, almost to our surprise, they enjoy a "voluptuous night" together (139). Boswell's immediate response is to complete the suspended self-portrait: "I have painted this night as well as I could. The description is faint; but I surely may be styled a Man of Pleasure" (140).

From this conscious artistry follow several unconscious corollaries. First, Boswell experiences a waning of passion, which he is content to interpret as a sign that his love for Louisa is "licentious," not "rational" (145), hence not conducing toward the permanence of marriage. Second, he soon detects in himself the symptoms of gonorrhea. Confident that "she could not have such a thing," Boswell nonetheless confronts Louisa with his condition, and when she denies being the source of the disease, he concludes that "she is in all probability a most consummate dissembling whore" (149, 160). The final evidence needed to confirm that Louisa is the kind of woman he has now decided she must be is monetary. Six weeks earlier, Boswell had been happy to lend Louisa some money to repay what he agreed was "a trifling debt" (97). His surgeon's bill now reminds him of the debt, and he writes to Louisa: "You cannot have forgot upon what footing I let you have it. I neither *paid* it for prostitution nor *gave* it in charity. If you are not rendered callous by a long course of disguised wickedness, I should think the consideration of your deceit and baseness, your corruption both of body and mind, would be a very severe punishment." He adds in his journal that "to such a creature as her a pecuniary punishment will give most pain" (175).

With these words Boswell successfully completes his simplifying recharacterization of Louisa as not wife but whore. Her reply a week later—"I opened it up and found my two guineas returned, without a single word written"—gives him momentary pause, and it is this entry that directly follows the character of the man of letters. "I felt a strange kind of mixed confusion," he remarks (187). Boswell's mixed confusion, the mirror inversion of his clarity on the double role of the man of letters, temporarily threatens his hard-won attainment of the role of man of pleasure because it complicates the unmixed character of Louisa, on which that role depends. But the conjunction of these two events also suggests that the mutilation of Louisa—and the crude type of the man of pleasure her mutilation facilitates—is instrumental in enabling Boswell to embrace the contradictory complexity of the man of letters. By projecting onto her the pecuniary vices of mere public self-sufficiency, he detoxifies the character of the man of economy enough to render it receptive to the private subjectivity of literary "genius." In Boswell's scenario, Louisa's final and predictable fulfillment of the traditional negative type of the professionalized subject—the duplicitous actress—is therefore inseparable from his own access to its innovative and positive alternative, the man of letters.

The second means by which Boswell entertains the view of himself as a professional writer is also exceedingly indirect. This is his relationship with Samuel Johnson, whom he meets three-quarters of the way through the journal. Johnson is now near the height of his renown, the most formidable and paradigmatic man of letters of his age. And for this reason, his famous advice to Boswell on keeping a journal helps reinforce the possibility of an internal integrity justly rewarded by external achievement: "He said indeed that I should keep it private.... There is nothing too little for so little a creature as man." "And now, O my journal!" writes Boswell, "Art thou not highly dignified?" (305).

But the real importance of the relationship with Johnson, at least in the *London Journal,* was not only that it provided Boswell with a pattern for identification but also that it offered, as in a family romance, an alternative genealogy. In fact, it is only the conjunction of these—the model character conjoined with the model plot—that gives to Boswell's autobiography its distinctively novelistic aura. Lord Auchinleck's distaste for his son's journal could not be further from Johnson's assessment. Yet Johnson also possessed an authority of social attainment and stature so antithetical to that of a Scots laird that it intimated a wholly alternative sort of paternal authority as well. When Boswell confides in him concerning his father, Johnson replies from the perspective of a father who has not forgotten what it was like to be a son: "Sir, a father and a son should part at a certain time of life. I never believed what my father said. I always thought that he spoke *ex officio,* as a priest does." When Boswell gives him an account of the family and the estate of Auchinleck, Johnson replies: "'I must be there, and we will live in the Old Castle; and if there is no room remaining, we will build one.' This was the most pleasing idea that I could possibly have," says Boswell, "to think of seeing this great man at the venerable seat of my ancestors" (331). And when Boswell asks, "if he was my father, and if I did well at the law, if he would be pleased with me," this is Johnson's reply: "Sir, ... I should be pleased with you whatever way of life you followed, since you are now in so good a way. Time will do all that is wanting" (326). Through such gentle encouragement, Johnson narrows the gulf between paternal patronage and self-determination. He enables Boswell to reconceive his inheritance—to reconcile his origins with his present state, his dependence with his independence, the man of consequence with the man of letters. It is therefore fitting that Boswell's status as man of letters should have been confirmed by the *Life of Johnson,* the last work with which I will be concerned.

III

At one point in the *Life,* Boswell records the following dinner-table remark by Johnson: "Why should the life of a literary man be less entertaining than the life of any other man? Are there not as interesting varieties in such a life? As *a literary life* it may be very entertaining."[12] The *Life of Johnson* is, of course, filled with details attesting to its status as a specifically *literary* life. But its extraordinary interest to us owes in large part to the way it captures, entirely by virtue of this special status, a general cultural type that the novel has been undertaking to represent for the better part of the century. In Boswell's *Life,* the human authority of the independent author becomes generalized to a fundamental condition of modern experience. In the process, Boswell turns some familiar conventions in new directions.

The outward shape of Johnson's life conformed closely to the pattern of one who, exemplifying the disjunction of externals and internals, lives to see his virtue rewarded. The son of a provincial bookseller, Johnson rose to a position of eminence in the metropolis, and Boswell's account of this rise lays heavy emphasis on Johnson's self-creation, on his personal responsibility for his own success as a man of letters. "No man who ever lived by literature," says Johnson at one point, "has lived more independently than I have done" (313). And as though to clarify this claim, he says at another: "No man but a blockhead ever wrote, except for money" (731)—that is, except for the public. The most celebrated evidence of Johnson's literary self-sufficiency is no doubt his deliciously patronizing refusal of Lord Chesterfield's belated offer of patronage: "Is not a Patron, my Lord, one who looks with unconcern on a man struggling for life in the water, and, when he has reached ground, encumbers him with help? . . . I hope it is no very cynical asperity not to confess obligations where no benefit has been received, or to be unwilling that the Publick should consider me as owing that to a Patron, which Providence has enabled me to do for myself" (185). Johnson's habits of composition and scholarship display his literary singularity in a compatible light. The sobriety and weight of his writings are belied, we learn from the *Life,* by the brilliance and impetuosity with which he dashes them off under the pressure of publication deadlines. And his remarkable learning is acquired not by diligent study, but, in Boswell's words, "by fits and starts, by violent irruptions into the regions of knowledge" (70) Thus, the expectation of the customary type of the private poet or the cloistered scholar is defied by the idiosyncratic individuality of the professional, and it is this experience of disjunction itself that comes to define the modern type of the man of letters.

But it is not only, or even primarily, in the field of letters that the basic pattern is established in the *Life of Johnson*. The very personage of Boswell's Johnson grows from the disparity between custom and individual, externals and internals, the squalor of circumstance and the sublimity of Mind. Boswell relates that when he first attended Johnson, "his apartment, and furniture, and morning dress, were sufficiently uncouth. His brown suit of cloaths looked very rusty; . . . his black worsted stockings [were] ill drawn up; and he had a pair of unbuckled shoes by way of slippers. But all these slovenly particularities were forgotten the moment he began to talk" (280–81). Bennet Langton, on first meeting Johnson, "was exceedingly surprised when the sage first appeared. . . . From perusing his writings, he fancied he should see a decent, well-drest, in short, a remarkably decorous philosopher. Instead of which, down from his bed-chamber about noon, came, as newly risen, a huge uncouth figure, with a little dark wig which scarcely covered his head, and his clothes hanging loose about him. But his conversation was so rich" (174).

Yet the true relationship between outward circumstance and inward mind is finally more complicated, in Johnson's case, than any simple antithesis between outward appearance and inward reality. Early on in the narrative, Boswell describes on several occasions and in close detail the grotesque bodily movements and gestures Johnson manifested for most of his life. According to Boswell, Sir Joshua Reynolds was convinced that such motions were not involuntary or convulsive: "My opinion is that [they] proceeded from a habit which he had indulged himself in, of accompanying his thoughts with certain untoward actions, and those actions always appeared to me as if they were meant to reprobate some part of his past conduct. Whenever he was not engaged in conversation, such thoughts were sure to rush into his mind; and, for this reason, any company, any employment whatever, he preferred to being alone. The great business of his life (he said) was to escape from himself; this disposition he considered as the disease of his mind, which nothing cured but company" (105–6).

By this account, Johnson's bodily quirks are a symptom not of mental sublimity but of mental anguish, a sign of the pain of being alone with himself. Johnson called these moments of solitude the "vacuities" of life, and he dreaded them as much as he dreaded anything. The creativity bred of solitude evident in Robinson Crusoe and Pamela has become hard to distinguish from the panic of solipsism. If solitude—the total disengagement from social dependence—is the precondition for modern authenticity (and it makes no difference if we are speaking now of the special type of the artist or the general type of the autonomous subject), it is also the state most to be feared. Reynolds's account throws into poignant relief the utter dependence of this self-sufficient, self-made man on the corroborative presence of others, a paradox captured by the crucial figure of speech "The business of his life was to escape from himself." For the modern type of the artist as man of letters is a contradiction held together by the fiction of an independence bred of the business of self-publication, a fiction whose effect is to constitute "the self" only in the act of disseminating it with the aid of a vast social network whose indispensability is expressly denied. In Reynolds's figure, the alienation of the artist converges with the alienation of the individual in commodity culture in the common and paradoxical experience of social activity that feels solitary.

Although the disparity between internals and externals remains an important feature of the modern type with which I have been concerned, Boswell's life of the writer also shows how fully that disparity has been internalized as a condition of mind. Throughout the *Life,* what Reynolds calls "the disease of his mind" preoccupies Johnson (and Boswell, on his own account) under the several alternative names available to eighteenth-century psychology: melancholy, hypochondria, the vapors, the English Malady, and so forth. Boswell adds: "I am aware that he himself was too ready to call such a complaint by the name of *madness*" (49). It would not be totally wrong, perhaps, for us to call this disease also by the name of "subjectivity," since it is only by constituting the self as a category unconditionally separable from its conditions that the problem of its internal self-alienation can become intelligible. Boswell's most famous figure for this modern psychomachia is the following: "His mind resembled the vast amphitheatre, the Colisaeum at Rome. In the centre stood his judgment, which, like a mighty gladiator, combated those apprehensions that, like the wild beasts of the *Arena,* were all around in cells, ready to be let out upon him. After a conflict, he drove them back into their dens; but not killing them, they were still assailing him" (427). The full internalization of the man of letters' contradictory state is the precondition for its self-consciously archaic externalization as heroic armed combat. The extremity of the figure owes in part to what occasioned it, one of Johnson's many declarations of his affecting but obsessive fear of death. Johnson's belief in an afterlife, although tortured, is not easily to be doubted. Nevertheless, it may be plausible to see in this obsessive fear of death an ambivalence of apprehension, the fear of damnation complicated by the fear of an absent afterlife—the fear that death is the ultimate and endless vacuity, an eternal condemnation to the company of one's own subjectivity.

The Samuel Johnson to whom I have thus been led is nothing if not "modern," and it may be wondered how this version of the man can be reconciled with the undeniable illiberalism of his well-known political, social, and religious opinions. The answer lies, I think, not far from the topic I have been treating, the fearsome specter of the subject unconstrained by external circumstance. I think Johnson's conservatism is really a very modern posture of provisional or suppositional belief in propositions not because they command implicit faith but because they have a certain pragmatic utility. For example, to the notion "that intrinsick merit *ought* to make the only distinction amongst mankind," Johnson replies: "Why, Sir, mankind have found that this cannot be. How shall we determine the proportion of intrinsick merit? Were that to be the only distinction amongst mankind, we should soon quarrel about the degrees of it. . . . There would be a perpetual struggle for precedence, were there no fixed invariable rules for the distinction of rank, which creates no jealousy, as it is allowed to be accidental" (312, 317). In matters of religion, Johnson based his preference for popery over Presbyterianism on the latter's lack of form and hierarchy, and he thought it dangerous to desert the faith in which one had been raised—as he puts it, "to choose a religion for yourself" (952). We can see in this expedient containment of the individual within the "rules" and "forms" of outward institutions something of the aesthetic attitude, as Johnson's metaphor in defense of social subordination implies: "I consider myself as acting a part in the great system of society. . . . I would behave to a nobleman as I should expect he would behave to me, were I a nobleman and he Sam. Johnson" (316). Thus, outward forms once implicitly effective in containing the anarchic force of the autonomous subject may be sustained, in the modern world, by a willing suspension of disbelief in them. They have become the instruments of a poetic justice—fictional, but nonetheless efficient for that. Johnson's conservatism is therefore a striking instance of the way the irreversible liberation of the subject from objective containment can paradoxically abet, through aesthetic detachment, the illusion of its continued subjugation.

IV

Let me end with a few words on a topic that could sustain many, the role of the author in the life of the writer. At the end of the *Life of Johnson*. Boswell acknowledges to readers the possibility that he may "have obtruded himself too much upon their attention" (1363). Although his authorial creativity is less obvious here than in the *London Journal,* no reader of the *Life* will deny a fairly continuous awareness of Boswell's presence—an effect that is intensified by, but does not depend on, his first-person participation in that life. In the present context, the most significant end of Boswell's obtrusive labors is the creation of reciprocal men of letters, Boswell and Johnson as mirror images. Episodes like the rebuke to Chesterfield owe their fame, of course, not to the intrinsic power of Johnson's letter (although it is very great), but to Boswell's artfully augmented presentation of it. In 1776, Boswell slyly manipulated Johnson into having dinner with a man whose principles he abhorred, the radical John Wilkes, and after its successful and peaceable conclusion, he is full of self-congratulation. But Johnson later reprimands him severely for this sort of behavior: "No man has a right to engage two people in a dispute by which their passions may be inflamed. . . . I would sooner keep company with a man from whom I must guard my pockets, than with a man who contrives to bring me into a dispute with somebody that he may hear it" (864)—and, we might add, that he may write it up.

Johnson's monetary figure is suggestive. The image of the biographer as pickpocket reminds us not only that Boswell aspired early on to the role of man of literary economy but also that if Boswell aims to become a man of letters through the artistic construction of Johnson as man of letters, the interests of the two cannot be expected to coincide always. Thus Boswell's "publication" of Johnson can sometimes recall the complex and suspect motives evident in Mr. B.'s "publication" of Pamela. And we may feel similar misgivings at the language of the "Advertisement to the Second Edition," where Johnson's fame seems a mechanical instrumentality of Boswell's: "I have been regaled with spontaneous praise of my work by many and various persons eminent for their rank, learning, talents and accomplishments. . . . An honourable and reverend friend speaking of the favourable reception of my volumes, even in the circles of fashion and elegance, said to me, 'you have made them all talk Johnson,'—Yes, I may add, I have *Johnsonised* the land; and I trust they will not only *talk,* but *think,* Johnson" (8).[13] At times like this, the alternative inheritance Johnson provides for Boswell in the *London Journal* seems to have been reduced, in the *Life,* to the status of a profitable literary property.

But on the other hand, the interests of the writer and the writer's author do not always conflict. Boswell the man of letters is not only the biographer of Johnson. He is also an extraordinarily various range of literary attitudes, an entire spectrum of receptive subjectivity whose presence registers a crucial response to the main object of our attention. If the biography is about Johnson, it must also be about him who perceives Johnson—at least for a culture that, like theirs and ours, has separated out the subjectivity of the perceiver. And in this respect, the reciprocity of writer and writer's author must be very close. This is perhaps only to repeat the modern truth that all biographies are in a sense also autobiographies, a truth that holds most of all for the writer's life, in which the story told is replicated at the level of form.

It is easy enough to maintain that the first great literary biography is the *Life of Johnson,* in part because of the fullness with which it vindicates this very truth. But I have also argued that the early novel anticipates the modern type of the writer because it intuits the writer's life as a cultural model for its own deepest concerns. And if we look toward the end of the eighteenth century for the *novel* that most explicitly fulfills this prefiguration once the type itself has obtained a cultural existence—if we look, that is, for the first great novel of the writer as hero—the obvious candidate is *Tristram Shandy,* a work that embraces so forcefully the self-creative autonomy of the subject that its story is nothing but its own abortive writing. The brilliant excess of Sterne's masterpiece may help explain what seems to me true of the modern history of the novel: that it is surprisingly deficient in great novels of the writer as hero. Not that they cannot be named; but the logic of my argument might have seemed to predict their imminent installation as a major subgenre of the nineteenth- and twentieth-century novel. Sterne's example, however, suggests that the liability of the novel of the writer as hero is precisely its redundancy, the supersaturated overdetermination of its central concerns. And it therefore may make sense that the novel should have announced its ties to the writer's life most insistently at its inception, through figurative evocations whose subtle efficacy is a matter of conjuring up, as a suggestive kindred presence, what had as yet no real historical substance.

But the example of *Tristram Shandy* is instructive in other ways as well, for it reminds us of alternative ways in which the concern of the genre with the problem of the subject comes to be overdetermined in its subsequent history. Tristram's inability to write his own story is a formal failure that recurs on the level of content through Sterne's complex satire of patrilineal inheritance. And this comprehensive concern with the failure of the line implies, fitfully but undeniably, a positive alternative model for organizing both narratives and families. Sterne's critique of linearity has an obvious relevance to his indulgence of sensibility. On the level of content, his new model of family cohesion substitutes for the traditional organizing principle of diachronic patrilineal inheritance the synchronic community of "originals," individual monads incapable of rational interaction but conjoined by the involuntary, accidental, and all-powerful force of sympathetic association. On the level of form, *Tristram Shandy* concentrates tendencies of continuing importance for both novelistic and biographical narrative: the replacement of a Theophrastan fixity of character type by a conception of character as continuous, extensive, and self-creative subjectivity (Boswell's *Journal* plays on the former to evoke a vision of the latter); the replacement of a preoccupation with the individual as a singular moment in the unraveling family lineage by a concern with the development of the individual "as such." It may be fair to say that the prefigurative project of the *Künstlerroman* is not so much sidetracked in the nineteenth century as taken over by the project of the *Bildungsroman.*

And what becomes of the problematically overdetermined figure of the novelistic heroine? The positive, even utopian, reading of Sterne's critique of patrilineage recalls a common interpretation of the cult of sensibility that is relevant to this final question. This is the view that sensibility depends on a fundamental and revolutionary inversion of gender roles whereby the passive and affective virtues traditionally attributed to women become normative also for men. Thus Uncle Toby, the representative man of feeling in *Tristram Shandy,* is explicitly accorded the modesty of a woman; and there is evidence to suggest that Sterne's championing of wit over judgment is figured also as a championing of "female" over "male" modes of knowledge. Indeed, within the ambit of sensibility, we can see the alienation of the writer as hero being reconceived in a modern direction: away from the Protestant model of industrious and worldly activity exemplified by Robinson Crusoe and Pamela and toward the sedentary retirement of the excessively sensitive "original" whose life model is the distinctively female condition.[14] Does the Age of Sensibility make good the merely strategic and self-interested alliance between progressive and protofeminist ideology evident in the Richardsonian apotheosis of "feminine virtue"?

Certainly, it is around now that the greatest explosion in the female authorship of novels begins, and the growing interest in novelistic "character development" (if not with the writer as hero) takes in female as much as male protagonists. Nevertheless, it seems mistaken to accord to this cultural episode and its implications a truly feminist impulse; once again, *Tristram Shandy* may help explain why. This is not to deny that the virtues we learn to recognize as normative in

Sterne's novel are also recognizably "female" virtues; it is rather to suggest that Sterne customarily reserves the right of their possession to men. However many likely literary exemplars we may be able to think of, it is no accident that the figure of the woman of feeling never attained the currency enjoyed by the category the man of feeling, which was quickly borrowed from the title of Henry Mackenzie's 1771 novel to name a veritable social type not unrelated to that of the man of letters. *Tristram Shandy* does not, like *Pamela,* discredit the male line by relocating value in the female mediator; it dispenses with mediation altogether and watches the men fend for themselves. Women recede into the background in Sterne's novel because it is an experiment in filling the vacuum created by the crisis in patrilineal authority without having recourse to the powerful model of autonomous female virtue that Richardson did so much to solidify. The real historical significance of the man of feeling is less that it augments the feminization of virtue than that it reclaims a recognizably female virtue as a distinctively male possession. Progressive ideology had exploited the idea of female virtue to its own ends by establishing the gender traits of the progressive heroine as an intersexual norm. The man of feeling improves on this dispensation by celebrating the feminized hero, who reincorporates the normative gender traits within what a patriarchal culture will persist in seeing as the normative sex.

Notes

1. Samuel Richardson, *Pamela: or, Virtue Rewarded,* ed. T. C. Duncan Eaves and Ben D. Kimpel (Boston, Mass.: Houghton Mifflin, 1971), 114. All further citations will be to this edition and will appear in the text. My treatment of *Pamela* and *Robinson Crusoe* in this essay is based on the fuller readings given in *The Origins of the English Novel, 1600–1740* (Baltimore, Md.: The Johns Hopkins University Press, 1987).

2. Daniel Defoe, *Robinson Crusoe,* ed. J. Donald Crowley (New York: Oxford University Press, 1981), 176. All further citations will be to this edition and will appear in the text.

3. "Postscript" to *Clarissa* (4th ed., 1751), 7:350–51, in Samuel Richardson, *Clarissa: Preface, Hints of Prefaces, and Postscript,* ed. R. F. Brissenden, Augustan Reprint Society, no. 103 (1964).

4. The terms are those of Alvin Kernan, who discusses the relationship between the commodification of the book trade, print technology, individual authorship, and other matters in *Samuel Johnson and the Impact of Print* (Princeton, N.J.: Princeton University Press, 1987), chap. 2 and passim.

5. *The Unlucky Citizen Experimentally Described in the Various Misfortunes Of an Unlucky Londoner . . .* (1673), 181–82.

6. The phrase "The Hero as Man of Letters" is Thomas Carlyle's: see *On Heroes, Hero-Worship and the Heroic in History* (1841). On the social dimensions of the type of the man of letters see Jerome Christensen, *Practicing Enlightenment: Hume and the Formation of a Literary Career* (Madison: University of Wisconsin Press, 1987). For an important discussion of this general subject, see also Robert Folkenflik, "The Artist As Hero in the Eighteenth Century," *Yearbook of English Studies* 12 (1982): 91–108.

7. On the historical circumstances underlying this effort, see *The Origins of the English Novel,* 156–58, 255–56.

8. For an instance of this double ambivalence, see Anne Bradstreet, "The Author to Her Book" (1666).

9. On the former, see John Mullan, "Hypochondria and Hysteria: Sensibility and the Physicians," *The Eighteenth Century* 25, no. 2 (1984): 153. On the latter, see *The Origins of the English Novel,* 205.

10. On Mary Carleton, see *The Origins of the English Novel,* 99–100, 241–44.

11. James Boswell, *Boswell's London Journal, 1762–1763,* ed. Frederick A. Pottle (New York: McGraw-Hill, 1950), 41. Further citations will be to this edition and will appear in the text.

12. James Boswell, *Life of Johnson,* ed. R. W. Chapman, rev. 3rd ed. (New York: Oxford University Press, 1980), 1141. All further citations will be to this edition and will appear in the text.

13. For related thoughts on this particular passage and on the larger concerns of this essay, see William H. Epstein, *Recognizing Biography* (Philadelphia: University of Pennsylvania Press, 1987), 90–137, especially 96, 108.

14. See Mullan, "Hypochondria and Hysteria," 146–51. Johnson's susceptibility to melancholy is therefore culturally consistent with the extraordinary sympathy women like Hester Thrale and Fanny Burney, no less than men like Boswell, felt to emanate from him.

Gordon Turnbull

Boswell and the Insistence of the Letter

Boswell's *Ebauche de ma vie* (5 December 1764), the carefully drafted and much revised "sketch" of his early life written to introduce himself to Rousseau, constitutes his first significant retrospective autobiographical self-appraisal, and the implied narrative of the *Ebauche,* this essay will argue, concerns the impact of implied narrative itself on the structure of Boswell's consciousness—its formation, its education.[1] The anxieties and distresses that compel Boswell to seek out Rousseau's analysis—some comical, some so severe they produced fleeting thoughts of self-castration and suicide—lead him to summarize himself as "an extraordinary example of the effects of a bad education."[2] Boswell's account of his "bad education" focuses on a sequence of preceptor figures of varying abilities and inadequacies in formative narrative positions (a sequence Rousseau is here being implicitly asked to join, i.e., to repeat, revise, and perhaps supplant) and moves to a detailed but guarded summary of an affair with a young married woman whom F. A. Pottle has identified as Jean Heron, daughter of the Scots jurist and author Henry Home, Lord Kames. That tale of sexual transgression, I suggest, registers the traces of his earliest encounters with the idea of narrative and its creation of gender-oriented desire, points ahead to much that is characteristic of Boswell's later illicit sexual conduct, and suggests some of the psychosexual forces behind his eventual emergence as the biographer of Johnson. The earliest and most radically formative of those early preceptor figures was his mother, the sensitive, pious, Calvinistic Euphemia (Erskine) Boswell, Lady Auchinleck. Much in Boswell's subsequent adolescent and adult behavior as it appears in his self-record discloses what the structuralist psychoanalysis of Jacques Lacan would see as the consequences of Boswell's acquisition of language, his earliest textual inscriptions. We find in the adolescent and adult Boswell a psychosexual repression of the mother as agency of cultural transmission and her incomplete erasure in favor of the authority of the father. The same paradigm informs the larger structure of Boswell's psychological and hence authorial career.

Boswell wrote confessionally and autobiographically all of the time, compulsively reinaugurating the textual narrative of himself, and the private diaries, letters, and legal papers out of which Boswell quarried at least in part his public biographies (of Paoli and Johnson) mark a continuing engagement with his own psychosocial points of origin. The conversion of himself into text in his diaries replicates the process of his earliest formations *by* textual structures. The *Ebauche* implies that textual narrative itself constitutes his most critical point of characterological origin. At important self-reflective moments in his later writings, Boswell himself will openly conceive of mind as a written thing. In a partly playful but frequently quoted remark on his own habit of journal keeping, his very life seems subordinated to the purpose of turning it into text: "I am fallen sadly behind in my journal. I should live no more than I can record, as one should not have more corn growing than one can get in. There is a waste of good if it be not preserved."[3] More explicitly, in an essay on the subject of diaries late in his series as "The Hypochondriack," the subject of diaries is precisely the letterlike quality of consciousness: "I have regretted that there is no invention for getting an immediate and exact transcript of the mind, like that instrument by which a copy of a letter is at once taken off".[4]

"The ancient philosopher certainly gave a wise counsel when he said, 'Know thyself.'"[5] Boswell opens his now-famous *London Journal 1762–1763* with some very old news from the Delphic oracle; he opens, thus, a quest for autobiographical originality with what is in fact the oldest of Western maxims, with the idea of language as both permanent inscription and prior to character. A flourish of autobiographical self-renewal, then, testifies to the power and force of prior inscription. And in the figure of the ancient oracle—a figure of language as lapidary, oracular, permanent—we find hints of some central Boswellian concerns, concerns that would lead him emotionally away from a career in law (everywhere a society's chief repository of culturally deployed written precedent) and into a career as biographer of the thunderously aphoristic Johnson, the first Boswellian records of whose lapidary discourse will appear, of course, in the later passages of the journal thus inaugurated.

"The unconscious is structured like a language," says Lacan in *his* most lapidary, or most frequently quoted and delphically oracular proposition.[6] Later he writes: "[W]hat the psychoanalytic experience discovers in the unconscious is the whole structure of language."[7] Fundamentally, Lacan's work and its subsequent applications have shifted the focus from the Freudian role of event in early experience to the question of what language has carried with it, culturally and ideologically, in its first acquisitions. In Lacan's much-discussed mirror stage, the Lacanian subject enters the Symbolic from the Imaginary, an entry linked to the acquisition of language and into a differential relation presided over by the law of the father. Feminist commentators on Lacan have stressed his contention that entry into language constitutes also entry into gender-oriented desire. According to Lacan, the child imagines itself to be the desire of the mother (a double genitive), but with the initiation of the child into the order of language, as Elizabeth Wright puts it, "the structures of language are marked with societal imperatives—the Father's rules, laws and definitions."[8] In Gregory Jay's useful gloss, when "Lacan rereads the Oedipal complex in terms of the Father's No and Name, he changes the sense of the transference, since now the relation to the father is seen in terms of the subject's assumption of a position in respect to the Symbolic order presided over by the discourse of the Father. It is the *desire* of the Father towards which the subject must be oriented, and which the subject incorporates through the socialization process."[9] In the Lacanian subject, there is an "unconscious conceptual grammar."[10] As Robert Con Davis explains, the Lacanian unconscious is "unconscious in the same way speakers are unconscious of grammar."[11]

Boswell accounts for himself, in his autobiographical memorial reconstruction of his psychic history, as formed by education, and claims: "I can recall the whole development of my existence since I was able to think" (1). Notably, as mentioned, the earliest major figure of narrative and thus conceptual formation is his mother. In a typical Lacanian paradigm, the relationship of the father to the family triad is one of authority and absence, and the father's voice enters via the mother's as law and prohibition. The young Boswell, he now confesses to Rousseau, was adept at working out ways to compensate for loss and separation by attracting his mother's attention during illnesses and consequently worked out ways of bringing on symptoms. Nonetheless it is surprising, Boswell writes, "that I did not often say that I was ill when I was actually well"—for before this time there had been paternal prohibition: "[M]y worthy father had impressed upon me a respect for the truth which has always remained firm in my mind" (2).

It seems at first in the *Ebauche* as though the mother is the law, not merely its agency, in the form of conventionally strict Scots Presbyterian piety:

> My mother was extremely pious. She inspired me with devotion. But unfortunately she taught me Calvinism. My catechism contained the gloomiest doctrines of that system. The eternity of punishment was the first great idea I ever formed. How it made me shudder! ...
>
> My mother was of that sect which believes that to be saved, each individual must experience a strong conversion. She therefore entreated me often to yield to the operations of Divine Grace; and she put in my hands a little book in which I read of the conversions of very young children. (2)

His father has "impressed" upon his mind, says Boswell, already a respect for truth; Boswell's *Ebauche,* and his later diaries, will therefore be candid. Boswell cannot hide from Rousseau what he calls his follies and crimes—presenting them for analysis to Rousseau, a new father who will forgive him (via the knowledge made possible by Enlightenment interrogations of feeling and sentiment), unlike the Calvinist God, whose fixed decrees send sinners into an eternity of hell. The image of eternal punishment was impressed upon Boswell's mind by his mother, acting as agency for the absent father, of whose absence we hear later in the *Ebauche:* "My father, who is one of the ablest and worthiest men in the world, was very busy and could not take much immediate care of my education" (3). Lord Auchinleck was, of course, busy at the law, agent of the religio-legist authority of Presbyterian Edinburgh, and thus a secular representative of the Calvinist divinity. Before the unseen Calvinist God, one has no choice of identity or character, as it is already preinscribed: to the "operations" of his grace one must simply "yield." Lord Auchinleck, who sits as a judge in the Scottish law courts, sends malefactors to irrevocable doom. Narrative comes to the young Boswell from his mother, yet she voices the father's laws and proscriptions (both secular father and divine). The mother, who comforted the boy in his illnesses, is also the bearer of his first feelings of terror, a terror of paternalistic retributive punishments.

Calvinism's text, moreover, is that agency of inscription and repetition, the catechism, through which a psychoreligious education textures the young mind through a repetitive impression of the letter of divine law. The young Boswell knows the divine law only through repetitive verbalization: from the age of eight to twelve, reports Boswell, he was happy, except on Sundays, "when I was made to remember the terrible Being whom those about me called God." He continues: "I was taken to Church, where I was obliged to hear three sermons in the same day, with a great many impromptu prayers and a great many sung psalms, all rendered in a stern and doleful manner. In the evening I was made to say my catechism and to repeat psalms translated into the vilest doggerel" (3).

For the young Boswell, the first moments of experiencing narrative bring simultaneous pleasure and terror—his mother's comforts and her education of his mind into a fear of hell. (Lower down the social scale, in a way suggestive of the young Brontës in Haworth parsonage in the next century, Boswell finds the pattern repeated at the level of Scots folkloric superstitions: "The servants diverted me with an infinity of stories about robbers, murderers, witches, and ghosts, so that my imagination was continually in a state of terror.") Maternal narrative has carried with it a deeper insistent grammar, the pleasure of feminine comfort along with the prohibitions of the (absent) father. The mother is as Jacqueline Rose summarizes "woman" in Lacan: "[A]s negative to the man, woman [is] elevated into the place of the Other and made to stand for its truth. [The] place of the Other is also the place of God. . . . [T]he woman becomes the support of [God's] symbolic place."[12] Held in imprisonment by the insistent letter of Scots Presbyterian law—the repeated doggerel psalms, the catechism, texturing his mind with punitive narrative—Boswell marks the result precisely as the disappearance of his freedom to be and to choose: "I was obliged by my religion 'not to do my own work, speak my own words, nor think my own thoughts on God's holy day.'" (The internal quotation marks are Boswell's, a sign of Boswell's point that he is marked by quotation.) "I tried," he continues, "in sincerity of heart to conform to that command; especially not to think my own thoughts. A fine exercise for a child's mind!" (3).

From his mother, he learns of a narrative of decisive and definitive peripeteia—conversion—and that the failure to achieve it results in eternal damnation, the permanent conversion of consciousness into torment. The child's desire for restorative identification with the mother's body (comforting in illness) is marked at the same time with a fear of punishment (by the father if he does not tell the truth, by God if he does not achieve conversion). The mother's discourse contains the twin emotions of the sublime, pleasure and fear, and of Aristotelian tragic katharsis, pity and terror—all of which underpin also the Christian master narrative of the Fall of Man. From those other narrative agencies in Lord Auchinleck's household, the servants, Boswell heard tales of similar perils: criminals in the sight of the law and of God ("robbers" and "murderers") and agencies of radical conversion—fairytale conversion, not religious conversion ("witches" and "ghosts")—all perils because they are agencies of loss, threats to deprive the mind of consciousness of itself, like the Presbyterian command to the child not to think its own thoughts.

Changes for the better in Boswell's boyhood, however, came between the ages of eight and twelve with the arrival of his tutor, the Reverend John Dun, the first important substitute parent in what over the course of Boswell's erratic life would be a long sequence (a sequence which, plainly, Rousseau is here being asked to join). Dun provided a more benign reformation of Boswell's mind. Not a severe Presbyterian with roots in the more ancient Scots pieties and superstitions, Dun (prefiguring Rousseau) has the Enlightenment virtues of "sentiment and sensibility."

> He began to form my mind in a manner that delighted me. He set me to reading *The Spectator;* and it was then that I acquired my first notions of taste for the fine arts and of the pleasure there is in considering the variety of human nature. I read the Roman poets, and I felt a classic enthusiasm in the romantic shades of our family's seat in the country. My governor sometimes spoke to me of religion, but in a simple and pleasing way. He told me that if I behaved well during my life, I should be happy in the other world. There I should hear beautiful music. There I should acquire the sublime knowledge that God will grant to the righteous; and there I should meet all the great men of whom I have read, and all the dear friends I had known. (2–3)

With this more genial preceptor, there enters sentiment and sensibility, a feminized father, a religious educator who gives Boswell religion without the terror, a narrative not of unattainable conversion but of justice and achievable reward. The language in which Dun speaks carries a different structure and a different grammar; the amiable Mr. Spectator (absent, in London) of Addison and Steele supplants the potency of the Whig, Lowland, Presbyterian authority of the absent Lord Auchinleck in Edinburgh's institutions of law and opens Boswell's mind to the fine arts, to taste, and to the attractions of London over what he would always condemn as narrow Scots provinciality. Textual encounters—reading of great men—now have eternal recompense: Boswellian heaven (it will not surprise anyone familiar with his later life) is an assembly of all the great men of whom he has read. Sublime emotions here involve no fear or terror but rather constitute a reward to the righteous. This heaven is an eternity of languid repose (like his pleasurable youthful illnesses), but it contains, importantly, (more on which below) no *female* source of terror or agency of guilt.

Here, then, was a pleasanter conversion narrative. The Reverend John Dun, voice of a benign divine order and of a benign parental order (the father's law but with the mother's comfort), provides a good education that supplants the bad. (Dun's virtues show up clearly against the description of his successor, Joseph Fergusson, who took over Boswell's education at the age of twelve when Dun was appointed minister of a parish. Fergusson marks a return to insistent repetition and is himself a figure of internalized inscription: "He had gone through the usual course of school and college. He had learned his lessons well, and all he had learned he had made part of himself." He is, consequently, a "dogmatist" who "felt and acted according to system" [3]). Dun had opened up a possible heaven to replace hell as the great idea. But this heaven is, of course, a boyhood heaven, full of music and admired great men—that is to say, without sexuality.

After a nervous collapse and recovery at Moffat, the Scottish spa, Boswell was sent to the university. With adolescence came sexual awareness—inevitably, because of his early maternal education, accompanied by religious terror. His "youthful desires," he tells Rousseau, "became strong," and "I was horrified because of the fear that I would sin and be damned. It came into my troubled mind that I ought to follow the example of Origen. But that madness passed." That madness passed so effectively indeed that, after a series of youthful experimentations with different religious and psychological systems—Methodism, Pythagoreanism, vegetarianism, then, at eighteen, Catholicism—which also passed, Boswell ran away to London, turned deist and eventually a "complete sceptic." By the time his father (now actively involved in his education and trying to force him into a career in the law) carried him back to Scotland, "I gave myself up to pleasure without limit. I was in a delirium of joy" (4–5).

Inevitably, sexual activity could not remain merely a delirium of joy. The legacies of his early initiations into pleasure and danger, comfort and prohibition, fear and guilt would of necessity appear. In the most detailed of the narratives with which he provides Rousseau to illustrate his newly dissolute life, Boswell tells the story of his adulterous affair with Jean Heron, daughter of the Scots jurist and literary theorist Henry Home, Lord Kames, and in the process provides the first of what in Boswell's later journals will be many accounts of his sexual life, in which woman figures as a source of both pleasure and danger, source of sexual adventures both thrilling and guilt-ridden.

> I was in love with the daughter of a man of the first distinction in Scotland.[13] She married a gentleman of great wealth. She let me see that she loved me more than she did her husband. She made no difficulty of granting me all. She was a subtle philosopher. She said, "I love my husband as a husband, and you as a lover, each in his own sphere. I perform for him all the duties of a good wife. With you I give myself up to

delicious pleasures. We keep our secret. Nature has so made me that I shall never bear children. No one suffers because of our loves. My conscience does not reproach me, and I am sure that God cannot be offended by them." (5)

Feminine discourse is again appealing: "Philosophy of that sort in the mouth of a charming woman," says Boswell, "seemed very attractive to me." This narrative offers a sexually seductive conversion and offers comfort in the form of a God (more benign than even the pleasant superintendent of the Reverend John Dun's musical and masculine heaven) who forgives sexual sin—a God not separable from individual conscience. This conversion, more comforting than the early maternal stories of Calvinistic conversion, is in important ways successful: "Sometimes even in my very transports I imagined that heaven could not but smile on so great a happiness between two mortals." But the structure of paternal prohibition soon enough emerges in Boswell's account, which plainly implies Boswell's sense of his crime as a crime against the patriarchal institutions of husband and father:

> But her father had heaped kindnesses on me. Her husband was one of the most amiable of men. He insisted that I mak extended visits at his seat in the country. I was seized with the bitterest remorse. I was unhappy. I was almost in despair, and often wished to confess everything to Mr. ———, so as to induce him to deprive my of my wretched life. But that would have been madness of the most fatal sort. (5)

The Boswell whose emergence into adolescence brought with it an Origen-like desire to emasculate himself would here, in a fleeting remorseful moment, confess his masculine guilt to Patrick Heron, to have himself killed. His very masculinity seems to him guilty. His response instead is to open his heart to Mrs. Heron, who was "affectionate and generous" but "reproached me for my weakness." Boswell continued his "criminal amour," and "the pleasures I tasted formed a counterpoise to my remorse." In a replication of maternal discourse, Mrs. Heron provides both comfort and moral reproach, but in inverted emphases. Paternal prohibition appears as Boswell's conscience, the father's law fully internalized, and the guilt with which his pleasures are counterpoised comes from a sense of crimes against husband and father. Boswell departs for London again, "glad to escape from Mrs. ———'s vicinity," to reinaugurate himself in his *London Journal* (in the way quoted above), and to realign himself with the most satisfactory of the later candidates for replacement of his father's prohibitive authority, Samuel Johnson. Boswell tells Rousseau, "I made the acquaintance of a famous scholar," who "proved to me the truth of the Christian religion" (5).

The point at which Boswell ends his *Ebauche* for Rousseau leaves him poised before the major directions his later life would follow—the legal career into which his father's desire would press him, a deepening acquaintance with Samuel Johnson (the more enduring substitute father, who would eventually supplant all other paternal candidates, including Rousseau), and a furtively libertinistic life in which his sexual partners would appear recurrently as both agents of comfort and sources of fear and guilt. The almost willfully self-punitive seeking out of venereal infection from daughters of the fallen Eve, recorded in the private diaries, will be counterpoised psychologically in Boswell's public authorial career by the Johnsonian biographies. Boswell's final inscription into permanence and immortality of Johnson's lapidary pronouncements resurrects the authority of the paternal word and represents a lifelong exertion to conquer feminine narrative, or the Word as sexually marked and thus (for the guilt-stricken libertine) seductive, corrupting, both pleasurable and a gateway to hell.

Notes

Boswell's papers are quoted with the kind permission of Edinburgh University Press and Yale University.

1. Boswell Papers, L1107. The papers preserved show Boswell working with great care through several outlines and earlier drafts. F. A. Pottle begins his *James Boswell: The Earlier Years 1740–1769* (New York: McGraw-Hill, 1966, repr. 1985) with his translation of Boswell's final draft of the *Ebauche* (see 1–6 and 449n). For the reader's convenience, I quote from the *Ebauche* in Pottle's translation in this essay.

2. Boswell's confessional summary, needless to say, bears sufficient resemblance to the modern psychoanalytic patient's report to an analyst to justify, if nothing else did, the use of psychoanalytic approaches to his life and writings. "Vous voyez un homme. Vous l'annalyserez. Vous le connoissez parfaitement," wrote Boswell in his first draft (Boswell Papers L1104).

Juliet Flower MacCannell points to the kind of connection this essay implies with the observation that for "Lacan, as for Rousseau, human experience is structured by the culture into which it is born far more than it is by the primary relation to . . . 'Nature' or the 'mother.'" See MacCannell, *Figuring Lacan: Criticism and the Cultural Unconscious* (Lincoln: University of Nebraska Press, 1986), 79. My account of Boswell and his mother emphasizes her role as a vehicle or agency of the culture of Scots Presbyterianism.

3. 17 March 1776. *Boswell: The Ominous Years, 1774–1776,* ed. Charles Ryskamp and F. A. Pottle (New York: McGraw-Hill, 1963), 265.

4. Hypochondriack no. 66, "On Diaries," March 1783. See *The Hypochondriack,* ed Margery Bailey, 2 vols. (Stanford, Calif.: Stanford University Press, 1928), 2:259.

5. *Boswell's London Journal 1762–1763,* ed. F. A. Pottle (New York: McGraw-Hill, 1950), 39.

6. Jacques Lacan, "The Unconscious and Repetition," *The Four Fundamental Concepts of Psycho-Analysis,* ed. Jacques-Alain Miller, trans. Alan Sheridan (New York, Norton, 1981), 20.

7. Lacan, *Ecrits: A Selection,* trans. Alan Sheridan (New York, Norton, 1977), 147.

8. Elizabeth Wright, *Psychoanalytic Criticism: Theory in Practice* (London and New York: Methuen, 1984), 109.

9. Gregory S. Jay, "The Subject of Pedagogy: Lessons in Psychoanalysis and Politics," *College English* 49, no. 7 (Nov. 1987): 787.

10. Jay, 789.

11. Robert Con Davis, "Pedagogy, Lacan, and the Freudian Subject," *College English* 49, no. 7 (Nov. 1987): 752.

12. *Feminine Sexuality: Jacques Lacan and the école freudienne,* ed. Juliet Mitchell and Jacqueline Rose, trans. Jacqueline Rose (New York: Norton, 1985), 50.

13. Boswell does not name the parties. For Pottle's establishment of their identities, see *Earlier Years,* 77-79.

Jerome Christensen

Ecce Homo

Biographical Acknowledgment,
the End of the French Revolution, and the
Romantic Reinvention of English Verse

Oedipus' answer to the Sphinx's riddle: "It is a man!" is the Enlightenment stereotype
repeatedly offered as information, irrespective of whether it is faced with a piece of
objective intelligence, a bare schematization, fear of evil powers, or hope of
redemption.
    —Max Horkheimer and Theodor Adorno, *The Dialectic of Enlightenment*

The old fascination with biography, given new impetus by an autobiographical com-
*placency (*Ecce Homo *underwriting Nietzsche's "madness"), and the old mechanism*
of exemplarity that was naively thought to be inoperative and out of use like the old
myths, continue to function. The desire for "figurality" has never been more powerful
or more constraining, thus forcing us—and this is the least of its consequences—to
return once more to philosophy and to its history, to the "score" and scansion imposed
upon it by those who thought they had passed beyond . . . the limits of the historical
and systematic field in which the subject held authority.
    —Philippe Lacoue-Labarthe, "The Echo of the Subject"

The Biography of the (Counter)Revolution

François Furet could venture to announce "the Revolution is over" by
virtue of his adoption of what he calls a "conceptual" relation to the
relevant historical materials, enabling him to break with those histo-
riographic practices that reproduce the experience of the French Revolution by rendering it as a spectacle that solicits political identification,
left or right. By rehabilitating the historiography of Alexis de Tocque-
ville and Auguste Cochin, Furet constructed a two-track interpretive
model that situated the French Revolution within a continuous political

development while giving full credit to its explosive character—the latter interpreted as the consequence of Rousseau's invention of a democratic ideology that invested sovereignty and power in the undivided will of the "people." Furet elaborated Cochin's view that the "people" was a mental representation of power generated by the discourse of philosophical societies that became political agents as they vied for the right to speak in its name.[1] From the "advent" of the Revolution, it was kept in continual agitation by real and supposed aristocratic threats and propelled by rivalry among factions for the "right to be the image of the people" (Furet, 74). Robespierre won the competition and, as "the final incarnation of that mythical identity," suffered his scripted fate by becoming "the scapegoat of the guillotine" (Furet, 57). This sacrificial embodiment of the people consummated the volatile revolutionary fusion of "political power and civil society." Thus, according to Furet, the Revolution was over.

Furet's "'story' of the Revolution," his account of it as "a specific dynamic of collective action," stands in relation to the account of the "historical process," the "set of causes and effects" in which the Revolution occurs, much as the practice of biography, which focuses on the contingent life course of an individual agent, stands in relation to a historiography that "sees the past as a field of possibilities within which 'what actually happened' appears *ex post facto* as the only future for that past" (Furet, 18-19). Furet's brilliant twist is to identify this latter "historical consciousness" *as* "revolutionary consciousness," a move that allows him to tell the story of the Revolution as the collective subordination of manifold, contingent individual life courses to the idea of an inevitable historical event, which is imagined as a massive effect that answers to a single, overpowering cause. We may conclude, then, that the biography of the Revolution is the story of the supersession of biography by typology—which is one way of explaining why it has always appeared so short-lived. Extending Furet, we might suppose that the end of the Revolution, considered not as a conceptual break occurring within the terrain of French historiography but as a moment of change executed by Englishmen whose history had been bound up with the course of the Revolution, might begin with the renewal of biography.

Furet's claim that the Revolution is over had its harbingers—most famously Napoleon Bonaparte, who repeatedly proclaimed the end of the Revolution. Earlier yet, however, there was Samuel Taylor Coleridge, writing to William Wordsworth on the eve of the Brumaire coup d'état: "I wish you would write a poem in blank verse, addressed to those who, in consequence of the complete failure of the French Revolution, have thrown up all hopes of the amelioration of mankind, and are sinking into an almost epicurean selfishness."[2] Coleridge's notion of a break with revolutionary discourse has, I shall argue, as much to do with Wordsworth's blank verse as with his elevating theme. For him, that is, the end of the Revolution will occur not only at the level of the concept but, more immediately, at the level of form—form radicalized to its elemental, sensuous insistence. To explain what he had in mind, Coleridge required, as we do, a biographical inventiveness; as we shall see, the vindication of romantic hope demanded that the spectacular appearance of revolutionary man be answered by the imagination of a new poetical character.

If Coleridge can be said to anticipate the concerns of Furet, Coleridge's own sense of biographical possibility was formed in response to the fierce precedent of Edmund Burke, who transformed both the English grammar for the formation of political statements and the code for recognizing a "new description of men."[3] Cochin's interpretation of the Revolution is embryonic in Burke's remarkable observation of September 1789 that

> it does not appear to me, that the National assembly have one Jot more power than the King; whilst they lead or follow the popular voice . . . ; I very much question, whether they are in a condition to exercise any function of decided authority—or even whether they are possessed of any real deliberative capacity . . . ; as [long as] there is a Mob of their constituents ready to Hang them if They should . . . in the least depart from the Spirit of those they represent.[4]

Not only the concepts that drive the Revolution but its whole life story is immediately visible to Burke's speculative eye. From the outset, he sees Rousseau's theory being enacted: he sees the emptying of the sphere of power; he sees the ignition of the engine of the "popular voice." And, earlier than Robespierre, he foresees the Revolution's destiny. "All these things have happend [*sic*] out of the ordinary Course of speculations," he writes. "One man may change all. But when and where and how is this man to appear" (*CEB,* 6:37). Burke's forecast of the return from the extraordinary to the ordinary through the agency of the coming man who will redeem the time is the first sounding of the "Ecce Homo" theme in English revolutionary discourse.

Burke could visualize the shape of the Revolution because he figured it as theatre. August 1789: "As to us here our thoughts of everything at home are suspended, by our astonishment at the wonderful Spectacle which is exhibited in a Neighbouring and rival Country—what Spectators, and what Actors! England gazing with astonishment at a French struggle for Liberty and not knowing whether to blame or to applaud!" *CEB,* 6:10). The sublime suspension of the English spectators' thought matches the interdiction of deliberation in the revolutionized National Assembly.[5] Each attests to the crucial revolutionary proscription of *thinking* in favor of *speaking*. The spectators' astonishment will, of course, soon be followed by "reflections." But reflection is not exactly *thinking;* it is not the kind of deliberation that goes on among duly elected representatives in Parliament, for example. Reflecting is the strategic equivalent of parliamentary deliberation; it is an imitation of thinking, generated by and answerable to the spectacle of the Revolution. For Burke the reflections of the spectator presuppose his leap across the footlights to become an actor himself.[6] If, as Furet writes, the "logic of revolutionary consciousness . . . by its very nature, tends to promote a Manichean explanation and to personify social phenomena," it is because the revolutionary "illusion of politics" is in truth a theatrical state, where all—actors and spectators—must speak and, speaking, struggle (Furet, 20, 26).

Rousseau is acclaimed by his ideological children as the father of the Revolution. Burke could legitimately claim authorship of the counterrevolution. Burke countered the Revolution's obliteration of the partition between the political and the social with a project equally totalizing. "The grounds upon which [he] went," Burke affirmed, were "the necessity of which this time imposed upon all men, of putting an end to differences of all sorts" (*CEB,* 7:312). The first step Burke took toward ending "differences of all sorts" was to condense differences into an antithesis of *one* sort, pro- or anti-Jacobin; the second, to personify difference as a general threat to an individual and national integrity that must be protected at all costs. Burke's strategic ambition entailed both the supersession of party politics in a counterrevolutionary coalition—which Burke engineered—and the dissolution of the partitions between theatre and world, the seat of government and seat of retirement—which he fantasized. "Foreign Politics," he claims, "are foreign only in name; for they are not only connected with our domestic Politics, but the domestic politics are actually included in them" (*CEB,* 7:305). The coalition that Burke formed with Pitt marks the invention of a new, incipiently totalitarian politics, christened "anti-Jacobin"—but one which, as Coleridge will argue, is anti-Jacobin only in name, for Jacobinism is not only connected with anti-Jacobinism but is actually included in it.

Burke and Robespierre were equally obsessed with the destruction of the "privileged *corps* of the Ancien Régime" (Furet, 50). Robespierre adopted the guillotine as the executive instrument of an animus against the many bodies of aristocrats, each thinking only of its own interest. Burke just as furiously denounced all challenges to the privileges of ancient corporations. John Brewer has demonstrated, however, that Burke's quasi-feudal model had little actual pertinence to Great Britain, where the administrative monarchy that was the future of postrevolutionary France was already in place and progressively undermining privilege by the steady expansion of a fine-grained network of financial and social regulations.[7] The supposed menace to corps and corporations was Burke's own anachronistic reflection of French affairs within the borders of Great Britain, his incorporation of a discorporated body politic into British political discourse. In revolutionary iconography, the severed head is that which cannot think but can be made to speak.[8]

AUX MÀNES DE NOS FRERES SACRIFIEZ PAR LE TRAITRE.

ECCE CUSTINE.

Son fang impur abreuva nos Sillons.

AINSI PÉRISE LES TRAITRES A LA PATRIE.

Courtesy Bibliothèque Nationale, Paris

The dismemberment of the human body and the severance of a natural life are supplied by a picture and caption that graphically present the type of a revolutionary life as a talking head. The caption

"Ecce Custine" satirizes both the man who lived under that name and the Christ to whom the phrase canonically refers. Yet it poaches on the Christological association to announce a new, amalgamated man— all the more powerful for being the product of a historical rupture and the political construction of the people. The mechanical reproduction and organized dispersion of this biographeme facilitated widespread recognition of the revolutionary subject.[9] In the figure of the talking head every man sees his own life typed as a life abridged. Under the dispensation of Enlightenment, guillotine and printing press alike perform as instruments of what Lacoue-Labarthe calls "mechanical exemplarity." Every man regards himself characterized as someone subject to the career of the Revolution, cut off from the corps, from the past, and from the possibility of autobiographical remembrance in order that the Revolution can come to speak through him as with his own voice. Burke answers meetly. If the difference between Jacobin Revolution and Burkean counterrevolution is negated by their shared ambition to abolish all differences, they are also positively leagued by the foresight that this cancellation of differences enables the reconstruction of an exemplary man: "I think Europe is recoverable yet. But it must be by a great and speedy Effort of *this Country*. This can never be done but by the extinction, or at least by the suspension, of Parties amongst us. Whatever our Sentiments or likings may be in this point we ought to act as if we were but one man" (*CEB,* 7:307). Taking advantage of the emergency he has called into being, Burke promotes the *extinction* of corporate interests and the deliberative function of the parliament as the precondition for the sovereignty of the counterrevolution, which speaks "as if" with one voice and acts "as if" one man—a legal fiction militant.

The French Revolution ended with the execution of Robespierre. The British counterrevolution, however, lasted until 1832, terminated only by the passage of the Reform Act, the political sphere's decisive recognition of new social arrangements.[10] The asymmetry can be assigned to a stray contingency. Robespierre's consummation was followed a week later by the consumptive death of Richard Burke. His father's mouthpiece to the European princes and French émigrés, the successor to his father's parliamentary seat, and the sole repository of his father's hopes—who Richard beheld his imag'd father saw. For Burke, the proximity of the deaths induced a symbolic connection. For the grief-stricken father, his son's death forever sealed the counterrevolution's incapacity to embody itself fully in a true hero who would redeem a Europe hell-bent on chaos. Burke's Thermidor, then, was a period of protracted mourning for Richard—not just for the son but for the ideal of the new, postrevolutionary man he was meant to embody. Although he resorted to a series of surrogates, such as the Earl of Fitzwilliam and William Windham, and even the vague prediction of a "military character" (*CEB*, 8:141), he never found the single figure that would triumphantly answer the galvanic threat of the revolutionary stereotype.

After 1794, under Pitt, the counterrevolution turned inward in a sustained campaign of self-inflicted violence, the so-called "repression." The repression was prosecuted under Pitt, but after Burke, who had always imagined the revolutionary war "as a war *on* my ideas and principles." The militant contradiction that is Burke's text can only be appreciated if the equivocalness of that "on" is acknowledged: a war *according* to Burke's principles must be a war *against* his principles. "It is with nations as with individuals."[11] And it was the crowning consequence of Burke's individuation of the counterrevolution, the fruit of his authorship, that he was able to personalize the moment by projecting the symptomatology (a word first used in 1798) of his own "old and infirm constitution" on the English nation (*CEB*, 8:253). The dynamic of the counterrevolution after 1794 was, as Coleridge saw, a continuing self-contradiction—an infliction of injury on the very body that the anti-Jacobin war was mounted to protect. Thus, the fierce vision of Burke's "Letter to a Noble Lord": "Why will they not let me remain in obscurity and inaction? Are they apprehensive, that if an atom of me remains the sect has something to fear? Must I be annihilated, lest, like old *John Ziska's,* my skin might be made into a drum, to animate Europe to eternal battle, against a tyranny that threatens to overwhelm all Europe, and all the human race?"[12] Behold Burke, who in default of the redemptive hero imagines himself cut off from thought in order that he might speak with power, who wills that he be flayed so that he might sound and resound the eternal alarm to everlasting battle!

Fathered by Burke, counterrevolutionary self-contradiction propagated itself in the distinctive neurotic form of melancholy. Thus the counterrevolution survived, despite the loss of its ambivalent object in Robespierre/Richard, by blaming itself both for the loss and for surviving the loss of that object which justified existence. After 1794 the "shadow of the object," in Freud's memorable phrase, "falls on the ego";[13] the one who survives—Burke, England—becomes the home front and is punished with renewed violence for a dangerous inclination toward foreign manners and "men of theory" (*Reflections,* 128). As Rousseau's theoretical rigor propelled Robespierre to the sacrificial embodiment of the general will, Burke's melancholy authorized Pitt's sorry repression of traditional voices and domestic hands in the name of "the little platoon." Pitt made war on Burke's principles. Defending against a perceived lapse in legitimacy, the government routinized itself as the serial administration of punishment to a subject people who could be said, sadly, to get what they deserved.

Coleridge and Suppositional Biography

Appearing in the glory year of his partnership with Wordsworth, Coleridge's thin quarto volume *Fears in Solitude, Written in April 1798, During the Alarm of an Invasion* separates itself from the collaboration that produced *Lyrical Ballads* materially (it was published by Joseph Johnson, the radical publisher of Godwin and Wollstonecraft, independently of Wordsworth), thematically (as the title announces), and tonally (conversational or meditative style tenses into high-strung declamation). The year 1798 marked not only the *annus mirabilis* but also the thunderous dawn of the Napoleonic threat and the heyday of Pitt's repression. If the publication of the volume seems to indicate Coleridge's assertion of a distinctive poetic identity, the poems movingly demonstrate that the claim for poetic identity is incoherent except in terms of a triple analogy between poetic, personal, and national identities. For the English poet responsive to his circumstances, the attempt to go his separate way does not demonstrate autonomy but its illusion; in these times, if the poetic must be personal, the personal is nonetheless fully political.

The title poem begins with the invocation of a place, "A green and silent spot, amid the hills, / A small and silent dell!" A description of the "heathy hills," a "swelling slope" covered by the golden "never-bloomless furze," and the "quiet spirit-healing nook" follows. It is a fluid, feminized, almost maternal landscape where one can peacefully organize a presexual innocence, the kind of place that all would love, "but chiefly he, the humble man, who, in his youthful years, / Knew just so much of folly, as had made / His early manhood more securely wise!" "In a half sleep," this man, too tranquil to actually desire anything, "dreams of better worlds." But the silence and dreams are soon dissipated:

> My God! it is a melancholy thing
> For such a man, who would full fain preserve
> His soul in calmness, yet perforce must feel
> For all his brethren—O my God!
> It weighs upon the heart, that he must think
> What uproar and what strife may now be stirring
> This way or that way o'er these silent hills—
> Invasion, and the thunder and the shout,

And all the crash of onset; fear and rage,
And undetermined conflict . . .

(ll. 1-38)

In the light of Burke, the similarity between the imagined invasion and a rape or primal scene fantasy looks less like Coleridge's confusion of the political with the sexual than an accurate rendering of the world as viewed from within the counterrevolution.[14] The historical facts negatively confirm the entanglement of the psychic and the political here: both kinds of invasion—sexual and military—were imaginary. The opening of the poem does not render some real event in terms of poetic fantasy, nor does it project a fantasy onto the political landscape; it represents "England" (place, poetry, and mind) as already invaded and occupied by a sexualized politics, afflicted by the prejudice that all domestic relations are secretly tainted, the suspicion that every touch disguises rape.

A corollary of this occupation is the curiously suppositional biography by which the poet makes his appearance. Unlike in "Frost at Midnight" and "Reflections on Having Left a Place on Retirement," the poet does not here speak autobiographically; instead he supposes "such a man"—a composite of the romantic type of a poet (recognizable from both Coleridge's and Wordsworth's earlier poetry) and the unitarian type of Christ (suffering his passion in the garden). The poem imagines a possible life (and that life the merest possible, little more than revery) whose private, blameless conduct is usurped by unwelcome thoughts of "uproar" and "strife" that erupt from the political unconscious. Plainly regressive, suppositional biography symptomatizes an inhibition on autobiographical meditation. The representation of a way that "such a man" *could* lead a life appears to be the precondition for the appearance of an "I" that can claim personal responsibility for its thoughts. But, as it happens, violation of the quiet tenor of "such a man"'s life by a political crisis triggers instead the abandonment of biographical narrative for fierce jeremiad, which turns on the apostrophic fiction that all men form a single man: "We have offended, Oh! my countrymen!" declaims the poet (l. 41).

That fiction answers to the metastasis of individual Englishmen into a sensation-hungry, counterrevolutionary public:

We, this whole people, have been clamorous
For war and bloodshed; animating sports,
The which we pay for as a thing to talk of,
Spectators and not combatants! No guess
Anticipative of a wrong unfelt,
No speculation on contingency,

> However dim and vague, too vague and dim
> To yield a justifying cause . . .
>
> (ll. 93-100)

The counterrevolution is, first of all, a discourse (the war is a "thing to talk of"). They who talk are "[t]his *whole* people"—the nation as a paying audience shaped and aroused by the systematically propagated illusion that the eventful pains of others are distantly staged for its pleasure. That pleasure may be designated political because it is immunized from moral reflection by the justifying postulate of a first cause: the foreign instigator, the conspiratorial plotter.

The theatricalism of the counterrevolution elaborates a long-standing governmental strategy for controlling civil society by scripting its speech. In the arena that is Great Britain,

> All individual dignity and power [is]
> Engulfed in Courts, Committees, Institutions,
> Associations and Societies,
> A vain, speech-mouthing, speech-reporting Guild.
>
> (ll. 54-57)

Here even "the sweet words / Of Christian promise . . . / Are muttered o'er by men, whose tones proclaim / How flat and wearisome they feel their trade. . . . " (ll. 63-67). Pursuing his critique of the regime as a repressive discursive formation, the poet assails the Test Act:

> Oh! blasphemous! the Book of Life is made
> A superstitious instrument, on which
> We gabble o'er the oaths we mean to break.
> For all must swear—all and in every place,
>
> . . . .
> All, all make up one scheme of perjury,
> That faith doth reel; the very name of God
> Sounds like a juggler's charm. . . .
>
> (ll. 70-80)

How can the Christian promise be credited if uttered by a perjured cleric, if eternal life is routinely jeopardized for the sake of a cozy living? The poet's diatribe recalls Coleridge's own detour from the moment of truth that awaited him on graduation from Cambridge and the application of the Test Act.[15] "Fears" assigns the suspension of Coleridge's life and living its full political significance. The poet sees that the transformation of the orders of French society into a "people," that voice which answers "yes" or "no" to propositions put to it by its spokesmen, has already been accomplished in England, where civil rights have long depended on a willingness to subscribe to the Thirty-nine Articles—whether or not one believed in them. In Great

Britain, where civil rights had not yet been extricated from a confessional submission, citizenship is the reward for paying lip service to a creed, acting as if (the fiction is Burkean) one believed in it. Hegemonic maintenance demands the dissociation of words—those that the newspapers report, those that one says—from their meaning: the outrages to which words refer, the beliefs to which they attest.[16]

The prophet avows that there *is* something that escapes the predictable violent antithesis of revolution and counterrevolution, something outside the generic conflicts staged within theater walls, something eventful not to be tagged to a personifiable cause. The "sweet influences of nature" may succumb to invasion by the abstract imperatives of the Revolution, but, the poet trusts, because abstraction is aberrant, it cannot long thwart the divine economy of meaning. The poet brandishes the threat that "Providence, / Strong and retributive, should make us know / The meaning of our words, force us to feel / The desolation and the agony / Of our fierce doings." Meaning involves bringing abstractions back to the body. The apocalyptic embodiment of meaning would destroy a counterrevolutionary polity that sustains its melancholy existence by doing injury to itself as to others.

Despite his indignation, the prophet seeks to forestall apocalypse. Relenting, he prays, "Spare us yet awhile, / Father and God! O spare us yet awhile!" (ll. 129-30). Aversion, not punishment, is the goal of the poem. The poet exhorts "Sons, brothers, husbands, all / Who ever gazed with fondness on the forms / Which grew up with you round the same fire-side" (ll. 134-36) to

> Stand forth! be men! repel an impious foe,
> Impious and false, a light yet cruel race,
> Who laugh away all virtue, mingling mirth
> With deeds of murder; and still promising
> Freedom, themselves too sensual to be free,
> Poison life's amities, and cheat the heart
> Of quiet hope, and all that soothes,
> And all that lifts the spirit! Stand we forth.
> (ll. 139-46)

This eloquence is not in the manner of Burke. The poet does not imagine a hero who comes to a tragic scene of oedipal conflict, threat, and triumph. His simple aim is to repel. A simple aim achieved by simple means: by stirring his reader (as himself) to a standing forth that will show a "sensual" enemy he is a man. The poet summons up the phallus for an apotropaic display that will ward off the evil of an invasion which was invited by doubts that Britons, supine before the provocative stimuli of their rulers, are really men. It is not the British female that the sensual French invader desires. In the intense climate of revolutionary conflict, there is no passion to spare for the "form" of the female. The British male dangerously opts for personifications of abstract ideas; the French revolutionist prefers the British male.

Standing forth, the British phallus will, however, deter the invader, who, in that most abstract of all personifications, will clearly behold the man. As a signifier of manhood with no body behind it, the juggled charm of the phallus is the exact counterpart to the Jacobinical severed head and all the more potent for its signal lack of meaning. Yet we might inquire how Coleridge hopes to get it to stand. If the best defense is a phallic standing forth—a proof that I am a man and therefore must repel your masculine desire—the poet must attempt to provoke a somatic response more primordial than that achieved by the powerful but mediated Burkean scenario of insulted queens, interdictory forefathers, and incestuous sons. Burke authored tragedy. Coleridge writes romance. He aims to distill his provocation to its volatile linguistic essence, a magical word. Written during the alarm of an invasion, the poem is designed as a watchword to alarm British men. The "Watch-word," as Coleridge elsewhere writes, is "some unmeaning term" that "acquires almost a mechanical power over his frame."[17] In the present war, there is reason of state to exploit the unreasoning body. And in "Fears in Solitude," the sexualization of politics refers aesthetic pleasure to its radical intimacy with power. As an antidote to the pictographic force of revolutionary iconography, this "unmeaning" poem aims to refashion the old mechanism of exemplarity in order to gain a pornographic, Geraldine-like power over the frame of the Englishman, to compel it to repel.

It nonetheless remains a question whether the watchword does not, in fact, constitute that evil which it averts. If the revolutionary pictograph renders the revolutionary subject as an instantaneously recognizable biographeme, Coleridge's "answer meet" is little more than the fabrication of an ideologeme capable of polarizing the world into good and evil, advents and consummations.[18] Despite his diagnosis of the antithetical illness that afflicts the disembodied polis, the poet cannot fully imagine an authentic alternative; he cannot conceive of a body that is not sexual or of a transition that would conduct him to someplace new. Although he wills a break with the counterrevolution, the poet nonetheless avails himself of a heightened counterrevolutionary rhetoric. His dread of rhetorical power fuels the desperate wish for that power, to use it just once. His fear of being abstracted energizes the dangerous wish to be objectified as irresistible charm, not a man but that mechanism which mans men by producing a single stiffening that will magically repulse invasion. The (counter)revolutionary poet dreams of things happening on time, pat on what Theodor Adorno calls the "cipher of catastrophe": punctual invasions, instant erections.[19] Such is the dream in which romantic poetry has always participated. Such is the dream which, by those native cadences that befall verse, romantic poetry continually falsifies.

Or so goes this poem's cadenza. Having vented his "filial fears," the poet says farewell to his solitary spot and winds his way "Homeward":

> and lo! recalled
> From bodings that have well-nigh wearied me,
> I find myself upon the brow, and pause
> Startled! And after lonely sojourning
> In such a quiet and surrounded nook,
> This burst of prospect, here the shadowy main,
> Dim-tinted, there the mighty majesty
> Of that huge amphitheatre of rich
> And elmy fields, seems like society—
> Conversing with the mind, and giving it
> A livelier impulse and a dance of thought!
> And now, beloved Stowey! I behold
> The church-tower, and, methinks the four huge elms
> Clustering, which mark the mansion of my friend;
> And close behind them, hidden from my view,
> Is my own lowly cottage, where my babe
> And my babe's mother dwell in peace! With light
> And quickened footsteps thitherward I tend.
>
> (ll. 210–27)

Home is the dreamer, home from the dell. Or almost. The poet (call him Coleridge) returns to the first person as he nears his own place. The suspension of biography is ended by a return to autobiography. Yet that appearance of progress is undermined by the failure of the autobiographical account to complete the homecoming it imagines. The narrative halts as the poet stops to overlook a cottage that remains visibly hidden from him. We might suspect that what gives his footsteps their tendency may very well be what gives him pause. Although he stands in Stowey, the poet observes a landscape uncannily Wordsworthian. In Wordsworth, the "four huge elms" spot a ruined cottage, haunted by the ghosts of an abandoned wife and children. Coleridge's prospect is also anticipated in "Adventures on Salisbury Plain," where it is said of the wandering sailor:

> Long had he fancied each successive slope
> Conceal'd some cottage, whither he might turn
> And rest.... [20]

In Wordsworth's poem, the price of the sailor's return is his discovery that he is a criminal forbidden entrance to his cottage and debarred from participation in a society proved kind by its exclusion of him.[21] The poem maps a series of uncanny transfers of agency and victimization between narrator and auditor—call them revolutions and counterrevolutions in the exercise of poetic power—a series that is only halted when the sailor, confronted with the wretched form of his abandoned wife, is identified by the assembled populace: "He is the man." That annunciation seals his criminal separation from domestic life and prepares for his suspension in an iron case as an example to all.

No wonder the poet halts. In the intertext through which Coleridge makes his anxious way, he is on the verge of returning to a home configured as the familiar Christological plot. Homecoming bodes the same old ending of recognition, indictment, and sacrifice, rendered meaningless for the modern as for the unitarian by virtue of its mechanical exemplarity. Worse, it is not just the same old plot: it is *Wordsworth's* plot in which Coleridge imagines himself inclined to take his appointed place as surrogate. On returning home after driving out the French invader, Coleridge finds his domestic space newly invaded and occupied by his brother poet, who has settled in as he stood forth. Later, in chapter 4 of the *Biographia Literaria,* Coleridge would identify his audition of the Salisbury Plain poems in 1795 as the occasion when he became as convinced of Wordsworth's genius as if it were the annunciation of his own destiny. In "Fears in Solitude," the resumption of autobiography is stigmatized as premature; it entails assumption of the biographical plot that Wordsworth has already written. For "such a man" to say "I" means assuming the penalty assigned to another thief of voice as his own. That uncanny effect is justified, however dimly, by this cause: in becoming the man who potently stood forth, he unthinkingly cut himself off from what was his own and became as another to those whom he served with a revolutionary fierceness. In any event, the watchman cannot enter the house or even risk the threshold. Better vagrancy than a homecoming. Another Wordsworthian figure puts it plainly: "Oh! dreadful price of being! to resign / All that is dear *in* being; better far / In Want's most lonely cave till death to pine / Unseen, unheard, unwatched by any star" ("Adventures," ll. 379-82). For the poet in search of his life, "home" is just another evil he must avert.

The poet's attempt to resolve "undetermined conflict" fails to do more than disclose its dread overdetermination—again. As Coleridge had already observed, the distress of England could not be ascribed to any single cause, except perhaps the ministerial obsession with a single, exclusively political cause. In his 1795 lecture "The Plot Discovered,"

Coleridge had already mockingly rehearsed Pitt's justification for the Sedition Act: "The outrage offered to his Majesty . . . is ascribed to 'the multitude of seditious pamphlets and speeches daily printed, published, and dispersed with unremitting industry and with a transcendant boldness.'" Coleridge answered that the "dispersion . . . of seditious pamphlets was not the cause: *that* was the cause which gave to sedition the colouring of truth, and made disaffection the dictate of hunger[—]the present unjust, unnecessary and calamitous War . . . !" (*LPR,* 287). The cause of seditious writing is hunger, the cause of hunger is "the PRESENT WAR." And of the war? "[I]ts total Causelessness must be proved," Coleridge urges, "—as if the War had been just and necessary, it might be thought disputable whether any Calamities could justify our abandonment of it" (*LPR,* 54).

Although neither just nor necessary, the war is nonetheless supplied with justification after justification by those who step forward to attest to Jacobinical plotters. The false witness men bear has political uses. Even so they do not lie for a political cause. They who swear do so for money. "POWER CAN PAY PERJURY" (*LPR,* 291) not because the minions of power are right- or left-wing but because they are hungry. Betrayal, like sedition, follows the "dictate of hunger," which has no author, presents no identifiable face. The "dictate of hunger" is the categorical imperative of self-maintenance. And perjury is the inevitable effect of the bias that the ministry of fear communicates to all professions by its command over the supply of food. Coleridge adapts the "dictate of hunger" to his own circumstances as a "hired paragraph-scribbler" in a letter to the industrialist and philanthropist Josiah Wedgwood in January 1798: "Something must be written & written immediately—if any important Truth, any striking beauty, occur to my mind, I feel a repugnance at sending it garbled to a newspaper: and if any idea of ludicrous personality, or apt anti-ministerial joke, crosses me, I feel a repugnance at rejecting it, because *something must be written,* and nothing else suitable occurs" (*CL,* 1:365). Coleridge convincingly vouches for his familiarity with a mode of social existence wholly subject to necessity and where the rhythm of production dictates the shape of opinion, where the ethical "ought" decisively yields to the economic "must."

It would be stretching a point, however, to describe Coleridge as completely degraded to the exigent status of the laboring poor; although he claims to be pressed by the need for "subsistence," he also fastidiously proclaims his desire to "preserve . . . delicacy of moral feeling"—a kind of capital, one assumes, not shared by the vast number of those who slave for wages in the capital. Moreover, the letter to Wedgwood is the vehicle for a frank exploration of vocational options—between pulpit and press—as well as a demonstration designed to appeal to a benefactor who aimed to give him "leisure for the improvement of [his] Talents at the same time that [his] mind should be preserved free from any professional Bias which might pervert, or at least hamper, the exertion of them" (*CL*, 1:364). Nonetheless, if "worker" does not accurately designate Coleridge's social identity, neither does "cleric," "poet," "journalist," or even "man of letters." The anachronistic label "bourgeois" is perhaps the least suitable tag for a man who veers between country and city, between "ministerial office" and journalistic "Trade," between a corporate existence lost and a class solidarity imaginable only as its spectral projection. The best description of this modern, low mimetic Adam (the world is all before him as a congeries of repugnant options) is that, like William Godwin's protean Caleb Williams, he corresponds to no description of man. And Coleridge will construct himself in that break of correspondence.

There was no necessity for him to do so. He had before his eyes the example—placed on earth as if to lesson him into prudence—of a man who ordered his parts into a machine of regular habits and estimable productivity, his brother-in-law, Robert Southey. Rather than follow Southey's lead, however, Coleridge counseled the former pantisocrat on the perils of his way:

> [M]y dear Southey! it goes grievously against the Grain with me, that *you* should be editing anthologies. I would to Heaven, that you could afford to write nothing, or at least, to publish nothing till the completion & publication of the Madoc.... Whereas Thalaba would gain you (for a time at least) more ridiculers than admirers—& the Madoc might in consequence be welcomed with an Ecce iterum. (*CL*, 1:546)[22]

The difference between "Ecce Iterum" and "Ecce Homo" captures Southey's exemplary accommodation to the endless daily piecework required to breathe a momentary, lackluster life into the old formulas by which hegemony is maintained. To behold the *iterum* rather than to behold the *homo* is to see the same *as* repetition—and to imagine the prudent author as a composite figure, constituted by a repetition that homogenizes one heroic poem with another as it merges authorship and anthologization. The career of Southey ("a man who has sacrificed all the energies of his heart and head—a splendid offering on the altar of Liberty" [*LPR*, 15]) exemplifies the routinization of counterrevolutionary melancholy into the specific form of alienation appropriate to a serial mode of cultural reproduction.

To break with the counterrevolutionary machine demands the release of a worth of words not determined by the market's pre-established codes of value. It requires writing for a future that cannot be clearly seen and that is not subject to a justifying cause. It requires imagining a biography of a man who has not yet been beheld: suppositional become *prefigural* biography. The Coleridgean prefigure is troped as transition:

> The death of a young person of high hopes and opening faculties impresses me less gloomily, than the Departure of the Old. To my more natural Reason, the former *appears* like a *transition;* there seems an *incompleteness* in the life of such a person, contrary to the general order of nature; and it makes the heart say, this is not all. But when an old man sinks into the grave, we have seen the bud, the blossom, and the fruit; and the unassisted mind droops in melancholy, as if *the Whole* had come and gone. (*CL,* 1:267)

"The good die young"—not because they are good—there is no fatality to goodness (or the insufferably decent Southey would have perished in his cradle)—but people are good *because* they die young. Because they live lives as yet unwritten, they are apparitions of a future as yet unknown. Like old, mad Burke, they die before they learn the meaning of their words. "Ecce Homo" is the caption for a severed head, a pictograph of the revolutionary subject. "Ecce iterum" captions the life of the Southeyean man who kept his head and made his living by trading in the stereotyped repetition of a period style. But what do we behold when transition appears?

The Cadence of the Future

Persuaded by Coleridge's diagnosis of his predicament, spellbound by Coleridge's promise, in early 1798 the industrialists Josiah and Thomas Wedgwood offered him a subsidy of one hundred fifty pounds a year, no strings attached, thus enabling him to avoid compromising his principles against "preaching for hire" and affording him what, in "Reflections on Having Left a Place of Retirement," he called the "luxury to be," that is, the luxury of having to write nothing. Being gifted by such unexampled bounty did not delude Coleridge into believing that the Revolution was over. "Fears in Solitude" may owe some of its moral conviction to Coleridge's newfound sense of financial well-being, but it also testifies that money cannot stop the rain. Furet has written of the impossibility even for a twentieth-century Frenchman of getting sufficiently outside the Revolution that he or she could see it for what exactly it *was,* for "one cannot practice ethnology in so familiar a landscape" (Furet, 10). Coleridge's historical perspective was similarly constrained by the counterrevolutionary genius that had usurped the English place. Staked by the Wedgwoods, however, Coleridge could resort to the terra incognita of Germany on a funded project of research into otherness to practice what we have come to call ethnography.

Germany was not, of course, a savage culture.[23] Nevertheless, the peculiarity of the place is registered by Coleridge's letters and journal entries. There he described the social world through which he moved in painstaking detail: from the shape of hats to the rules of card games. Walter Jackson Bate has astutely suggested that Coleridge, suffering from a "floating anxiety," fled to Germany in search of a "purified self or 'body-image.'"[24] I want to redefine "floating" as a *biographical* anxiety in order to indicate that the breakdowns, felt and observed, of the partitions between the private and the public, between the psyche and the polity, between the felt and the observed, were the occasion of Coleridge's search for a biographical paradigm purified of revolutionary and counterrevolutionary stereotyping. The synthesis of a "purified self" awaited (not logically, but historically) a new description of "man" on which Coleridge could hope to improvise—he sought, that is, a biography fit for autobiography. As we have seen, Coleridge's anxiety was aggravated by the well-founded sense that biographical embodiment according to any available model would end with the objectification of the self in an image framed, captioned, and suitable for hanging.[25]

Coleridge's ethnographical and biographical impulses were in uneasy harness. On the one hand, he displayed a scrupulous attention to the fine grain of German society. On the other, he attempted to fulfill a promise to the Wedgwoods by preparing the ground for a comprehensive biography of the celebrated Lessing. Compounded of a desire to meet the conventional expectations of his patrons and a need to satisfy his own craving for a companionable form, Coleridge's biographical impulse expressed itself in a hunt for observable correspondences. He thus sought resemblances between the physiognomies of renowned writers and his own; he remarked on the possible parallels between pictures of the famous and their countenances, between their countenances and their characters. Here is Coleridge at the house of the younger brother of the poet Friedrich Gottlieb Klopstock:

> We saw at his house a fine Bust of his Brother—there was a solemn and heavy Greatness in the Countenance which corresponded with my preconceptions of his style & genius.—I saw likewise there a very, very fine picture of Lessing. His eyes were uncommonly like mine—if any thing, rather larger & more prominent—But the lower part of his face & his nose—O what an exquisite expression of elegance and sensibility! (*CL*, 1:437)

The bust not only presupposes an encoding of the inside by the outside but, because it is a portrait of a living man, is also a promise of a correspondence between representation and a reality, a kind of foresight of the future.

The bust's promise proved unreliable, as Coleridge makes clear in his artful account of his later meeting with the poet: "The Poet entered.—I was much disappointed in his countenance. I saw no likeness to the Bust.—. There was no *comprehension* in the Forehead—no *weight* over the eyebrows—no expression of peculiarity, either moral or intellectual, in the eyes;—there was no *massiveness* in the general Countenance." The biographical aim ends in negation. But the ethnographer's hand continues writing: "He is not quite so tall as I am—his upper jaw is toothless, his under jaw all black Teeth; and he wore very large half-boots, which his legs completely filled. They were enormously swelled.—He was lively, kind and courteous. He talked in French with Wordsworth—&, with difficulty, spoke a few sentences to me in English." Coleridge notes Klopstock's "rapture" at the surrender of the French in Ireland and his presentation of himself as a "vehement Anti-Gallican." But then,

> The Subject changed to Poetry—& I enquired, in Latin, concerning the history of German Poetry, & of the elder German Poets.—To my great astonishment he confessed, he knew very little on the subject—he had indeed read occasionally one or two of their elder writers—but not as to be able to speak of their merits. . . . He talked of Milton & Glover; & thought, Glover's blank Verse superior to Milton's!—Wordsworth & myself expressed our surprize—& Wordsworth explained his definition & ideas of harmonious Verse, that it consisted in the arrangement of pauses & cadences, & not in the even flow of single Lines—Klopstock assented, & said that he meant only in single Lines that Glover was the Superior. . . . He spoke with great Indignation of the English Prose Translation of his Messiah. . . . Wordsworth told him that *I* intended to translate a few of his Odes as specimens of German Lyrics—"I wish, you would render into English some select Passages of the Messiah, & *revenge* me of your Countryman." . . . I looked at him with much emotion—I considered him as the venerable Father of German Poetry; as a good man; as a Christian; with legs enormously swelled; seventy four years old; yet active and lively in his motions, as a boy; active, lively, chearful and kind and communicative—and the Tears swelled into my eyes; and could I have made myself invisible and inaudible I should have wept outright. (*CL,* 1:442–43)

The ethnographic character of this moment is identified by the interview format, by Coleridge's scribal posture, and by the prevailing sense of Klopstock as a "specimen"—a specimen father, as vengeful as venerable; a specimen body image, albeit bathetic rather than exemplary. Ethnography requires a nontheatrical distance. Because Coleridge and Wordsworth did not have the advantage of either the invisibility or the inaudibility of the audience in a darkened theatre, they could not weep outright. The Englishmen could pay their respects without submitting to the Burkean prescription of acting as if in the presence of a canonized forefather.[26] Klopstock's gouty legs are not Priam's wounded heart. Tragedy tears unshed are ethnographic disappointments transcribed.[27] This specimen poet, complete to the point of overripeness, is, as Coleridge says of his poetry, "sad stuff"—surprisingly out of touch with that national past which could grace him with authenticity. All of Europe has gone into the making of a poet already invaded by revolutionary discourse, already suffering from the anxiety of influence.

Yet if the cosmopolized Klopstock is degraded from the Teutonic purity that would make his life worth writing and his poetry worth reading, there remains a significant difference between him and his interviewers. Unlike the self-conscious and mobile English ethnographer, the German poet does not seem able to take strategic advantage of his alienation; for him, to change his mind means simply shifting from one position to another (French to English, Homer to Milton, Glover to Homer) according to what, in the "Advertisement" to *Lyrical Ballads*, Wordsworth calls "pre-established codes of decision." Yet even so, Klopstock performs his shifts clumsily, *Germanically*. There is, in James Clifford's terms, something tellingly "offcenter" about this encounter, which is registered in Klopstock's blunder about Glover and in his failed adaptation of Homeric hexameters to German heroic verse.[28] The offcenteredness advantageously turns a potential standoff between Self and Other or between anxious sons and "venerable" father into a blessedly oblique communication between brother English poets: Wordsworth gets to lay out his theory, and Coleridge gets to overhear, record, and transmit it. Poetry, Wordsworth instructs, is not the *iterum* of a flowing line, what anyone can see, but cadences and pauses, those contrivances that are off the center of translatable meaning but that articulate the historical authenticity of English verse—of Milton and beyond.

Coleridge goes on to catch Klopstock in a lie about the date of his exposure to Milton. The facts prove that Klopstock's majesty is altogether derived, his Messiah the offspring of an English divinity. Thus Klopstock's life story differs in no fundamental regard from the biography of anxiety and repression by which every post-Miltonic poet is presupposed. Nonetheless, although meeting Klopstock is no encounter with the new, Coleridge's disappointment crystallizes the conditions for its appearance. In wedding a mechanical anti-Gallicanism to a paralyzed anti-Miltonism, the Klopstockian crux suggests a possible means of getting beyond both. By determining the radical character that gives English, and therefore Miltonic, verse its identity and its allegorical strength, Coleridge can hope to transform the condition for past majesty into the occasion of future glory.

Having detected Klopstock's untruth, Coleridge evenhandedly goes on to admit to a lie of his own about his knowledge of German hexameters. Only Coleridge's falsehood was remediable. And he diligently applied himself to the remedy in Ratzeburg, where he dug in alone, William and his sister Dorothy having departed for Goslar, an isolation deeper far. The above letter to Poole remarks on Coleridge's receipt, after six weeks, of the first words from William, whose "violent hatred of letter-writing had caused his ominous silence [and] for which he accuses himself in severe terms" (*CL,* 1:445). What, exactly, Wordsworth had been doing at Goslar is not clear. "Dorothy says— 'William works hard, but not very much at the German.'—This is strange—I work at nothing else, from morning to night—/—It is very difficult to combine & arrange the German Sentences" (*CL,* 1:445). If Wordsworth had turned strange, Coleridge's labors became increasingly, even acutely, definite. Absent from family and friends, disappointed with the countenance of German poetry, anxious to discover a lifeline that would be something other than a "joyless form," Coleridge took a decisively linguistic turn. His notebooks record his intense application to the combination and arrangement of German sentences and to his classification of German vocabulary. But the pages are also crowded with notations of a staggering array of poetic meters, clouds of diacritical marks combined and arranged into the phantom of verse.[29]

As if clinging to the formalities of their erstwhile collaboration strangely disparted, Coleridge labored in strict accord with Wordsworth's supervisory mandate. For if writing "harmonious verse" consists in "the arrangement of pauses & cadences," the solitary Coleridge concentrated on the cadence, the modulation or fall of voice that accents poetic language. In his analysis of the German hexameter, the preferred vehicle of Klopstock's epic aspirations, he specifically identified its characteristic failing as a falling, albeit fortunate: "Is the German, in truth, adapted to these metres? I grievously suspect that it is all pure pedantry. Some advantages there, doubtless, are, for we cannot fall foul of any thing without advantages" (*CL,* 1:450). That observation, in theme and tenor, epitomizes what I mean by

"Coleridgean."[30] Here he notices that in falling afoul of the heroic hexameter, the peculiar cadence of the German appears. Thus begins the breakthrough.

Soon Coleridge Englishes the effect in a remarkable prosodic exercise sent to the Wordsworths. His demonstration hexameters begin with the representation of a technique for marking the regularity of the beat:

> William, my teacher, my friend! dear William and dear Dorothea!
> Smooth out the folds of my letter, and place it on desk or on table;
> Place it on table or desk; and your right hands loosely half-closing,
> Gently sustain them in air, and extending the digit didactic,
> Rest it a moment on each of the forks of the five-forked left hand,
> Twice on the breadth of the thumb, and once on the tip of each finger;
> Read with a nod of the head in a humouring recitativo;
> And, as I live, you will see my hexameters hopping before you.

Beat on yourself as do I. As we (he, they, you, and I) read with body English, beating out the time, so Coleridge lives, sensuously at hand. It is a milder fate than Burke's vision of being flayed, stretched, and drummed. Not yet subject to a figure, he lives according to a characteristically tactful rhythm. But though materialized physically before us by the handreading of his handwriting, it is at the cost of self-control:

> I would full fain pull in my hard-mouthed runaway hunter;
> But our English Spondeans are clumsy yet impotent curb-reins;
> And so to make him go slowly, no way have I left but to lame him.

No centaur the English hexameter, but an idiot man on a runaway horse. Although the English is no more suitable for the heroic pace of the classical mount than the German, each language falls afoul of the Homeric antecedent in its own way. Here the meter runs because of a lack of fit between the quantities of the Greek and the quality of the English. Only the dead weight of lumpen monosyllables finally lames the hunter's legs and brings the race to a dead stop. Coleridge has not learned—will never learn—to arrange pauses, which invariably come upon him as momentous separations, violent breaks, guilt-ridden betrayals—overdetermined, melodramatic. This laming, as is so often the case with Coleridge's verse, has the force of a self-infliction—oedipal damage done to the legs of his own poetry—even as it hints at a castrative aggressivity released both against clippity Klopstock and against Wordsworth, whose "digit didactic," extended and animated in response to Coleridge's beat, is momentarily blocked.

Yet Klopstock is not a father; verse is not a man; a finger is not the body. Nor is collaboration identity. The "laming" of the verse is the occasion of an apostrophe that turns away from the heroic strain, that unhands Wordsworth and brings the note of English pathos in: "William, my head and my heart!" The exercise plunges into ten lines of physical complaint—the same old pitiable Coleridge—and then a textual break, and then a startling turn:

> . . . my eyes are a burthen,
> Now unwillingly closed, now open and aching with darkness.
> O! what a life is the eye! what a strange and inscrutable essence!
> Him that is utterly blind, nor glimpses the fire that warms him;
> Him that never beheld the swelling breast of his mother;
> Him that smiled in his gladness as a babe that smiles in its slumber;
> Even for him it exists, it moves and stirs in its prison;
> Lives with a separate life, and 'Is it a Spirit?' he murmurs:
> 'Sure it has thoughts of its own, and to see is only a language.'

It is as if the laming of the hunter has blankened Coleridge's sight, allowing him to imagine the life of the eye as the story of what it does before it sees. He imagines a pre-Homeric, pre-Miltonic, pre-oedipal, and, most importantly, *prefigural* "separate life" that "stirs" the murmurous supposition that the self and all it sees are contingent codes, a "language." This "separate life," then, is the suppositional biography of the "eye" (that it could be deciphered equally plausibly as Wordsworth's or Coleridge's is just the point) logically precedent to the integrated, insightful "I" on which autobiography will mount its vexed and vexatious mountings.

Although a prisoner that sees not, the "eye" is not sequestered in a noumenal isolation, for somehow it befalls that the prisoner makes its absence felt; somehow it befalls that, though blind to the schemata by which sight grammaticizes the world into sense, the "eye" nonetheless stirs a murmur, which affects to respond in kind. Hear it:

> William, my head and my heart! dear William and dear Dorothea!
> You have all in each other; but I am lonely, and want you!

The closing cadence is not visible but audible, and then only to the ear of an English speaker. Indeed, hearing here we learn now (as, after so much labor, Coleridge heard and learned there and then) that the real self-contradiction of Klopstock was not that he lied about the age at which he read Milton, but that he could have imagined he *read* Milton at all, when his only access was to a prose translation.[31] Without English, Klopstock could easily prefer Glover to Milton, since without English Klopstock could not hear the Miltonic voice. His foreign eye was not alive to its parochial stirring, to the way the modulation of verse falls on an English ear; hence like the untutored child of Coleridge's "Nightingale," Klopstock "mars all things with his imitative lisp." Klopstock's self-contradiction is only a German version of the deafness that disabled the response of the eighteenth century to Milton, which read his blank verse as prose because it could only read with its bodily eye.

Coleridge's trip to Germany allowed him to imagine a transition to the future—a new century and a new poetry—in terms of his acquired understanding of the past as a foreign country. And the Augustans' prosaical insensitivity to the cadenced music of blank verse was remedied in large part by Coleridge, the poet with the nicest ear for cadences, those falls dying or desiring that are the accidents and the peculiar distinction of English verse.[32] We hear that remedy in this renegotiation of the relations between the classical model and the English instance, no longer considered in terms of revival or correspondence but as a lapse into a personal speech whose historicity is exactly the note of a pathos previously unheard.[33] The pain of absence has been articulated as the slight slippage between the manly beats of the heroic spondee, steadfast in the assertion of its timeless objectivity, and the soulful falling off of the final, ever-diminishing trochee ("want you"). Coleridge makes audible what the physical eye cannot see.[34] Without trope or figure he hopes to move one with whom he no longer corresponds.[35] Having escaped apocalyptic consummation on the altar of (counter)revolutionary spectacle, the abstracted "I" returns to the body in the sensuous detail of its breathings. It is in its cadences that English escapes polarization with the French or appropriation by the German. It is by the English tongue's delicate fallings off from brute symmetry that the "loss of national character" (*LPR,* 60), hastened by the murderous tradeoffs between revolution and counterrevolution, is obstinately questioned. It is in its falling off that the advantage of English as a language for pathos, and thus its genius for poetry, appears. Having fallen off from Wordsworth, the decadent Coleridge has acquired the singular advantage of hearing the vital music in the blankest of verse.[36]

As Coleridge refined the cadence, so his collaborator mastered the pause. It was Wordsworth who insisted on the separation; and Wordsworth gave that space its own slow time by protracting the interval between his departure and his first letter, thereby suspending the responsive exchange of collaborators each to each with an "ominous silence" that mocked his correspondent's best skill. Coleridge has thought and will think again of "a man who should lose his companion in a desart of sand where his weary Halloos drop down in the air without an echo" (*CL,* 1:471). But this time, his voice drops down to find not its echo but something else. It is Wordsworth, on whose heart

Coleridge's cadence has gently fallen, who arranges cadences and pauses into a responsive passage that both answers and incorporates the moving call. To Coleridge, for whom every interval is an absence and every absence a pain, Wordsworth replies with a letter of instruction in the management of pauses. We know it only from Coleridge's response:

> The blank lines gave me as much direct pleasure as was possible in the general bustle of pleasure with which I received and read your letter. I observed, I remember, that the 'fingers woven,' &c., only puzzled me; and though I liked the twelve or fourteen first lines very well, yet I like the remainder much better. Well, now I have read them again, they are very beautiful, and leave an affecting impression. That
>
> > Uncertain heaven received
> > Into the bosom of the steady lake,
>
> I should have recognised any where; and had I met these lines running wild in the deserts of Arabia, I should have instantly screamed out 'Wordsworth!' (*CL,* 1:452-53)

This is what the silence, the suspension of all correspondence, has omened. Transition appears. Something completely unforeseen and providentially incomplete falls to him who has hung listening. Neither a body nor a joyless form but living lines—lines that have a peculiar music and give a peculiar, unidentifiable pleasure. This then, retrieved from the dinning revolution of hoots and counterhoots, is the figure of biography: the impression of a transient affect that continues, transiently, to be affecting; a life written as the cadenced suspension of the identity we know it "must" become. And we may take for our own the moral or "theoretical consequence" that Phillipe Lacoue-Labarthe points out: "[T]he figure is never *one.* Not only is it the Other, but there is no unity or stability of the figural; the imago has no fixity or proper being. There is no 'proper image' with which to identify totally, no essence of the imaginary."[37] What has fallen by chance is received across a pause that suspends, that *uncertains,* all past determinations of who or what "I" must be. These lines about a boy coming to be as one-who-was render poetry's cadence and pause as a transition to a future as yet unseen.

It is given to Coleridge to name that future. His Arabia is not the world historical desert where, in the fall of 1798, fearlessly prowls the solitary Bonaparte. It is a romantic, textual wilderness where, after the Revolution, language invisibly changes into something new and strange, with a glory which Coleridge says he immediately apprehended. But then *after* the instantaneous moment of apprehension, Coleridge freely acknowledges what appeared to him by the name of

"Wordsworth." We do not know what in fact Coleridge perceived it *as,* if anything. No doubt Coleridge—separated from his friend's physical presence, with ample time to read and analyze—could have shouted some other name: "Behold Milton!" (thinking of "Lycidas") or even "Behold Coleridge" (thinking of "The Nightingale")—but it might as well be "Wordsworth," that name which capitally allegorizes the surplus value that language acquires by the fiction of authorial attribution.

Wordsworth, to be sure, will repay this gift as if Coleridge's acknowledgment were nothing but his echoic due, hollowly resounding the sublime note of his own noble soul. He will close the biography of "a boy" with a death, as if it were the story of a person, say a rival poet, who has generously departed the world in order that another, more gifted one might stage his life in all the glory of its dialectical progress toward dominion. But there is nothing personal about the essential music of this cadenced pause, nor is there anything personal in Coleridge's acknowledgment of Wordsworth as the hybrid figure of this coinstantive labor, this radical meter of transition. And in truth, Wordsworth's autobiography will, despite itself, unfold as the allegorical understanding of this image of meter's destabilization of the imaginary. Coleridge's greeting heralds a "philosophical poem" that will begin as a meditation on the cadences with which the mind steadies its footing in the suspenseful world. It is a text that Coleridge names and can in good faith profess.

After the Revolution, Coleridge does not in fact die; but he does fall off from poetry. And that falling becomes his calling: criticism. In one of his early and enthusiastic letters home from Germany, Coleridge mentioned a visit to "Professor Ebeling." He added, "Now what a *Professor* is, I know not," and promised to "enquire & inform" his wife in a subsequent "account of the German Universities & the condition of their Literary Men" (*CL,* 1:436). Once again, Coleridge's aim answers to an act of counterrevolutionary closure, brutally voiced by Burke: "Here the Magistrate must stand in the place of the Professor. They who cannot or will not be taught must be coerced" (22 July 1791; *CLB,* 6:304). Like so many of Coleridge's promises, this one was only partially fulfilled.[38] Yet the demonstration of "what a *Professor* is" occurs in the letter we have been reviewing, where, outside of the coercive kingdom, professing Wordsworth supersedes confessing Coleridge. We might be inclined to describe this moment as an epochal transfer of powers: that moment when Wordsworth, who has since ruled the modern poetic imagination, finally impressed his dominion on the subjected Coleridge. But Coleridge's acknowledgment of the Wordsworthian text presupposes that power is lodged in the kind of affective transfer that disables mastery's dialectic.[39] The personal may be the political, but this transitive arrangement of cadences and pauses suspends persons as it renews the vitality of English verse in order to frame new social bodies, based not on a mythic contract (only adults can engage in those) but on a continued metrical contact: "I am sure I need not say how you are incorporated into the better part of my being," Coleridge writes to his friend, "whenever I spring forward into the future with noble affections, I always alight by your side" (*CL,* 1:453).

Notes

1. François Furet, *Interpreting the French Revolution,* trans. Elborg Forster (Cambridge: Cambridge University Press, 1981), 48. Hereafter cited as Furet in the text.

2. *Collected Letters of Samuel Taylor Coleridge,* ed. Earl Leslie Griggs, 6 vols. (New York: Oxford University Press, 1956, 1971), 1:527. Hereafter cited as *CL* in the text. Coleridge anticipates Furet's characterization of revolutionary politics in the first of his letters "To Mr. Fox" published in *The Morning Post* in November 1802. "Let a free country be, or be supposed to be, in danger," he writes, "and Jacobinism is the necessary consequence. All men promiscuously, not according to rank or property, but by the superiority of popular talents, and the impulse of superior restlessness, will take an active part in politics. And this is itself Jacobinism, a political disease." (*Essays on His Times,* ed. David V. Erdman, *The Collected Works of Samuel Taylor Coleridge,* 3, Kathleen Coburn, general editor [Princeton, N.J.: Princeton University Press, 1978], 1:382).

3. Edmund Burke, *Reflections on the Revolution in France* (London: Penguin, 1968), 211.

4. *The Correspondence of Edmund Burke,* 10 vols., ed. T. L. Copeland, et al. (Cambridge: Cambridge University Press, 1958–78), 6:25. Hereafter cited as *CEB* in the text.

5. On Burke's application of the sublime and its associated oedipal scenario to the French Revolution, see Ronald Paulson, *Representations of Revolution (1789–1820)* (New Haven, Conn.: Yale University Press, 1983), 57–73. For a discussion of the place of theatricality in Burke's work, see Paul Hindson and Tim Gray, *Burke's Dramatic Theory of Politics* (Aldershot: Avebury, 1988).

6. "Our principles are antijacobin. We cannot be neuter. We are on the Stage: and cannot occasionally jump into the Pitt or Boxes to make observations on our brother actors" (*CEB* 7:461).

7. John Brewer, *The Sinews of Power: War, Money, and the English State, 1688–1783* (New York: Knopf, 1988) 3–24 and passim.

8. Reproduced from *French Caricature and the French Revolution, 1789-1799* (Los Angeles, Calif.: Grunewald Center for the Graphic Arts, 1988), 194.

9. On the recognition of the biographical subject, see William H. Epstein, *Recognizing Biography* (Philadelphia: University of Pennsylvania Press, 1988), 71–89.

10. See J. C. D. Clark, *English Society: 1688-1832* (Cambridge: Cambridge University Press, 1985), 38–45.

11. "Four Letters on the Proposals for Peace with the Regicide Directory of France," Letter 1, *Selected Writings of Edmund Burke,* ed. Walter J. Bate (New York: Random House, 1960), 476.

12. *Selected Writings,* 486.

13. Sigmund Freud, "Mourning and Melancholia," *General Psychological Theory: Papers on Metapsychology,* ed. Philip Rieff (New York: Collier Books, 1963), 170.

14. For a recent useful discussion of the poem, which, however, does not engage its sexual implications, see Nicholas Roe, *Wordsworth and Coleridge: The Radical Years* (Oxford: Clarendon Press, 1988), 263–68.

15. For a discussion of the Test Act in the context of political turmoil during the 1790s, see Clark, *English Society,* 341–46.

16. The canonical instance of the theatricalization of counterrevolutionary ideology is the passage in *Reflections* where Burke celebrates the English "theatre [as] a better school of moral sentiments than churches" (*Reflections,* 176); but see also his comment, late in life, to the Shakespearean editor Edmond Malone that "[y]our admiration of Shakspeare would be ill sorted indeed, if your Taste . . . did not lead you to a perfect abhorrence of the French Revolution, and all its Works" (*CEB,* 8:456). For accounts of the ideological usage of Shakespeare in British society, see Terence Hawkes, *That Shakespeherian Rag: Essays on a Cultural Process* (New York: Methuen, 1986); Graham Holderness, *Shakespeare's History* (New York: St. Martin's, 1985); and Jonathan Bate, *Shakespearean Constitutions, Politics, Theater, Criticism, 1730-1830* (Oxford: Oxford University Press, 1989).

17. Samuel Taylor Coleridge, *Lectures 1795 on Politics and Religion,* ed. Lewis Patton and Peter Mann), vol. 1 of the *Collected Coleridge,* Kathleen Coburn, general editor (Princeton, N.J.: Princeton University Press, 1971), 52. Hereafter cited as *LPR* in the text.

18. See Fredric Jameson, *The Political Unconscious: Narrative as a Socially Symbolic Act* (Ithaca, N.Y.: Cornell University Press, 1981), 115–19.

19. Theodor Adorno, *Aesthetic Theory,* trans. C. Lenhardt (London: Routledge & Kegan Paul, 1970), 48.

20. "Adventures on Salisbury Plain," ll. 64–66, *The Salisbury Plain Poems of William Wordsworth,* ed. Stephen Gill (Ithaca, N.Y.: Cornell University Press, 1975), 125.

21. For the best discussion of the various transactions that occur in Wordsworth's poem, see Karen Swann, "Public Transport: Adventuring on Wordsworth's Salisbury Plain," *ELH* 55 (Winter 1988): 811–34.

22. Short for "Ecce Iterum Crispinus!" from Juvenal's *Satire IV* (l. 1). As Leslie Marchand translates it: "Lo, Crispin again (I revert to the topic I have mentioned so often before)." *Byron's Letters and Journals,* 12 vols. (Cambridge, Mass.: Harvard University Press, 1973-82), 1:194 n.

23. There is, however, the curious fact that in Hamburg Coleridge found himself lodged—by Wordsworth's arrangement—at "Der Wilder [*sic*] Man i.e. The Savage—an hotel not of the genteelest Class" (*CL,* 1:433).

24. Walter Jackson Bate, *Coleridge* (New York: MacMillan, 1968), 88 and 95.

25. An outcome that is represented, although not fully dramatized, in act 3 of Coleridge's *Osorio: A Tragedy,* in *The Complete Poetical Works of Samuel Taylor Coleridge,* ed. E. H. Coleridge, 2 vols. (Oxford: Oxford University Press, 1912), 2:554-56. Cf. the pictorialism of "Reflections on Having Left a Place of Retirement."

26. In De Quincey's version of the scene, Wordsworth is dragged back within the oedipal orbit: "[H]appening to look down at Klopstock's swollen legs, and recollecting his age, [Wordsworth] felt touched," according to De Quincey, "be a sort of filial pity for his helplessness" ("Samuel Taylor Coleridge," *De Quincey's Collected Writings,* ed. David Masson, 14 vols. [London: 1896], 2:170).

27. The literary model for this paratragical scene is Pope's translation of the passage in book 24 of the *Iliad,* where the venerable Priam appears before Achilles to plead for the corpse of Hector. The scene ends awash in tears. Burke's citation of the passage in his *Enquiry* had made it a touchstone for discussions of sublimity (see Burke, *A Philosophical Enquiry into the Origin of Our Ideas of the Sublime and Beautiful* [Notre Dame, Ind.: University of Notre Dame Press, 1968], 64; for recent discussions, see Thomas Weiskel, *The Romantic Sublime: A Study in Transcendance* (Baltimore, Md.: The Johns Hopkins University Press, 1976), 89 and Jerome Christensen, "'Thoughts That Do Often Lie Too Deep for Tears': Toward a Romantic Concept of Lyrical Drama," *The Wordsworth Circle* 12 [Winter 1981]: 54-56).

28. James Clifford, *The Predicament of Culture: Twentieth-Century Ethnography, Literature, and Art* (Cambridge, Mass.: Harvard University Press, 1988), 9. Coleridge sums it up: "They call him the German Milton—a very *German* Milton indeed!" (*CL,* 1:445).

29. *The Notebooks of Samuel Taylor Coleridge,* ed. Kathleen Coburn, 4 vols. (Princeton, N.J.: Princeton University Press, 1957-), 1:372, 373.

30. Cf. the inverted, Augustan formulation of the sentiment in a letter to John Thelwall: "[W]hatever a man's excellence is, that will likewise be his fault" (*CL,* 1:279). On Coleridge and falling, see Jerome Christensen, "'Like a Guilty Thing Surprised:' Coleridge, Deconstruction, and the Apostasy of Criticism," *Coleridge's Biographia Literaria,* ed. Frederick Burwick (Columbus: Ohio State University Press, 1989), 171-90.

31. A similar suspicion attaches to Coleridge's scene. How is it that Coleridge, who spoke no French, could have imagined he heard Wordsworth's prosodic instruction of Klopstock, which was conducted in French? The crucial prosodic instruction does not appear in Coleridge's detailed account of the interview in his notebooks (*Notebook,* 1:339). Did Coleridge's recollection improve during the composition of the letter? Or did he ventriloquize Wordsworth?

32. On Samuel Johnson's "characteristically Augustan (and aesthetically, rather paradoxical) failure to feel accents strongly [as an] explanation of his customary deprecation of blank verse," see Paul Fussell, Jr., *Theory of Prosody in Eighteenth-Century England* (1954: rpt. Archon Books, 1966), 155. Fussell credits Coleridge's experimentation with accentual verse in *Christabel* as being the watershed in the "Discovery of the Force of English Accent," *Theory,* 151–53). It is clear that *Christabel,* although (or perhaps because) unpublished, was the most powerful poetic precedent of 1798—its meter signally influencing and deforming the poetic enterprises of Scott, Byron, and Southey, as well as Wordsworth and Coleridge himself. Wordsworth's remarks explaining his decision to exclude *Christabel* from the 1800 *Lyrical Ballads* are well known: "I found that the Style of this Poem was so discordant from my own that it could not be printed along with my poems with any propriety" (quoted in *CL,* 1:643). Wordsworth's exclusion registers the threat that *Christabel* represented as *text* (and, in the character of Geraldine, as performative theory of the rhetorical power of texts) to the *Lyrical Ballads* as *book*—an exclusion that was in fact the echo of Coleridge's own attempt to make *Fears in Solitude* a book by quarantining dangerous romance in *Christabel.* But, alarmingly, *Christabel* kept coming back: it is disseminated throughout "Fears" and its companion poems, as well as throughout the writings of Coleridge's contemporaries. A full account of the postrevolutionary and non-Miltonic line of *Christabel*'s metrical influence remains to be written. The two essays most attentive to the unsettling "style" of *Christabel,* Karen Swann's superb "'Christabel': The Wandering Mother and the Enigma of Form" (*Studies in Romanticism* 23 [Winter 1984]: 533–53) and "Literary Gentlemen and Lovely Ladies: The Debate on the Character of *Christabel* (*ELH* 52 [Spring 1985]: 397–418), disregard meter in favor of generic issues involving the supernatural and the feminine. A supplementary account would build on John Hollander's illuminating remarks about "meter" as a "curiously strong indication or emblem of genre" in order to argue the way in which the irregularity of *Christabel* at once announces what Hollander calls a "metrical contract" and disables the contract form (Hollander, *Vision and Resonance: Two Senses of Poetic Form* (New York: Oxford University Press, 1975), 192–96.

33. I rely on Hollander's fine discussion of the *ethos* of the hexameter in *Vision and Resonance,* 190–91. Paul Magnuson discusses Coleridge's "attempt to recover the audibility of a natural language" in *Coleridge & Wordsworth: A Lyrical Dialogue* (Princeton, N.J.: Princeton University Press, 1988), 188.

34. On Coleridge's problems with descriptive writing, see his 17 May 1799 letter to his wife, where he complains, "I see what I write / but alas [! I cannot] write what I see" (*CL,* 1:503).

35. The theoretical implications of this hope for a kind of transference without trope are referred to a de Manian and psychoanalytic vocabulary and analyzed with exemplary subtlety by Cynthia Chase in her essay "'Transference' as Trope and Persuasion," in *Discourse in Psychoanalysis and Literature,* ed. Schlomith Rimmon-Kennan (New York: Methuen, 1987), 211–33.

36. Hollander remarks that "it is with Romantic poetry that we begin to get a poetic confrontation of the realms of the two reigning senses." His historical analysis suggests that Coleridge's momentous engagement with Greek hexameters is at once a unique confrontation and the repetition of a struggle that has always occurred at the articulation of modernity with the classical Greek: "The superimposition of schemata for the poetry of one language upon the hostile realities of another engender[s] grave complexities. . . . [I]t was with the adaptation of Greek meters to Latin that poetry, originally inseparable from music, began to grow away from it. And it was then that poetry began to develop, in its meter, a seeming music of its own" (*Vision and Resonance,* 23 and 11).

37. Phillipe Lacoue-Labarthe, "The Echo of the Subject," in *Typography: Mimesis, Philosophy, Politics,* ed. Christopher Fynsk (Cambridge, Mass: Harvard University Press, 1989), 175. For a remarkable and graphic synthesis of this dynamism in "The Boy of Winander" passage, see Neil Hertz, *The End of the Line* (New York: Columbia University Press, 1985), 217–19.

38. Having completed his inquiries, Coleridge did duly report on the function of professing in Germany. "*A Professor,*" he wrote, "is one who has received from the Government & University that especial Degree which authorizes him to teach publickly in the particular department or faculty, of which he is Professor" (*CL,* 1:477). Unfortunately, Coleridge's letter survives only in fragmentary form.

39. For a critique of liberalism as requiring a "net transfer of powers," see C. B. Macpherson, "The Maximization of Democracy," in *Democratic Theory: Essays in Retrieval* (Oxford: Clarendon Press, 1973), 3–23.

Alison Booth

Biographical Criticism and the "Great" Woman of Letters

The Example of George Eliot and Virginia Woolf

In a 1941 collaborative obituary of Virginia Woolf, the novelist Rose Macaulay recorded Woolf's mimickry of a Victorian voice: "'Is this a great age?' [Woolf would ask] or, 'can there be Grand Old Women of literature, or only Grand Old Men? I think I shall prepare to be the Grand Old Woman of English letters. Or would you like to be?'" (317). This possibly invented biographical vignette captures the self-mocking, elusive, brilliant, and ambitious Woolf we have come to know from her published letters, diaries, essays, and, at an interpretive stretch, from her novels. We can readily believe that the "real" Virginia Woolf acknowledged, in private conversation, her peculiar role as the leading *woman* writer of her age. She had succeeded to the title that only George Eliot had won before her, that of The Grand Old Woman of English Letters. The title, as Woolf's remark suggests, was deeply ironic, since the grandeur or greatness seemed calibrated with the writer's ability to suppress the disqualification of womanhood. The female laureate might as well be male, she has become so representative of the age.[1]

The humor of the remark is due not only to the idea of a woman masquerading as a man but also to the recognized absurdity of the cult of literary genius: everyone knows that the Great Man of Letters is a figment of lingering hero-worship. Biographies in Woolf's day had debunked the notion of flawless public figures—the "Shining Ones," as Eliot ironically calls them in *Middlemarch* (109)—whose rise to greatness is supposedly undimmed by the sordid detail of personal life-stories. Besides this irony toward greatness in general and toward the masculine norm of greatness in particular, Woolf's comment finally may expose a tension that has strained literary criticism at least since T. S. Eliot proclaimed the impersonality of the artist (a tension that persisted in Wimsatt and Beardsley's denunciation of "The Intentional Fallacy" and Barthes's and Foucault's pronouncement of "The Death of the Author").[2] During an extended period in which literary biography and biographical criticism have flourished, there have been persistent attempts to "free" literature from historical context and personal origins.

For Woolf, George Eliot was the most important—indeed the only complete—exemplar of the Grand Old Woman of English Letters. The acceptance of Eliot and Woolf into the canon as great writers in spite of their womanhood—i.e., their success in fulfilling the requirement that great art be impersonal—to me offers the most compelling reason for reading these two different figures together. Indeed, it solicits a new, more wary kind of biographical criticism of "Eliot" and "Woolf," the sort of biographical criticism that feminists such as Cheryl Walker and Nancy Miller have proposed. I would like to examine the justification for such a feminist biographical criticism, which would take into account poststructuralist assaults on textual referentiality and authorial presence while reenvisioning the historical contextuality of literature as well as the possibility of agency or voice, which women like George Eliot and Virginia Woolf struggled so hard to earn (Walker, 560).

The moment I name these writers and refer to their struggle, I place my own criticism within a context of Anglo-American feminist readings of "the" female literary tradition. In doing so, I also want to gain perspective on that body of criticism and its biographical bias, recalling the difficulty writers like Eliot and Woolf faced in trying to *escape* biographical criticism. Just as women themselves have been conventionally accused of being too personal—always personal—so criticism of women's writings has been almost invariably biographical, whether or not the critic shares in the feminist revalorization of the personal as political.

The intersecting biographies of the two "great" women of letters afford an example of the benefits and drawbacks of feminist biographical criticism particularly because they conceived their own quests for greatness in terms of an escape from female personality. (To focus, as I do here, on writers whose biographies are famous should also remind us of writers less privileged, the obscure who have no canonical personality to escape.) Eliot and Woolf, though themselves biographical critics and narrators of collective biographical histories in their novels, nevertheless devised narrative personae to deflect readers' inquiries into the actual authorial origin of their own work. These personae, the omniscient philosopher "George Eliot" and the disembodied reflector of impressions in Woolf's novels, never succeeded in discouraging widespread interest in the real Marian Evans Lewes or Virginia Woolf, nor perhaps did these ambitious women truly wish to deflect such interest. But the impersonal personae did gain ground for the works of Eliot and Woolf to be deemed great by prevailing standards and hence did win laurels for the great women of letters themselves. What Eliot would have considered an impertinence and Woolf an irrelevance—the probing of the author's life for the sake of insight into the work—appears to me crucial to a developing interpretation of diverse women's roles in cultural production. In what follows, I will first explore the alternative approaches to feminist biographical criticism before following the Woolfian path, certainly the most *beaten* path, to a reading of the Grand Old Women of English Letters, with a detour through their readings of other women writers. I hope to emerge from this labyrinth with a map for further exploration: a model of the divided plots that have heretofore determined most biographical criticism of women writers.

The Strains of Feminist Biographical Criticism

That post-modern proclamations of the death of the author should coincide with the "second wave" of feminism and a burgeoning interest in female authorship is perhaps no accident. Feminism itself owes much to humanism and the long historical movement toward an elaborated concept of the individual, but it quickly emerges as a challenge to notions of autonomy and authority underwritten by patriarchy. Instead of equality for the unified *female* subject, many feminists turn to an ideal of selflessness or deconstruction of the subject; instead of working to insert more women's biographies in a single cultural history, they advocate an overthrow of the specious narrative coherence implied in the concepts of a "life" and a "universal" history. Yet as the word itself indicates, selflessness might range from a subversive jouissance to a coerced submission; the Angel in the House, after all, is conceived as essentially selfless. Moreover, many theorists' insistence on the breakdown of all grounds for authority and identity may reveal an unconscious resistance to sharing cultural privilege with the marginalized groups who are beginning to grasp at it (Morgan, 6; Jardine, 45–46). In any case, much as feminist thought has been enhanced by a distrust of models of identity and authority, feminist literary criticism (like feminist scholarship generally) could hardly have launched itself without regard for the existence of certain individual, historical women, such as those in the supposedly dead role of "author." Finally, whereas some feminist theorists with good reason have attacked conventions of biographical criticism, all feminist criticism, however chastely textual, ultimately refers to the specificity of female experience; the "feminine" is never simply a writing effect, but also registers the living effects of female human beings.

Anglo-American feminist criticism, in its so-called second stage, the study of the female literary tradition (Showalter, "Feminist Criticism," 248), has been most openly biographical in its approach to works by women. At times this approach does draw too direct a correspondence between a woman's sexual identity and her authorship; it is a deterministic prejudice as old as men's criticism of women's writing. I hear the echo of Leslie Stephen's reading of Eliot that "in spite of her learning and her philosophy, George Eliot is always preeminently feminine" (74). To restore value to the writing of women does not necessarily challenge the mode of thought that defined the feminine other in the first place. Thus Peggy Kamuf charges feminist critics who are preoccupied with "women's language, literature, style or experience" with reinstating humanistic epistemology, "with its faith in the universal truth of man" (44). Toril Moi admonishes readers of American biographical feminist criticism: "For the patriarchal critic, the author is the source, origin and meaning of the text. If we are to undo this patriarchal practice of *authority,* we must take one further step and proclaim, with Roland Barthes, the death of the author" (62–63).[3] Similarly, Mary Jacobus scorns the American feminist "flight toward empiricism" as part of the obsession with origins and authority that constitutes Western metaphysics. Yet Jacobus concedes, "the category of 'women's writing' remains as strategically and politically important in classroom, curriculum, or interpretative community as the specificity of women's oppression is to the women's movement" ("Woman in This Text?" 138).

We will not go far, I think, with a premature Foucauldian dismissal of the category "woman" along with the category "man" because in practice that is to deny the "specificity of women's oppression," including the distinctive burden of personality that arises when we modify "author" with "woman." From this more pragmatic angle, Nancy Miller counters Kamuf's antiauthorial stance: "to foreclose . . . discussions of the author as sexually gendered subject in a socially gendered exchange" may be to deny the material context of our theoretical discourse. Text-centered approaches, whether New Critical or poststructuralist, have been used to evade the political context of the choice of text, which always entails the privileging of one kind of authorship (or particular author[s]) over another. Feminist critics may retain a concern with the signature or sexual identity of the author, Miller hopes, without naive empiricism or a demand for positive role models: "the author can now be rethought *beyond* traditional notions of biography" ("Text's Heroine," 50).[4] This is my hope, as well. Like Eliot and Woolf, we risk appearing simple-mindedly *personal* unless we show ourselves capable of mastering theory (or any dominant cultural discourse), but we should resist the temptation to betray what Woolf, in her famous "elegy" for George Eliot, calls the "difference of view" (160; Jacobus, "Difference," 27–28). Like the women novelists, we may be damned if we do invoke biography or the personal, but we will be damned if we do not: the personal is always attributed to texts written by women, whether or not the authors strove to write in an impersonal mode. With Walker, I would advocate the inclusion of the author's biography and of historical context(s) as contributing, unfolding *texts,* not reified entities, in an alert intertextuality (560).[5]

This said, I would nevertheless insist on the rewards of an occasional experiment in conflating author and work in order to witness the vocational difficulties facing women writers and to challenge an aesthetics of impersonality that devalues the feminine. Many feminist critics have traced the historical effects of this enforced intimacy between women and their writing. Writer and text are liable to be mistaken for each other and to be read aesthetically as trivial and morally as loose (Ellmann, 29). The public has a traditional preoccupation with female origins of a text; access to the privacy of the author seems more intensely desired when the author is a woman, given the charged cultural value of a woman's privacy. It would seem, then, to be a sign of progress that women writers be accorded the ability to distance themselves from their work as men generally are allowed to do.[6] Such distancing, however, has its drawbacks for women: to place the author at an aesthetic remove—indifferent, paring *his* fingernails—may not be for a woman quite what it is for a man. Obscurity and self-effacement for her may be qualities that preclude authorship rather than help her assume godlike authority. It has been the task of many literary women to invent ways to display exceptional powers that seem to transcend ordinary identity (mere womanhood) yet never to claim the self-determined authority of masculine hero or author.

A standard model of female biography guides criticism of women writers, a model that I will trace primarily in Woolf's response to Eliot as Great Woman of English Letters but also in a sampling of these novelists' criticism of other women writers. Briefly, this biographical model prescribes a division between the art and the life in terms of an ideal of feminine self-sacrifice. More is at stake here than the prescription of impersonality—more than T. S. Eliot's separation of "the man who suffers" from "the mind which creates" ("Tradition," 54); what is most at stake is the separation of gendered spheres. As though to naturalize the different social destinies of men and women, criticism of women writers enforces the same biographical convention that shapes heroines in novels. This dividing and duplicitous convention, for example, denies Maggie Tulliver the "world outside" of love that her brother finds (*Mill,* 361); it frustrates her modest attempts to earn a living as he does; and it necessitates her ultimate sacrifice to bring him back within her world of love. This same convention determines that Dorothea Brooke is worshipped as a "poem" (*Middlemarch,* 166) and Mrs. Ramsay as an absent madonna, while their husbands become the reformer or philosopher.

Nancy Miller has characterized this novelistic convention as a differentiation between "ambitious" and "erotic" plots (Miller adapts these terms from Freud's "The Relation of the Poet to Daydreaming" [345–46]). For heroines, the plot of education or vocation must yield to the "natural" demands of the plot of love and marriage, upon pain of failure and death. Biography, of course, must somewhat accommodate actual exceptions, such as Eliot's or Woolf's good fortune in both career and marriage, but exceptions can be made to prove a rule. Thus biographical criticism of women writers, obeying dichotomous convention, assumes that behind the great creative mind must be a woman who suffers, and, conversely, that the more the woman comes forward in the work (unless with a covert display of agony), the less great the work. Corollaries of this principle are that the married mother cannot be a truly great writer, that autobiographical writing by women is inherently flawed (though all female work is inherently autobiographical), and that a female author's claims to independence from the sacrificial destiny of womanhood are punishable by the death of the text. A woman cannot help but write her self, and her self cannot help but be a woman.

Biographical Criticism and the "Great" Woman Writer

The most fundamental challenges, then, to the woman who wishes to become a "great writer" are, on the one hand, to suppress the modifier "woman"—though how this is done remains mysterious even in the instances of literary women's acknowledged "greatness"[7]—and, on the other hand, to come to terms with the masculine norm inherent in the individualistic concepts of greatness and authority. No woman writer, of course, has ever successfully proven the complete irrelevance of her womanhood, but at the height of her reputation for greatness, her sex must somehow seem either incidental, intriguing, or all the more cause for admiring her transcendence of ordinary life. In other words, the ambitious plot must be released from the expectations of the erotic plot.

Women writers face not only the obstacle of preconceived womanhood but also the perhaps more daunting problem of the conception of greatness itself. To be great, in patriarchal culture, is to resemble the male hero; in modern, post-Romantic European culture, to be great is to embody an individualistic ideal. The great artist, at least in most popular accounts, is urged to forfeit all conscious "thinking in common"; *he* must be *original*. Woolf's vision of tradition as a "thinking back through" rejects the artist as self-made solitary, especially by urging women to think back through "our mothers," since mothers are notorious for threatening the dissolution of the ego. At the same time, the high modernist cult of the artist as impersonal catalyst, while apparently encouraging thinking in common, stresses the purity of an exclusive tradition that would be horribly muddied by poetry for ladies, by the personal emotions of mothers, by the vulgar indiscriminacy of the masses. Compared to the strictures of Joyce, T. S. Eliot, and other male modernists, Woolf's vision of a common tradition ends up on the sentimental, populist, feminine side almost in spite of herself. While Woolf more than anyone before labored to restore a female literary tradition and explicitly honored a number of female predecessors, most notably the Brontës and Austen besides Eliot, she nevertheless labored to be beautiful in a tradition that regarded itself as beyond gender or personality.

Woolf's biographical criticism contends with the model that determines irreconcilable erotic and ambitious plots for women. At times she seems to accept uncritically the standards of female greatness associated with this model, as in her Mt. Rushmore of Jane Austen, Charlotte and Emily Brontë, and George Eliot, none of whom led the conventional life of wife and mother (whether this exemption from the usual domesticity was the condition of their being taken seriously or of their being *able* to undertake a vocation is impossible to determine, and probably both effects played a part in their recognized achievement). In *A Room of One's Own,* Austen and Emily Brontë earn Woolf's most wholehearted praise because they have only minimal biographies: readers know little about them, and their personal grievances never intrude upon the page. Charlotte Brontë and Eliot, on the other hand, are more easily criticized because they became notorious—their lives became matter for public debate. Whereas Charlotte offends Woolf's aesthetics of impersonality by allowing autobiographical protest about woman's lot to encroach on her novels, Eliot utters no personal outcry, though Woolf reads Eliot's heroines as awkward self-portraits. It might almost seem that Eliot achieved the self-effacement Woolf sought in the woman writer; escaping the woman's sphere of the novel of manners, Eliot, according to Woolf, was "one of the first English novelists to discover that men and women think as well as feel" ("George Eliot" [1921]). Yet Eliot's command of the unfeminine realm of thought and her masculine pseudonym and style seem to strike Woolf as biographical monstrosities ("George Eliot" [1919], 160; *Room,* 70-80). Given this personal criticism, why was George Eliot so fundamental to Woolf's definition of her own role as great woman of letters? Because Eliot's rejection of the charming-lady role was the necessary precondition of her success as the preeminent, sibylline woman of letters, largely escaping the usual patronizing criticism of female writers.

No female writer besides Eliot had held the place in London intellectual circles that Woolf could claim, and none was so nearly family as Eliot. Both Woolf's father, Leslie Stephen, and his sister-in-law, the novelist Anne Thackeray Ritchie, visited Marian and George Henry Lewes during Sunday author-worship at the Priory,[8] and both father and "aunt" provided biographical portraits of George Eliot, on which Woolf based her centenary reassessment, the 1919 "George Eliot." To some extent, then, Woolf inherited her reading of Eliot, especially from Leslie Stephen's 1902 biography for the English Men of Letters series. This inherited reading stresses the erotic plot, or the suffering-woman-behind-the-book. Woolf reiterates her father's criticism of the novelist's womanly faults; in *George Eliot,* Stephen attributes Eliot's limitations to a natural feminine diffidence and desire for respectability. Woolf, more generous, assumes that those limitations were culturally imposed: Eliot's narrow range (as compared to Tolstoy's, for example) is due to the enforced "suburban seclusion" of a woman living with a married man. Yet at the same time, Woolf seems to hold Eliot's struggles with her reputation against her, as a kind of self-imposed handicap, "which, inevitably, had the worst possible effects upon her work" ("Women and Fiction," *Women,* 47; *Room,* 73–74).

Eliot is difficult to pity as feminine victim, though Woolf eventually devises a way to do so. The greatest obstacles for the biographical critic of Eliot, Woolf finds, are the masculine narrative persona and the ambition and charmlessness of the historical woman. The textual George Eliot is obviously too manly; she "committed atrocities

with" the "man's sentence" (*Room,* 79–80). The imposing stature
granted to her by the Victorians as an exception among women—
Herbert Spencer admitted her novels, "as if they were not novels," to
the London Library ("George Eliot" [1919], 150–51)—frustrates an
impulse to love and pity the woman, but it helps that she is dead and
has come to be laughed at. More useful still is the indescribable ugliness (physical appearance usually rears *its* ugly head in criticism of a
woman's work):

> Her big nose, her little eyes, her heavy, horsey head loom from behind
> the printed page and make a critic of the other sex uneasy. Praise he
> must, but love he cannot; and however absolute and austere his devotion
> to the principle that art has no truck with personality it is not George
> Eliot he would like to pour out tea. On the other hand, . . . Jane Austen
> pours, and as she pours, smiles, charms.

A critic of the same sex, Woolf is uneasy until she can treat Eliot as
"an Aunt": "So treated she drops the apparatus of masculinity which
Herbert Spencer necessitated; indulges herself in memory; and pours
forth . . . the genial stores of her youth, the greatness and profundity
of her soul" ("Indiscretions," *Women,* 72–76).

Woolf needs to discover a precursor at once truly great, by standards she is unwilling to abandon, and truly feminine. Thus she claims
that the mind which created was one and the same as the woman who
suffered; a false patriarchal convention divided the personality that the
female successor can reunite. "I can see already that no one else has
ever known her as I know her. . . . I think she is a highly feminine and
attractive character—most impulsive and ill-balanced . . . and I only
wish she had lived nowadays, and so been saved all that nonsense. . . .
It was an unfortunate thing to be the first woman of the age" (*VW
Letters,* 2: 321–22). Perhaps "nowadays" an ambitious woman might
avoid monstrous disguises. But Woolf's own resolution of the two plots
was not easy and no more clearcut than the equivocations I have been
tracing in her criticism of Eliot the woman and Eliot the works.

In keeping with her need to confirm the *woman's* feminine personality, Woolf recreated a Victorian image of the *works* as chronicles
of rural life. She shared many early readers' preference for the works
that drew on "the genial stores" of Eliot's upbringing in Warwickshire,
Scenes of Clerical Life, Adam Bede, The Mill on the Floss, and *Silas
Marner* ("George Eliot" [1919], 154; Carroll, *Critical Heritage,* 2, 16–
20). Though the author of robust country scenes might be viewed as
more masculine than feminine, the details of a homey past inevitably
carry feminine associations; in emulating Dutch realism, Eliot could
gratify nostalgia for the maternal and for a lost sense of community

(Graver, 250–55) while defying the classical artistic order and gender hierarchy that trivialize domestic detail (Carroll, *Heritage,* 17; Schor).

The nostalgic reading of Eliot was not enough for Woolf, however; she refused to "confine her to village life and lament the book-learned period which produced *Middlemarch* and *Romola.*" In other words, Woolf rescues the woman writer from the feminine sphere of letters, condoning her fulfillment of an ambitious plot. Woolf insists that the later novels forfeit the early charm for the sake not of blue-stocking pedantry but of "wider scope" for the author and her heroines ("George Eliot" [1921]). The loss of the charm associated with home and the past is thus no repudiation of the authority of feminine experience but a means of expanding its influence.

For Woolf, as for Eliot, the challenge is to command "wider scope" without assimilating the masculine norm of human experience; indeed, in their writings the feminine seems to approximate an ideal universality. It is for raising the feminine to the level of the universal that Woolf values Eliot most of all: for having expressed not only everyman's "ordinary joys and sorrows" but also the stifled sufferings of women. "The romance of the past" fades from the novels after *The Mill on the Floss,* but they gain power to express "the ancient consciousness of woman, charged with suffering and sensibility, and for so many ages dumb." Eliot's heroines, presumed by the biographical critic to be autobiographical figures, come to represent the yearning of all women torn between romantic confinement and an unfulfilled desire for some less personal object; this yearning

> brimmed and overflowed and uttered a demand for something . . . that is perhaps incompatible with the facts of human existence. George Eliot had far too strong an intelligence to tamper with those facts. . . . Save for the supreme courage of their endeavour, the struggle ends, for her heroines, in tragedy, or in a compromise that is even more melancholy.

The heroines' story of feminine self-sacrifice "is the incomplete version of the story of George Eliot herself." Eliot, unlike her heroines, found fulfillment in "learning" and "in the wider service of [her] kind," "confronting her feminine aspirations with the real world of men." In short, she transcended her fated personality as a woman, though "the body . . . sank worn out" ("George Eliot" [1919], 154–60). While Woolf certainly wished to attain Eliot's wide range of cultural achievement through other means than Eliot's, she honors the "triumphant" great writer and loves the woman who sank under the burden of personality; she decks her *visited* tomb with "laurel and rose" (160). She portrays the Victorian author as the incomplete version of the story of

Virginia Woolf herself, without directly questioning the "facts" that necessitate that incompleteness.

Woolf's heroines are also incomplete versions of their author's own story, though she does grant artistic fulfillment to the unmarried, childless Lily Briscoe and Miss La Trobe, as well as improbable fame and family fulfillment to her magical, aristocratic poet, Orlando. Both authors' heroines must typify feminine "suffering and sensibility," they must remain in womanly silence, so that Eliot and Woolf may articulate the untold story of universal feminine experience. The story is generated in the gap between the female characters' potential and their achievement, in their struggle with the supposedly incompatible plots of female personality and ambition. As feminist biographical critics, we may repeat this move; our subjects, the women writers, become heroines in a plot of women's education and ambition necessitating self-sacrifice and suffering because of the "facts" of oppression. *We* presumably never end in Woolf's tragedy or Eliot's melancholy compromise.

A Biographical Sketch of Eliot and Woolf

We have seen how Woolf devised a biographical reading of her predecessor that offered a possible reconciliation of the woman who suffers with the mind that creates, thus freeing herself to think back through Eliot. She would not have to repeat the mistakes of the woman or the writer: the mask of pedantry, the not-quite ladylike ugliness of the "grand-daughter of a carpenter" ("George Eliot" [1921]) were no threat to a beautiful heiress of the intellectual aristocracy whose fictional narrators generally appear androgynous, Paterian, unpersonified. Or was Woolf's own development also a response to the threat that an ambitious greatness spelled a denial of femininity? If Woolf's criticism of Eliot takes pains to reveal the woman behind the masculine persona that made the works of "George Eliot" possible in the first place, what prophecy could she have read to a woman writer (like herself) who tried to do without that enabling persona? She must strive to efface herself in works somehow beyond gender—without the masks of Austen's charm or Eliot's rigor. The body and mind of the woman must sink worn out by the effort; she must become a tragic heroine of an ambition plot though a triumphant Great Woman of Letters. Biographical criticism appears to confirm such prophecy; the facts assembled about Eliot and Woolf seem to arrange themselves in suspiciously similar patterns.

Criticism of both canonized authors has been fascinated with their personalities, as though to read their works, not unusually autobiographical, were to read a woman. Both idolatry—of Eliot in her own day and Woolf in ours—and repudiation have fixated in either case on the author's appearance. Woolf's mournfully serene face has been reproduced so often in the photographs, and Bloomsbury has been so thoroughly palpated, that we confront a popular legend when we approach her work (Rose, 249–51). The few portraits of Eliot reveal, in spite of the disproportion of nose and chin, a face as evocative as Woolf's: the serenely mournful expression, the head elegantly tilted, the hair plainly drawn back (compare the illustrations in Bell and in Haight). Most interpreters of both writers seem unable to distinguish the embodied woman from her narrative style. Defenders must compensate by uncovering a feminine Marian Evans Lewes and a masculine Virginia Woolf; one variation of the latter is the robust, political Woolf exhumed by feminists. Ugly and instructively wise, Eliot must be certified to be gentle (Haight entitles a chapter of his biography "Someone to Lean Upon"). Beautiful, cultivated, and charming, Woolf must overcome the role of Invalid Lady of Bloomsbury (Bell, 2:146, 210; Plomer, 324; Caramagno).

Different as their origins certainly were, Eliot and Woolf can be read as heroines struggling against much the same odds with much the same success. Both women overcame the pieties of their upbringing, whether Evangelical or humanist (and Leslie Stephen's humanism owes much to Eliot), to consort with the freethinkers of their day; both triumphed over their educational disadvantages as girls to master classical and contemporary learning and literature. Both dutiful daughters understood that nursing the sick and pouring the tea must always supersede the translation project or the literary reviewing—until they escaped to homes of their own. Both lost their somewhat remote mothers while they were in their teens. They were both strongly attached to their fathers, who, though they encouraged their clever daughters, expected them to lend domestic service. Each woman viewed her father as an inhibiting power. Mary Ann, before Evans's death, wrote: "What shall I be without my Father? It will seem as if a part of my moral nature were gone. I had a horrid vision of myself last night becoming earthly sensual and devilish for want of that purifying restraining influence" (*GE Letters,* 1:284). As a measure of the distance Woolf has traveled from Eliot's (and her own) early filial piety, her comment in 1928 on her father's death expresses no horror at her own propensities, but only a sense of release: his "life would have entirely ended mine. . . . No writing, no books" (*VW Diary,* 3:208).[10] After their fathers' deaths (and supported by small inheritances), they were able to begin careers in earnest, publishing translations or reviews and essays before building up confidence to write and publish eight or nine novels as well as biographies, poetry, or stories while they kept up their correspondence and amassed notebooks and journals.

This might be the pattern narrative of success, but it would be dull without a hint of the great woman's suffering, and certainly we must not omit the love interest. Eminence took its toll: Eliot was often ill and despondent as she wrote her novels; Woolf went into severe depressions after every novel appeared. The suffering was mitigated for each woman by a fortunate union with a loving man of letters capable of tending her career, supplying confidence when she despaired.

I would not want to exaggerate the woman writer's dependence on the tolerance of the men around her, but it seems certain that without some release from the conventional roles of daughter, wife, and mother, neither Eliot nor Woolf would have excelled as they did. In spite of their famous departures from convention (Eliot's alliance with Lewes, Woolf's briefer one with Vita Sackville-West), both led quiet domestic lives, forfeiting with regret the right to have children (Haight, 205, 413; Showalter, *Literature,* 272–73). The ban on childbearing suggests a similarity between the status of the mistress and the madwoman. An unmarried woman and a woman liable to suicidal bouts with insanity were equally denied the full status of motherhood, although Eliot welcomed the role of "Madonna" and "Mutter" to Lewes's sons and others (Beer, 27, 109–12; Homans, 22), while Woolf, though vicariously engaged in Vanessa's mothering, tended to designate other women to mother her (Marcus, 96–114). Woolf herself points out that "the four great women novelists" bore no children ("Women and Fiction," *Women,* 45); while literary creation and childbirth were welcome analogies, they seemed to be antinomies in most women's lives.

Perhaps because of their unusual domestic circumstances, Eliot and Woolf were able to combine a reclusive private life with public prominence and wide access to culture. Woolf noted that Eliot played the retiring sibyl, and Rose Macaulay observed the same of Woolf, in spite of the fact that both hobnobbed with the rich and famous. Yet both strove to make a virtue out of the enforced privatization of a woman's life; Woolf urged the woman writer to find a room of her own (Showalter, *Literature,* 285, 297; *Room,* 24), while Eliot expressed gratitude for her involuntary isolation from polite female society, which afforded her a kind of room of her own. Whatever the cost, a certain retreat from the world seems to have been necessary for both Eliot and Woolf, perhaps because the personality of a famous woman seems especially assailable.

The very definition of "greatness," according to George Henry Lewes, entails a self-determination and disregard of personal judgments that are culturally withheld from women: "A magisterial subjection of all dispersive influences, a concentration of the mind upon the thing that has to be done . . . these are the rare qualities which mark out the man of genius. In men of lesser calibre the mind is more constantly open to determination from extrinsic influences." Socialized as women, Eliot and Woolf easily could be marked out as less than men of genius because they could not concentrate wholly on the work, finding themselves open to "dispersive influences," the validated demands of others. In compensation, they devised impersonal narrative personae that make a virtue out of susceptibility to others, to the extrinsic and distracting. "Dispersed are we," intones the audience-narrator of *Between the Acts*. The historian of Middlemarch, claiming to be dwarfed by the "great" predecessor Fielding, struggles like Lewes's lesser man against distraction: "[A]ll the light I can command must be concentrated on this particular web, and not dispersed over that tempting range of relevancies called the universe" (105). But, like the playwright Miss La Trobe's self-effacement, this is no genuine expression of modesty but a claim to greatness—to universal insight—through selflessness, beyond gender, beyond the cult of personality and genius. The pose of masculine objectivity of Eliot's narrators and the masquerade of androgynous interpersonality in Woolf's fictions both strive for the same end of distancing the biographical woman from her creations without at the same time concurring in the egotistical model of the "impersonal" man of genius.

Eliot and Woolf as Biographical Critics

In spite of their best efforts, both Eliot and Woolf faced the highly personal biographical criticism of their day, which defined greatness according to the model of the imperial masculine self. Perhaps surprisingly, they turn around and apply the same tools in their criticism of other writers; in their cultural judgments they often sound like the voice of tradition. Women writers who seemed untrue to their innate "vocation" as well as women writers who appeared too womanly both met with their disapproval: the unwomanly and the womanly were incompatible with greatness.

Woolf herself laid a foundation for feminist biographical criticism with her emphasis on the material and ideological conditions that have constrained women's writing. In one sense, this was true to her heritage; the biographical mode dominated nineteenth-century criticism, including Eliot's essays. As we would expect, Woolf's biographical criticism probes further than Eliot's would have done into private details and physical circumstances, while taking a more phenomenological approach to identity ("The New Biography," *VW*

Essays, 4:229–35). Yet both authors preferred reticence about the writer's intentions, doubting the relevance of biography to criticism of the novel.

Eliot repudiates curiosity about authors in severe moral terms:

> I am thoroughly opposed in principle (quite apart from any personal reference to myself) to the system of *contemporary* biography. . . . [T]he mass of the public will read any quantity of trivial details about a writer. . . . Even posthumous biography is, I think, increasingly perverted into [a time-wasting] indulgence. . . . It seems to me that just my works and the order in which they appeared is what the part of the public which cares about me may most usefully know. (*GE Letters,* 6:67–68)

Woolf characteristically grants that personal details may not be trivial (and Eliot's narrators often insist on their importance) and often likes to defend popular appetites against a disapproving elite (as Marian Lewes would not). Unlike Eliot, Woolf condones a reader's interest in the "truth" behind the fiction ("nothing is more fascinating"). But she clearly dissociates the novel from the author, who can tell us about *himself* but who is probably unable to "say anything about his own work" ("Introduction," v–vi). The author is one thing, a very interesting thing, and the canon of "his" works is another.

Though Eliot and Woolf both engaged in biographical criticism themselves, it would not have been news to them that the living being who becomes an author has little final say as to what the book becomes in the hands of readers, and that he or she is profoundly unknowable, like Lydgate "a cluster of signs for his neighbours' false suppositions" (*Middlemarch,* 105). Yet both authors share a model of character as a developing process largely determined by milieu; Woolf's three pieces on Eliot, for example, confidently enlist the circumstances of her predecessor's life as determinants of the works. In spite of her reliance on biographical detail, Woolf as critic passes harshest judgment where personalities and circumstances are too well known; she is most lenient with the most obscure or with the great whose "lives" are lost. "The people whom we admire most as writers, then, have something . . . impersonal about them." We know too much about the Victorians, she claims: it is impossible to imagine "George Eliot gathering her skirts about her and leaping from a cliff" as Sappho did ("Personalities," *VW Essays,* 2:275, 274). Though we know almost too much about Woolf's most private life, we still can romanticize her as having taken such a plunge—perhaps because narrative conventions are stronger than unglamorous details.

Eliot and Woolf rely on these narrative conventions in judging other women writers; in spite of their different orientations toward women, they apply the divided-plot biographical model in much the same way. They both assumed that a woman's disadvantage—which must become her strength—lay in her confinement to the romantic plot; her expertise must be in the detail of domestic experience, from counterpanes to courtship. It is fatal to the woman writer to write like a man, it only adds fuel to the male critics' inevitable ridicule if she pretends to learning or theology, and if she overindulges her imagination or raises a protest, she positively fails in her duty. In short, if she is in every way as much like Jane Austen as she can be, she may do fine things as a novelist; otherwise, she is a woman thrown entirely on her own resources, like Jane Eyre in the wild.

This rendition of Eliot's and Woolf's counsel to women writers might also paraphrase the critical doctrine of George Henry Lewes and Leslie Stephen; it is not, however, a complete account of what Eliot and Woolf had to say about women writers. Eliot, for example, greatly admired Harriet Beecher Stowe and Charlotte Brontë, both of whom diverge markedly from Austen in their use of melodrama and social protest. Woolf similarly swerves from the Austen model by encouraging the Mary Carmichaels, the twentieth-century women novelists who write of women's relations to each other and to their work outside the home, as well as those writers of the future who will disregard altogether the injunction that women should write novels if they must write (*Room,* 95, 80–81).

A thorough consideration of Eliot's and Woolf's criticism of women writers is, of course, impossible here, but I will touch on a few examples where their biographical prescriptions take similar effects. Generally speaking, Eliot sought to discourage "silly" lady novelists, whereas Woolf promoted many a woman writer from obscurity—a difference perhaps biographically traceable to Eliot's own expressed preference for men and Woolf's for women. As late as *Theophrastus Such,* Eliot appears to wish that a minor lady writer had never published a word ("Diseases of Small Authorship," 155), whereas Woolf stresses the "ghosts" and "prejudices" that women writers face before they can perfect or even publish that word ("Professions for Women," *Women,* 61–62). Yet, like Eliot, Woolf subscribes to certain prejudiced expectations of women writers. She censures almost as strictly as Eliot does the women writers who recklessly promote their own personalities or opinions—or, worst of all, their partisanship of womanhood. Woolf warns: "It is fatal for a woman to lay the least stress on any grievance . . . ; in any way to speak consciously as a woman" (*Room,* 108). Must all who aspire to greatness emulate George Eliot, uncomplaining, unselfconscious, full of manly wisdom? Yet both Woolf and Eliot mock the manly female writer who struts "like a bad actress in male attire" ("Woman in France," *GE Essays,* 53).

Eliot and Woolf at times seem to imply that they alone of all women shared the perch with men of letters, yet they did find some contemporaries and predecessors to admire. They were not unwilling to grant the excellence of literary women such as Elizabeth Barrett Browning and Mary Wollstonecraft, either because these authors were able to reconcile artistic calling and womanhood or because they refused to reach a compromise. Barrett Browning, for example, impressed both Eliot and Woolf as a distinctly feminine writer who seized a masculine artistic freedom. In her 1857 review of *Aurora Leigh,* Eliot calls Barrett Browning "all the greater poet because she is intensely a poetess," one who exhibits "all the peculiar powers without the negations of her sex." As Gillian Beer explains in citing this review, however, Eliot believes the feminine writer must, like Barrett Browning, incorporate masculinity along with femininity in order to achieve "liberty *from* sexual type: 'there is simply a full mind pouring itself out in song as its natural and easiest medium'" (16). Woolf's similar reading of *Aurora Leigh* expresses stronger misgivings about the feminine personality displayed in the work. Barrett Browning, according to Woolf, "was one of those rare writers [whose] . . . imaginative life . . . demands to be considered apart from personalities." Yet the *poem* is too personal: "the connexion between a woman's art and a woman's life was unnaturally close." In *Aurora Leigh,* the feminine "genius," then, remains "in some pre-natal stage waiting the final stroke of creative power" because the woman poet cannot escape her personality after all ("Aurora Leigh," *Women,* 137-44). Both great women of letters find in Barrett Browning, lauded as the greatest English woman poet in her day, the incomplete version of their own stories: a somewhat too easy, personal, feminine artist, though a great venturer in the poetic territory of the drawing-room that Eliot and Woolf were to mine so profitably.

Like Woolf, Eliot viewed other women writers through the lens of personality, at times empathizing with suffering and admiring fidelity to womanly duty while praising the escape from the "negations" of personality. Eliot compared her own career with those of Harriet Beecher Stowe and Margaret Fuller, and though Eliot might not entirely concur with their reforming zeal, she admired the combination of public mission and ladylike private life. Eliot sustained a long friendship in letters with Stowe, acknowledging her as one who properly fulfilled a dual vocation of womanhood and art (outdoing Eliot in the former at least): "you have had longer experience than I as a writer, and fuller experience as a woman, since you have borne children and known the mother's history from the beginning" (*GE Letters,* 5:29–31). She praised Stowe's "rare genius," belonging to "that highest rank of novelists who can give us a national life in all its phases" ("[Three Novels]," *GE Essays,* 326). The example of Fuller seems to have illustrated a conflict between vocations—as explicator of the national life and as woman—that was closer to Eliot's experience: "It is a help to read such a life as Margaret Fuller's," Eliot wrote in 1852 (before her union with Lewes); "I am thankful, as if for myself, that [the life] was sweet at last" (*GE Letters,* 2:15; Pinney, 199). Eliot perceived that the postponed romance plot in Wollstonecraft's and Fuller's ambitious lives was similar to her own; the late loving marriage after literary endeavor comes to Barrett Browning and Aurora Leigh as well. Fuller could be seen as a heroine who smooths over the clash of competing plots, a crusader who does no harm to Tennysonian "distinctive womanhood" ("Fuller and Wollstonecraft," *GE Essays,* 200). Indeed, Fuller's brother, in the edition of *Woman in the Nineteenth Century* that Eliot reviewed, reassures us (as Gaskell did in her biography of Brontë) that "literary women" and female reformers do not necessarily "neglect the domestic concerns of life" (Ossoli, Preface, iv–v). Fuller's belated marriage and sudden death soon after make her a heroine like Gaskell's Brontë, while her drowning has a fortuitous literary respectability; Eliot recalls Wollstonecraft's earlier attempt to drown herself (*GE Letters,* 5: 160–61) and rewrites aspects of these exemplary lives in Maggie Tulliver's drowning and Mirah Lapidoth's attempted suicide. It is difficult not to believe that Woolf was trying to write the closure of her own life into such a tradition.

Woolf as much as Eliot tries to read her literary women as heroines, linking text and personality, and she, too, perceives womanly greatness in Mary Wollstonecraft. But while both Eliot and Woolf rediscover the "loving woman's heart" in the legendary hyena in petticoats ("Fuller and Wollstonecraft," *GE Essays,* 201), Woolf is not certain that feminine susceptibility is to the credit of the great reforming author. With her "reformer's love [and hatred] of humanity," Wollstonecraft "won fame and independence and the right to live her own life" but, according to Woolf, she was always brought up short by her desire for domestic love. The woman herself embodies conflict: "these contradictions [show] . . . in her face, at once so resolute and so dreamy, so sensual and so intelligent, and beautiful into the bargain." Ultimately, like Dorothea Brooke, "she has her revenge. . . . [O]ne form of immortality is hers . . . we hear her voice and trace her influence even now among the living" ("Wollstonecraft," *Women,* 98–99, 103).

In other portraits of female predecessors, Woolf is less tolerant of the conflict between womanhood and ambition, though it is clear that to compromise in favor of womanhood is to forfeit all claim to greatness. Mrs. Humphry Ward, whose books "we never wish to open" again, chose the route of "compromise"; she displayed no disinterested devotion to art, though she was active in public causes, including the ignoble antisuffrage campaign. The worst is that "her imagination always . . . agrees to perch"; she has become mere historical personality ("The Compromise," *Women,* 171-72). In contrast, Olive Schreiner would seem to have some of Wollstonecraft's vision and to share the honor of tragedy (in ultimate obscurity and isolation) rather than compromise, but her egotism prevents her from measuring up to Woolf's standard for greatness. Schreiner's *Story of an African Farm* "has the limitations" of the Brontës' "egotistical masterpieces without a full measure of their strength. The writer's interests are local, her passions personal." Nevertheless, like a reverse of Mrs. Humphry Ward, Schreiner earns "pity and respect" as one of "those martyrs" to "the cause . . . [of] the emancipation of women." If she is "one half of a great writer" ("Schreiner," *Women,* 180–83), the other half is marred by politics and egotism.

Apparently, Eliot's and Woolf's ideal of greatness for the woman writer would be almost impossible to fulfill if one must be both genius and angel, must live *down* and live *by* one's personality as a woman. The woman writer's only hope, perhaps, was to suppress the gender bias of biographical criticism by offering up work so authoritative as to constitute a kind of reinvention of the personality of the author. The hope has never been fulfilled, and, as I have suggested, the attempt to escape feminine personality might prove more treacherous than enabling. Few now would wish to posit an unproblematic identity for any author, male or female. Instead, a continual revision of literary history in light of the narratives of authorial personality that have always guided readings of women authors should yield some perspective on current critical practice—putting a stop, at least, to the obvious abuses of the divided-plot convention. We must try to steer clear of the pitfalls of prescriptive biographical criticism of women writers without resorting to some safer zone of undifferentiated textuality.

The great woman of letters, like a newer vision of the heroine Antigone, is in danger of being buried alive in her youth. If we primarily aim at preventing her misguided sacrifice to the deities of authorship and greatness, we side with Creon against the new Antigone's defiance of the state of literature. Instead, though we no longer need to believe in these classical myths except as effective (and often dangerous) literary conventions, we should seize whatever power is left in them, if only for satire or parody. There are plenty of other voices, besides those of the well-intentioned cultural critic opposed to the imperial subject, that are ready to silence the ambitious woman.

Notes

Adapted from Alison Booth: *Greatness Engendered: George Eliot and Virginia Woolf.* Forthcoming from Cornell University Press, 1992. Used by permission of the publisher.

1. Such is the logic implied in T. S. Eliot's contribution to the same tribute (which appeared in *Horizon* 3 [1941]: 313–406); Woolf belongs to the masculine category of "great writer," becoming "the centre . . . of the literary life of London," "the symbol" of the "Victorian upper middle-class" cultural tradition.

2. Cheryl Walker traces the tradition of attacks on author-centered criticism, including Jan Montefiore's anti-intentionalist argument that cites Wimsatt, Beardsley, and Barthes (Walker, 563). T. S. Eliot crystallized a doctrine that George Eliot and others in the nineteenth century already shared; her Herr Klesmer (based on Liszt) might have told Gwendolen Harleth, "The progress of an artist is a continual self-sacrifice, a continual extinction of personality" ("Tradition and the Individual Talent," 53).

3. See Walker's critique of Moi's denial of authorship. Moi continues to rely on false dichotomies, including that between "creative and critical discourse"; for Moi, critics, unlike creative writers, can be read biographically as authors (557–59).

4. Miller has continued to pursue the goal of a political yet deconstructed idea of writing and the author. "So why remember Barthes . . . ?" she slyly asks, recalling his 1968 "The Death of the Author" ("Changing the Subject," 104–5). See *Subject to Change,* 16.

5. For convenience, I use "we" to refer to feminist critics, in the hope that diversity will be allowed within the plural pronoun. By the same token, my claims about the dilemmas of two "great" women of letters are not meant to suppress the diversity of writers who are biologically female.

6. The industry of biographical criticism has provided even the Bard with a boyhood—such criticism is not reserved for women—but Shakespeare is considered great (as Woolf says) because he evokes universal, not his own, experience (*Room,* 58). Women's writing is more insistently and consistently read through authorial experience than men's.

7. Ellen Moers illustrates this difficulty, faced even by the female feminist critic, when she begins her preface to *Literary Women: The Great Writers:* "The subject of this book is the major women writers, writers we read and shall always read whether interested or not in the fact that they happened to be women" (ix).

8. Stephen noted in his *Mausoleum Book* that "one had to be ready to discuss metaphysics . . . and offer an acceptable worship" at the Priory; Lady Ritchie wrote, "[T]he shrine was so serene and kind that this authoress felt like a wretch for having refused to worship there before" (quoted in Showalter, "The Greening of Sister George," 293).

9. In quoting this passage, I have omitted a piece of the sort of gossip Woolf treasured for casting predecessors as suffering heroines (the editors swiftly put down the charge as "quite unfounded"): "(Mrs Prothero once told me that she—George Eliot that is—had a child by a Professor in Edinburgh . . . the child is a well known Professor somewhere else—)." Was the great writer but a woman after all?

10. In *Three Guineas,* Woolf writes of the "infantile fixation" of fathers who claim complete possession of their daughters. Nevertheless, "[i]t was the woman, the human being whose sex made it her sacred duty to sacrifice herself to the father, whom Charlotte Brontë and Elizabeth Barrett had to kill"—not the father himself (134–35).

Works Cited

Beer, Gillian. *George Eliot.* Key Woman Writers. Brighton: Harvester, 1986.

Bell, Quentin. *Virginia Woolf: A Biography.* 2 vols. New York: Harcourt Brace Jovanovich, 1972.

Caramagno, Thomas C. "Manic-Depressive Psychosis and Critical Approaches to Virginia Woolf's Life and Work." *PMLA* 103 (1988): 10–23.

Carroll, David. *George Eliot: The Critical Heritage.* London: Routledge & Kegan Paul, 1971.

Eliot, George. *Essays of George Eliot.* Edited by Thomas Pinney. London: Routledge & Kegan Paul, 1963.

———. *The George Eliot Letters.* Edited by Gordon S. Haight. 9 vols. New Haven, Conn.: Yale University Press, 1954–1978.

———. *Middlemarch.* Boston: Houghton Mifflin, 1956.

———. *The Mill on the Floss.* Boston: Houghton Mifflin, 1961.

———. *Impressions of Theophrastus Such.* Vol. 21 of *The Complete Works of George Eliot.* New York: Harper & Brothers, n.d. [1910].

Eliot, T. S. "Tradition and the Individual Talent." *The Sacred Wood: Essays on Poetry and Criticism,* 47–59. London: Methuen, 1960.

———. "Virginia Woolf I." *Horizon: A Review of Literature and Art* 3 (1941): 313–16.

Ellmann, Mary. *Thinking About Women.* New York: Harcourt, 1968.

Gaskell, Elizabeth. *The Life of Charlotte Brontë.* Harmondsworth, Middlesex: Penguin, 1975.

Graver, Suzanne. *George Eliot and Community: A Study in Social Theory and Fictional Form.* Berkeley and Los Angeles: University of California Press, 1984.

Haight, Gordon S. *George Eliot: A Biography.* New York: Oxford University Press, 1968.

Helsinger, Elizabeth K., Robin Lauterbach Sheets, and William Veeder. *The Woman Question: Literary Issues 1837–1883.* Vol. 3 of *The Woman Question: Society and Literature in Britain and America, 1837–1883.* 3 vols. New York: Garland, 1983.

Homans, Margaret. *Bearing the Word: Language and Female Experience in Nineteenth-Century Women's Writing.* Chicago, Ill.: University of Chicago Press, 1986.

Jacobus, Mary. "The Difference of View." *Reading Woman: Essays in Feminist Criticism,* 27–40. New York: Columbia University Press, 1986.

———. "Is There a Woman in this Text?" *New Literary History* 14 (1982): 117–41.

Jardine, Alice A. *Gynesis: Configurations of Woman and Modernity.* Ithaca, N.Y.: Cornell University Press, 1985.

Kamuf, Peggy. "Replacing Feminist Criticism." *Diacritics* 12 (1982): 42–47.

Lewes, George Henry. "The Lady Novelists." *Essays and Reviews of George Eliot.* Edited by Mrs. S. B. Herrick, 7–24. Boston: Aldine, 1887.

Macaulay, Rose. "Virginia Woolf, II." *Horizon: A Review of Literature and Art* 3 (1941): 316–18.

Marcus, Jane. *Virginia Woolf and the Languages of Patriarchy.* Bloomington: Indiana University Press, 1987.

Miller, Nancy K. "Changing the Subject: Authorship, Writing, and the Reader." *Feminist Studies/Critical Studies.* Edited by Teresa de Lauretis, 102–20. Bloomington: Indiana University Press, 1986.

———. "Emphasis Added: Plots and Plausibilities in Women's Fiction." *The New Feminist Criticism.* Edited by Elaine Showalter, 339–60. New York: Pantheon, 1985.

———. *Subject to Change: Reading Feminist Writing.* New York: Columbia, 1988.

———. "The Text's Heroine: A Feminist Critic and Her Fictions." *Diacritics* 12 (1982): 48–53.

Moers, Ellen. *Literary Women: The Great Writers.* New York: Oxford University Press, 1985.

Moi, Toril. *Sexual/Textual Politics: Feminist Literary Theory.* New York: Methuen, 1985.

Montefiore, Jan. *Feminism and Poetry: Language, Experience, Identity in Women's Writing.* London: Pandora, 1987.

Morgan, Susan. *Sisters in Time: Imagining Gender in Nineteenth-Century British Fiction.* New York: Oxford University Press, 1989.

Ossoli, Margaret Fuller. *Woman in the Nineteenth Century, and Kindred Papers Relating to the Sphere, Condition and Duties, of Woman.* Edited by Arthur B. Fuller. Boston: Jewett, 1855.

Pinney, Thomas, ed. *Essays of George Eliot.* London: Routledge & Kegan Paul, 1963.

Plomer, William. "Virginia Woolf, IV." *Horizon* 3 (1941): 323–27.

Rose, Phyllis. *Woman of Letters: A Life of Virginia Woolf.* New York: Oxford University Press, 1978.

Schor, Naomi. *Reading in Detail: Aesthetics and the Feminine.* New York: Methuen, 1987.

Showalter, Elaine. "Feminist Criticism in the Wilderness." *The New Feminist Criticism.* Edited by Elaine Showalter, 243–70. New York: Pantheon, 1985.

———. "The Greening of Sister George." *Nineteenth-Century Fiction* 35 (1980): 292–311.

———. *A Literature of Their Own: British Women Novelists from Brontë to Lessing.* Princeton, N.J.: Princeton University Press, 1977.

Stephen, Leslie. *George Eliot.* London: Macmillan, 1902.

Walker, Cheryl. "Feminist Literary Criticism and the Author." *Critical Inquiry* 16 (1990): 551–71.

Woolf, Virginia. *Collected Essays.* 4 vols. New York: Harcourt Brace & World, 1967.

———. *The Diary of Virginia Woolf.* 5 vols. Edited by Anne Olivier Bell and Andrew McNeillie. New York: Harcourt Brace Jovanovich, 1977–1984.

———. "George Eliot." 1919. *Women and Writing.* Edited by Michèle Barrett, 150–60. New York: Harcourt Brace Jovanovich, 1979.

———. "George Eliot (1818–1880)." *London Daily Herald.* 9 March 1921. 7.

———. "Introduction." *Mrs. Dalloway,* v–ix. New York: Modern Library, 1928.

———. *The Letters of Virginia Woolf.* Edited by Nigel Nicolson and Joanne Trautmann. 6 vols. New York: Harcourt Brace Jovanovich, 1975–1980.

———. *Women and Writing.* Edited by Michèle Barrett. New York: Harcourt Brace Jovanovich, 1979.

———. *A Room of One's Own.* 1929. New York: Harcourt Brace Jovanovich, 1957.

———. *Three Guineas.* 1938. New York: Harcourt Brace and World, 1966.

Cheryl Walker

Persona Criticism and the Death of the Author

The difficulty with doing biographical criticism today is that the figure of the author has increasingly come under attack, almost as if the author's portrait, which at one time routinely accompanied critical works, were being atomized, dissolved in an acid bath of scorn and distrust.[1] Though "death of the author" critics have made a number of important points about the rigidity and naiveté of certain earlier forms of biographical criticism, I find that in my own practice I am loath to give up all vestiges of the author. The strategy I have chosen is what I call persona criticism, a form of analysis that focuses on patterns of ideation, voice, and sensibility linked together by a connection to the author. Yet persona criticism allows one to speak of authorship as multiple, involving culture, psyche, and intertextuality, as well as biographical data about the writer.

Persona criticism will not pass muster with those who, following Roland Barthes, believe that the critic's job should be recognized as that of "ceaselessly posit[ing] meaning [only] ceaselessly to evaporate it"[2] because this critical stance aspires to hold its place long enough to suggest connections between cultural, psychological, and literary history, connections that presume to rearrange our conception of the real. Persona criticism represents a compromise between those who will have no truck at all with authorship and those for whom the author is always and everywhere an ascertainable reference limiting what a text can and should mean. It is, as I have said, a strategy; but by calling it a strategy, I do not mean to suggest that its motivation is simple expedience.

Though biographical criticism was a respected genre forty years ago, contemporary attacks upon it force one to have recourse to some set of strategies in order to continue connecting authorial biography to textual meaning. Today the question of what role the author can claim to perform in writing a poem or a novel is deeply enmeshed in ontological uncertainties that first began to be registered a century ago, when anxieties about authorship also began to surface. Philosophically, this question has become entangled with concerns about the status of the will and intentionality. What do I do when I put my fingers on the computer keys? And who am "I" anyway?

In our frustration with the Romantic notion of the artist as supreme originator, towering above "his" time and igniting "his" text with primitive bolts of genius, we are now skeptical of both unified subjectivities and newness. Materialist critical theories remind us that historical circumstances in many ways determine the literary product. Critics of language insist that authors are always already inscribed in a linguistic situation drenched with the past and with ideology. Post-Freudians, too, are rightly skeptical about claims to conscious control over the "finished" product, control that has in the past often been seen as essential to the notion of the artist.[3]

Though all these are important considerations, as a feminist I find myself dissatisfied with the abstract indeterminacy of "textuality," which has, in many cases, come to replace authorship in critical discourse. It continues to seem to me important to identify the circumstances that govern relations between authors and texts, as between texts and readers, because without such material we are in danger of seeing gender disappear or become transformed into a feature of textuality that cannot be persuasively connected to real women.

Of course, it should be said that the main proponents of "death of the author" criticism—Roland Barthes, Michel Foucault, and Jacques Derrida—were never so extreme as to deny all attempts to discuss the author, and even the most rigorous opponents of biographical criticism may wish to make use of some form of what Foucault calls "the author function."[4] Often, however, it is assumed that critics like Barthes and Foucault would disapprove of any extended usage of biographical material.

To correct this assumption, I have elsewhere noted that Barthes's real target in "The Death of the Author" was not so much biographical criticism per se as any practice that sought "to impose a limit on [the] text, to furnish it with a final signified, to close the writing."[5] "Death of the author" critics are united in rejecting the notion that behind the text stands a subject called the author to whom all questions about the text should be referred and by whom (literally or figuratively) all confusions will be resolved.

I have no difficulty in accepting the notion that our understanding of "the author" must always be open to reconsideration, just as the text itself finds its meanings in readers who, because they are potentially infinite in number, might be said (à la Barthes) to be "without [any particular] history, biography, psychology" (DA, 148). But this is useful only when one is considering the *potential* of the text to assume significance in the multiple contexts of its reception.

Foucault is more specific about other contexts that might be interesting to explore. Though in his essay he says that "one has already called back into question the absolute character and founding role of the subject" as author, he goes on to say: "Still, perhaps one must return to this question, not in order to reestablish the theme of an originating subject, but to grasp the subject's points of insertion, modes of functioning, and system of dependencies."[6] In other words, Foucault is quite ready to allow that exploring interconnections between what he calls, in other sections of the essay, the "scriptor" and the text might be both interesting and productive.

In his view, of course, it is also possible to extend authorship to a variety of subjects who, for one reason or another, might appropriate the text. These subject-readers might also be considered authors, according to Foucault. Here again I concur as I do when Derrida, in "Signature Event Context," says that "the sign possesses the characteristic of being readable even if the moment of its production is irrevocably lost and even if I do not know what its alleged author-scriptor consciously intended to say at the moment he wrote it, i.e. abandoned it to its essential drift."[7] Rather than examine the essential nature of what is readable, however, I prefer to appropriate Nancy K. Miller's strategy of "changing the subject"[8] in order to reflect on why it seems important to me to reconstitute the author in these contestatory times.

One of the useful insights of feminist criticism is that much totalizing theory is designed to obscure difference. In the past twenty years, women have been resisting the tendency of many masculinist theorists to assume that the male can speak for the species without finding out if what is claimed works equally well for both sexes. In fact, gender has been obscured as an important consideration in most modern critical practices in their formative stages. In psychoanalytic criticism, for instance, male experience has often been considered normative. In much historical criticism, history has been defined narrowly as the ideas and experiences of men. In myth criticism, male myths (often of the hero) seemed at first more central than divergent or complementary female myths. These are merely three of many areas that have been targets of recent feminist revisions. It now seems absurd to act as if female experience is somehow deviant or exceptional and male experience is typical or normative.

Applying the techniques of feminist resistance to such old-fashioned assumptions, one might now ask if the following statement in Foucault's "What Is an Author?" is as universal as it claims to be. Foucault insists: "Using all the contrivances that he sets up between himself and what he writes, the writing subject cancels out the signs of his particular individuality. As a result, the mark of the writer is reduced to nothing more than the singularity of his absence; he must assume the role of the dead man in the game of writing" (WIA, 102–3). It is the word "must" that I puzzle over. In its claim to be true for all cases, I suspect it is hiding something and that what it is hiding may well be enormously significant.

Presumably, given the direction of other remarks, Foucault means that stylistic conventions and the iterability of language itself enforce a kind of impersonality (the translator Josué Harari calls it, significantly, *indifference*) that will always mock any pretense of particular identity in the writer.[9] "He must assume the role of the dead man ... ," etc. But should we interpret this statement as meaning that the writer *must assume* that he must assume this role? In other words, does this seek to address the writer's understanding of the nature of "his" own performance?

Or is Foucault pointing to the way readers respond to a piece of writing—the fact, long recognized, that the writer cannot control the response of the reader, that the writer becomes *for the reader* a function of the way the text is structured rather than vice versa? The writer thus dies into art, and the text itself takes its promiscuous way indifferent to the feelings, the aims, the arrogance of its author. If the latter is what Foucault's text is suggesting, then one of the issues that is obscured with this word "must" is that the gender of the author, which—one would assume—would count as a particularizing aspect, has had and continues to have a great impact on the way readers actually encounter texts. Assertions about what a text means, especially if the writer is female, frequently depend for their logic upon widely shared assumptions about gender differences. Many women writers would gladly have accepted the role of "a dead man" in the game of writing only to find themselves treated by male critics as "a live woman" instead.

At the end of Foucault's essay, he asks the question: "What difference does it make who is speaking?" For Foucault, in 1969, subjects as historically limited individuals seem far less important than the infinite texts in which "writing unfolds like a game (jeu) that invariably goes beyond its own rules and transgresses its limits" (WIA, 102). Women have long been aware, however, that it makes a good deal of difference who is preceived as speaking. For example, research has shown that women are more frequently interrupted than men, most frequently *by* men.[10] Indeed, women have only comparatively recently been allowed the privilege of speaking in public at all. Toril Moi coins an effective phrase to indicate the way men have thought themselves capable of speaking *for* women when she refers to "the ventriloquism of patriarchy."[11]

In the past, women have become writers partly to create substantive identities. Too often such women have found themselves ignored, drowned out, spoken for, or spoken against with the result that they have even lost contact with what they might be inclined to think, should they ever have the opportunity. At the level of her own understanding about her role as an author, therefore, it is fatal for such a woman to choose the role of self-sacrifice Foucault describes as characteristic of contemporary *écriture*. Self-sacrifice, as Nancy K. Miller suggests, may well be a phase in the development of authorial consciousness not appropriate to such female authors.[12] But, of course, all of this is only relevant at the level of the author's positionality and intentions, concerns that are frequently ruled out of court by "death of the author" critics.

On the issue of the text itself, there are still other problems to contend with. What about the ethical considerations of reading a woman's writing as writing written by a woman, for instance? Would it not be better to avoid the kind of derogatory, patronizing, or cooptive commentary women writers have been subjected to (even by women) by simply treating all texts without reference to the historical particularities of their authors? Though sometimes recommended by critics who think of themselves as sympathetic to the claims of feminism, this mode mimics, it seems to me, the universalizing tendencies of patriarchal criticism by claiming to be able to transcend culture and gender entirely, at least at the level of authorship. This approach has always resulted in the masking of oppression of various kinds. As long as gender, class, race, sexual orientation, and other forms of difference are constituted hierarchically by power politics, they will remain important features of both writing and reading. The choice to ignore such issues, in the end, serves the status quo.

From my point of view, it seems far better to bring to the fore those ways in which readers and writers differ than to dwell at length upon the essentialist properties of textuality. If what legibility means is that a semantic sequence must be able to be made sense of irrespective of particularities among readers or writers, this tells us nothing about what actually happens in textual relations connecting author and text, reader and text, author and reader. Though I am not "against theory"[13] that focuses on the nature of language and textuality (indeed I find such theory fascinating), I find other investigations interesting as well. Readings that make clear what is at stake for the reader seem to me especially valuable because they clarify their own limits and thus help us to orient ourselves as readers.[14]

Rather than erasing the author in favor of an abstract textuality, I prefer a critical practice that both expands and limits the role of the author, in my case by finding in the text an author-persona but relating this functionary to psychological, historical, and literary intersections quite beyond the scope of any scriptor's intentions, either conscious or unconscious.[15] The persona functions more like a form of sensibility in the text than a directional marker pointing back toward some monolithic authorial presence.

The strategy of persona criticism is aimed at reconceiving the author function. The persona is a mask that may be related simultaneously to the biographical data available about the author and to other cultural and literary voices. It is particularly relevant to lyric poets in the modern period in whose work it *appears* that we have access to something approximating the author's voice. However, many novelists, such as Nathaniel Hawthorne, Herman Melville, George Eliot, and William Faulkner (not to mention more contemporary writers like Margaret Drabble and Milan Kundera), project a similar illusion of definition and accessibility in their fictions and could be addressed productively by means of this form of analysis. Hawthorne's narrators, Ishmael in *Moby-Dick,* Eliot's authorial intrusions, and Gavin Stevens in Faulkner all offer versions or masks of their authors for consideration. The mask may well be at odds with some information we have about the author. However, the significance of the persona goes beyond its congruence with or divergence from typical authorial moods and meditations.

Rather than locating the grounds for deciding between interpretations in the historical subjectivity of the writer, persona criticism alerts us to the diversity of possible investments in the text. First, it is necessary to identify the characteristics of an author-mask in a range of related texts in order to establish the significance of this contruct. One searches for a pattern, a constellation of effects.

The second phase of persona analysis explores the way these effects (this voice or character) come out of a particular time and place at the intersection of psychological and cultural history. Often (though not always) the mask functions as an organizing feature of the text.

Thus the mask of the skeptic is not only a subject in *The Education of Henry Adams* but also a structuring device. Similarly, in Emily Dickinson's poetry, the cheshire cat persona—prone to ironic dissolve—often makes voice into poetic pattern. Of course, fissures in the mask become significant as well. One should always pay attention to contrary evidence or slippage.

What makes the mask preferable to the author as a focus of analysis is the fact that the mask is unlike a human being. It is limited, identifiable, constructed, and without intentions. Indeed, in my understanding, the persona is almost precisely opposite to the historical subject-author in that it functions like an outline, a potentiality, rather than a fullness which is always already depleted as it renders itself in discourse. One might even call the persona a *thin description,* in the sense that it acts simply as a structuring mechanism, a predisposition that takes on substance as it becomes embedded in particular contexts. The persona may well appear various in these contexts, but these variations cannot be said to be the result of persona intentions. Furthermore, the mask is not a limit on what the text can mean. It is simply a feature of the text like a node from which meaning can be seen to radiate in many directions.

To use an example from my own research, my reading of Elinor Wylie's work focuses on the persona of the woman warrior.[16] This figure is often the speaker or the subject of Wylie's poetry. Furthermore, its lethal combination of aggression against others and abjection of self is particularly seductive for females, I believe, and can be connected to both culture and psyche in the historical situation of early twentieth-century American women writers.

Elinor Wylie (1885–1928) was a highly respected poet in her day whose work often prompted critics to indulge in a simpler form of biographical criticism. Her poems were read straightforwardly as autobiographical statements. One reason for this is that Wylie wrote so many self-portrait poems in which she speculated, often ironically, about the strengths and weaknesses of her own character. A second reason has to do with the highly colored nature of her life. The scandal of Wylie's desertion of her first husband, her three much-publicized marriages, the many suicides in her family—all served to inspire speculation about the relation between the pain so palpable in her poetry and her own experiences.

On the other hand, Wylie was not primarily interested in confession, and some found her work overly cold and artificial. As the *Norton Anthology of American Literature* puts it: "She appears to have assessed her talent coolly, and she continued to write the elegant, formally conservative, decorative poems that she preferred,"[17] despite the pressures of modernism. The challenge of interpreting her work is posed by the tension between its violence and its control, the dry ice of its language.

I have found the persona of the woman warrior a productive way of contextualizing that dry ice with reference to Wylie's time and gender. Focusing upon this mask appears to me preferable to undertaking the kind of biographical analysis characteristic of her critics in the twenties and thirties. Is Elinor Wylie's particular personal experience relevant to the creation of the woman warrior persona? Absolutely. Yet from the perspective of persona criticism, all such experience can be seen in contexts broader than the personal. Even the exceptional fact of Wylie's upper-class status and scandal-ridden life, even these particularities, though not normative, are representative. In her case, they connect her with the "band of outsiders" also deeply significant to the poet H. D., with whom she shares a great deal, both culturally and psychologically.

At this point I suspect some of my readers will want to ask: What about the *uniqueness* of Wylie's work? If everything is seen as representative, does this not undermine the special value of the poet and her poetry? Though the process of persona analysis tends to relate the poetry to contexts outside itself, the way a given text is representative is always peculiar to that text. Presumably one chooses to work on a writer whom one respects and whose work one feels to be enriched by the kinds of readings the critic can bring to bear.

However, it is true that notions of individual genius and exceptionalism are weakened by this process. Unlike some critics on the left with whom I share other assumptions, I do not think it is necessary to set aside the notion of genius entirely, as long as it is not being used to do the kind of ideological work that has resulted in oppression (particularly of women) in the past. The genius (one thinks of Milton) may be an unusually powerful writer, but the genius is not always a reliable source of ideas about politics and gender. It is dangerous to make authors into cultural icons.

Furthermore, though I am still willing to say Emily Dickinson was a genius, I am not willing to leave it at that. The fact that she had special talents and peculiarities does not mean that she should be read in isolation, even from the other American women poets of her day who were not as talented.

By the same token, I am interested in Elinor Wylie as a separate entity, but I am also interested in the way her literary persona takes shape in a particular cultural gestalt that binds her to others of her time and gender. I prefer this mode of appreciation to one that would elevate her to the status of an eagle isolated on its mountaintop. The very fact that she was so envious of the eagle, for example in her poem "The Eagle and the Mole,"[18] leads us back to the assault upon female subjectivity experienced by the woman warrior. Indeed, by shifting primary attention from author to persona, one is participating in the contemporary move away from genius and toward culture, away from presence and toward representation.

In another era (our own, perhaps), it is unlikely that Wylie would have chosen the woman warrior for her preferred mask. In the United States today, it is mostly women of color and lesbians who seem attracted to the warrior persona, a fact that itself might be productively analyzed.[19] By tracing the forms of Wylie's self-representation, one must also take into account the grammar of her cultural context in which her choices were embedded. The "author" as she appears in her novels and poems is as much the world of late nineteenth- and early twentieth-century social change as it is any particular subjectivity named Elinor Wylie. The woman warrior was a favorite with white, comparatively privileged, and ambitious women around the turn of the century who saw themselves fighting for new modes of self-expression.[20]

But what about Wylie's intentions? Surely she did not see herself as representing such hypostases as the New Woman, the Victorian aesthetes, or Julia Kristeva's suicidal "abject."[21] To this one must respond by saying that in persona criticism Wylie's intentions are relevant, but they are in no way definitive. Indeed, Wylie was herself suspicious of intentionality, claiming that authors adopt deceptive strategies to avoid both "the bitterness of being understood" and "the bitterness of [self-] understanding."[22] If I feel that my conception of what Wylie's work is up to is enriched by investigating the hostility and self-hatred that puts it at the crossroads of culture and psyche, gender and genre, I need not believe that Wylie herself would have thought so.

Strangely, however, the very fact that Wylie *could not have* understood her poems the way I understand them makes the kind of readings I advocate unpalatable to some. For others, the attempt to get at the circumstances governing textual production is liable to be condemned as historical rather than critical, as though it were important to keep history outside of criticism. In contemplating my own insistence on uniting the two, I have also come to a further conclusion regarding my own type of analysis, and this is what I mean when I say that I have not adopted the strategy of persona criticism for the sake of mere expedience.

Serious criticism, it seems to me, always emerges from deep and complex sources in both the culture and the critic. When I consider what a subject is, when I consider what I am and how the self-that-I-can-use-in-writing[23] connects to my texts, I am convinced that the best exploration of my role as author would take into account my psychological development, gender, race and class affiliations, cultural experience, reading habits, and intellectual and political concerns. It seems particularly relevant to the shaping of my own critical practice, for instance, that I grew up poor, in a female-headed household, profoundly isolated in the fifties and sixties in Midwest suburbia. I thus failed to realize until my college years that I had *any* relation to history whatever. Like many of the women I study, the wider world of social, economic, and political life seemed to have nothing to do with me. Therefore, it later became extremely important to begin to connect psyche with culture, gender with literary history, even to see my mother's 1920s love poetry as the signature of a certain form of nascent female consciousness in that era. Making these connections gave me a way into the historical conversation, made it possible for me to write. I can now see that I am/not my mother, and, whereas she stopped writing, I can (must?) continue.

But I also feel confident in saying that a text itself is an encoding of history in which one may find traces of both culture and psyche without the prior context of biography. Part of the project of cultural criticism, to which persona criticism essentially belongs, is the uncovering of such lost mediations in the text. Alan Trachtenberg provides the following illumination of this project where he says:

> "Culture" distances the reader from the "text" pure and simple—and calls attention to what is absent, the missing mediation of the text's history, or as we might put it, the texture of transactions by and through which we know it as a cultural artifact. Thus does culture replace the familiar literary object with an unfamiliar reading, . . . the aim of such a distanced reading being not to understand the presumed text in its presumed autonomy, but the network of relations into which the cultural text subsumes and reconstitutes the literary text.[24]

Persona criticism is an attempt to connect what is peculiar in a writer's work to what is shared with others. That I am motivated because of my special life experiences to value such connections is neither irrelevant to my work nor the whole truth about it. Instead of saying this aspect of the writer's work is important *because and only because* it relates to something the writer experienced or something we know he or she thought about, the persona critic must reflect on the way the forms of authorial representation available in the text open it to other kinds of texts from the same time period or to other texts produced under similar circumstances.

Choosing to concentrate on a composite persona removes the difficulty of having to decide who the writer "really" was and what she "really" meant, an irritating tendency of some psychological criticism. The persona is a mask, necessarily artificial and therefore unlike human subjectivity, which, with all its artificiality, also produces the genuine as one of its descriptive binaries. Limited and identifiable, the persona inevitably represents history, for the mask is embedded in ritual and culture. Like the masks used in dramatic tribal rituals, the persona always invokes the past as well as its particular moment.

Of course, it must be said that persona criticism cannot legitimate the introduction of biographical material in critical practice for those who would prefer not to think of texts as having authors at all. It can, however, be an appealing strategy for those who are committed to talking about the author but do not wish to fall into the trap of limiting the text to the author's experience. For me, persona criticism has provided a way to go on talking about the combination of forces that impinge on the text without sacrificing my sense of psychological complexity, my notions of intertextuality, or my commitment to cultural history. Rather than functioning as a way to "close the writing," persona criticism multiplies the critical horizons, suggesting not limits of possible significance but avenues of potentiality and new worlds to explore.

Notes

1. As one example of a piece of recent critical theory that takes a hard line concerning authors, see Toril Moi's *Sexual/Textual Politics,* in which she exclaims: "For the patriarchal critic, the author is the source, origin and meaning of the text. If we are to undo this patriarchal practice of *authority,* we must take one further step and proclaim with Roland Barthes the death of the author" (62–63). She therefore disdains the attempt of Jane Marcus to take into consideration Virginia Woolf's state of mind as she was composing her texts. See Moi, *Sexual/Textual Politics: Feminist Literary Theory* (New York: Methuen, 1985).

2. See Roland Barthes, "The Death of the Author," *Image, Music, Text,* trans. Stephen Heath (New York: Hill and Wang, 1977), 147.

3. For a typical example of the way the artist role has been associated with control over the text, see Sylvano Arieti, *Creativity: The Magic Synthesis* (New York: Basic Books, 1976). Arieti compares schizophrenics who "appear to be" creative with those he feels are truly creative because, unlike mental patients, they can make conscious decisions about their art.

4. In "What Is an Author?" Michel Foucault uses the term "author function" to signify the way a "mode of being of discourse" is characterized,

often through the use of the author's name: "the name seems always to be present, marking off the edges of the text, revealing, or at least characterizing, its mode of being." See Foucault, "What Is an Author?" trans. Josué Harari, in *The Foucault Reader,* ed. Paul Rabinow (New York: Pantheon), 107.

5. Barthes, 147. Further references to Barthes will appear in the text as DA, page reference following. My essay "Feminist Literary Criticism and the Author" appears in *Critical Inquiry* 16 (Spring 1990): 551–71.

6. Foucault, 118. References to this text will henceforth appear in the text as WIA, page reference following quotation.

7. Jacques Derrida, "Signature Event Context" first printed in *Glyph I* (Baltimore, Md.: The Johns Hopkins University Press, 1977), 182. This essay also appears in Derrida's *Margins of Philosophy* (Chicago, Ill.: University of Chicago Press, 1982), 307–30.

8. See Nancy K. Miller, "Changing the Subject: Authorship, Writing, and the Reader" in *Feminist Studies, Critical Studies,* ed. Teresa de Lauretis (Bloomington: Indiana University Press, 1986), 102–20.

9. On the issue of iterability see Derrida, "Signature Event Context" and *Limited Inc* (Evanston, Ill.: Northwestern University Press, 1988).

10. Widely known in psychological circles, studies confirming these tendencies are discussed in Wendy Wood, "Meta-Analytic Review of Sex Differences in Group Performance," *Psychological Bulletin* 12 (1987): 53–71. Also see Nancy Henley, *Body Politics: Power, Sex and Non-Verbal Communication* (Englewood Cliffs, N.J.: Prentice-Hall, 1977).

11. See Moi, 68.

12. See Miller, 105.

13. The allusion here is to two essays by Steven Knapp and Walter Benn Michaels: "Against Theory," in *Against Theory: Literary Studies and the New Pragmatism,* ed. W. J. T. Mitchell (Chicago, Ill.: University of Chicago Press, 1985), 11–30 and "Against Theory 2: Hermeneutics and Deconstruction," *Critical Inquiry* 14 (Autumn 1987): 49–68. Knapp and Michaels argue that since the text must be construed as meaning something in order to function as a text, its meaning must also be limited and ascertainable; that limit, they feel, is furnished by the author.

14. For a good example of a critic who tells us what is at stake for her in her readings, see Cora Kaplan, *Sea Changes: Essays on Culture and Feminism* (London: Verso, 1986).

15. Though similar in some ways to Paul Jay's work, *Being in the Text: Self-Representation from Wordsworth to Roland Barthes* (Ithaca, N.Y.: Cornell University Press, 1984), my work does not concentrate on prose autobiography, and my sense of persona is expanded to include more than psychological and epistemological issues.

16. My most extended discussion of Elinor Wylie's work occurs in *Masks Outrageous and Austere: Culture, Psyche and Persona in Modern Women Poets* (Bloomington: Indiana University Press, 1991), chapter 4.

17. *The Norton Anthology of American Literature,* ed. Nina Baym et al. (New York: Norton, 1989), 2:1197.

18. See "The Eagle and the Mole" in *Collected Poems of Elinor Wylie* (New York: Knopf, 1971), 4, which begins:

> Avoid the reeking herd,
> Shun the polluted flock,
> Live like that stoic bird,
> The eagle of the rock.

19. For examples of contemporary women who use the woman warrior persona, see Audre Lorde (almost any of her works), *Writing and Art by North American Indian Women,* ed. Beth Brant (Sinister Wisdom Books, 1984), and Maxine Hong Kingston's novel *The Woman Warrior: Memoirs of a Girlhood among Ghosts* (New York: Alfred Knopf, 1976).

20. For discussions of the use of the woman warrior motif around the turn of the century, see T. J. Jackson Lears, *No Place of Grace: Antimodernism and the Transformation of American Culture 1880–1920* (New York: Pantheon, 1981), Carroll Smith-Rosenberg, *Disorderly Conduct: Visions of Gender in Victorian America* (New York: Oxford University Press, 1986), and Sandra M. Gilbert and Susan Gubar, *No Man's Land: The Place of the Woman Writer in the Twentieth Century,* vol. 1 *The War of the Words* (New Haven, Conn.: Yale University Press, 1988).

21. Wylie's use of the woman warrior converges with the image of the abject as discussed by Julia Kristeva, *Powers of Horror: An Essay on Abjection* (New York: Columbia University Press, 1982).

22. See Wylie, "Symbols in Literature," *Collected Prose of Elinor Wylie* (New York: Knopf, 1933), 878–89.

23. In *Sea Changes,* Cora Kaplan talks about "the 'self' that occupies the place-from-which-I-can-write," an idea I have borrowed from her. See Kaplan, 225.

24. Alan Trachtenberg, "Comments on Evan Watkins' 'Cultural Criticism and the Literary Intellectual,'" *Works and Days* 3 (Spring 1985): 37.

Sharon O'Brien

Feminist Theory and Literary Biography

Before we can explore the compatibilities and contradictions between feminist theory (or, to be more precise, feminist *theories*) and literary biography, we need to consider a broader problem: the tensions between contemporary critical theory and the traditional assumption that biography can convey in language what Leon Edel terms the "essence" of a self.[1] The ability to name and to analyze these tensions is hampered, however, by the contradictory expectations that many contemporary readers and reviewers bring to biography. So I would like to begin by examining these contradictions.

Contemporary critical and cultural theory has challenged the traditional epistemology underlying both history and biography: the belief, as Gordon Wood has phrased it, that "the past is real and that the truth of it can be recovered through story-telling."[2] Theoretical developments in psychoanalysis and semiotics as well as poststructuralism and deconstruction have led many of us to question (if not to discard) beliefs in the transparency of language, in the possibility of objectivity, in the explanatory power of narrative, and in the self as a unified, knowable, and recoverable entity.

And yet, outside of the interpretive communities that embrace such views—academic communities for the most part, and, in contrast to general readers of biographies, not very populous—people hold very different assumptions about epistemology and thus about biography. Most biographers and, I suspect, most readers assume that the biographer's task is to arrive at the "truth" about his or her subject; that the biographer must maintain objectivity (a difficult but not impossible task); and that the biographer must not approach the subject through limiting or reductive interpretive frameworks (like feminism).

Such beliefs posit that it is possible for the biographer to dispense with all interpretive frameworks, except those ultimately suggested by the data—never imposed by the biographer. According to this traditional view, a good biographer is able to "know the true shape of another's experience, to capture it in the face of all resistance," as Marc Pachter writes in his introduction to *Telling Lives: The Biographer's Art*. In Pachter's view, the biographer's self-conscious use of theory can only distort the "true shape" of the subject's life. The one "unforgivable sin," according to Pachter, is the biographer's violation of the spirit of the life by "introducing his theories upon its meaning."[3] From this perspective, the "meaning" of the subject's life is, somehow, already there before the biographer begins his or her investigation. So the biographer's task—like that of the Puritan seeking to read the spiritual significance of a natural event such as a thunderstorm or a drought—is to uncover the meaning that exists, not to create it. But the Puritans believed that God was the Author of all earthly scripts, the Creator of meaning: one problem with the traditional view of biography is the question of who is the author. One might assume that the subject is the author of the biography, and the biographer the medium or interpreter who reveals meaning but does not construct it.

But another, contradictory strain in the traditional view of biography invests the biographer with the novelist's shaping power—as Pachter's subtitle, "The Biographer's Art," suggests. The "biography as fiction" metaphor is commonplace, even if its implications are not fully acknowledged. Many biographers think of themselves as storytellers and draw on novelistic techniques (scene-painting, foreshadowing, juxtaposition, even dialogue) as well as employing that staple of traditional fiction, the linear, chronological plot. It is high praise for a reviewer to say of a biography that "it reads like a novel," just as it is damning to declare that the subject/central character "never really comes to life." "Camerado, this is no book," wrote Walt Whitman, "who touches this touches a man," and those who subscribe to the biography-as-fiction model also want to believe that when they pick up a biography they are touching a man (or woman), not a book (certainly not a text).[4] The traditional biographer must make the subject's spirit manifest in language, performing the miracle of incarnation. Given these assumptions, I can understand Marc Pachter's disappointment when he failed to find the "real" Willa Cather living and breathing in the pages of my biography, regretfully observing that "Miss O'Brien has not delivered to us the presence of Willa Cather."[5] But Ms. O'Brien, who was writing from a different set of assumptions about theory, gender, biography, and the self, never intended to deliver the real Willa Cather to the reader.

These contradictory strains in the traditional view of biography—at once truth and story, objective and fictional—may perhaps be reconciled when we realize that the kind of novel imagined as the model for biography is the nineteenth-century novel. The biographer's art is patterned on Austen, Thackeray, or Eliot, not on Beckett, Faulkner, or DeLillo. The model here is realism, not modernism or postmodernism, and the assumptions made about biography accord with those made by the readers and writers of realistic fiction: language is a transparent medium capable of representing the world; character and the self are knowable; the cause-and-effect linearity implied by the chronological plot is a reliable way of ordering reality; and the author is a trustworthy narrator who understands the relationship between the private self and the public world. Given these assumptions, it is easy to see why a traditional biographer or critic would distrust the presence of *any* acknowledged theory in biography; this presence not only exposes the framework the biographer is using to interpret the subject, situating the biographer historically and undermining the pretense of objectivity, but the self-reflexivity implied by the overt use of theory moves biography into the realm of the modernist or postmodernist novel, a fictional world in which characters do not "come to life" according to the conventions of nineteenth-century realism. (Don DeLillo's cartoonlike characters in *White Noise* are not constructed with the same assumptions about social and psychological realism as were Jane Austen's.)

While the biographer's acknowledgment of a theoretical perspective—whether feminist, psychoanalytic, or Marxist—is the "unforgivable sin" according to the traditional view of biography, new challenges to the notion of the self now coming from a variety of theoretical directions—primarily deconstruction and Lacanian psychoanalysis—question the very existence of biography as a genre. Leaving aside the question of language and representation, if the self is considered decentered, multiple, or unknowable, how can any genre purport to give us the "presence," "essence," or meaning of a self? Is not biography then inevitably naive—if not downright dangerous—insofar as it promotes the outmoded and bourgeois ideology of the individual? Certainly we can see the links between biography and humanism in the Western context and between biography and individualism in the American context. The metaphors of unveiling and revealing that we associate with biographers (so and so has "revealed" the "inner" life of an author) suggest that the biographer, firmly standing on the untroubled ground of nineteenth-century romanticism, can display to us the core, essential (if hidden) self of the subject. For critics who no longer accept the notion of a core, continuous self, such an assumption is problematic, to say the least.

One historian's solution to this collision between contemporary critical theory and biography has been to create a radical new form of biography consistent with theory—a form that so dismantles conventional biography that David Nye calls his work an "anti-biography." Attacking the outworn conceptions of traditional biography—the notion that a linear, chronological, unified narrative can present us with an essential self—Nye offers an alternative in his anti-biography of Thomas Edison.[6] Drawing on semiotics and structuralism, Nye abandons chronology and linearity: friendly to poststructuralist challenges to the unified self, he offers us many Edisons rather than "the" Thomas Edison, and he refuses to recombine his sources and insights into a higher level of synthesis. The result is an interesting experiment in biographical form, although it poses problems for the reader, since Nye has denied us the pleasures of narration along with the problems.

It is interesting that no feminist biographer as yet has taken up the notion or form of anti-biography, since on the surface it offers an escape from traditional biography, a form feminist readers connect with patriarchal as well as Western humanist definitions of the individual self—a self imagined, although frequently not admitted, to be male. The fact that feminist biographers have not yet begun to write poststructuralist anti-biographies is connected, I think, with current tensions and contradictions in feminist theory. Some strains in feminist theory challenge the assumptions of traditional biography, while others support those assumptions; some strains are compatible with notions of the decentered or multiple self, others are not. These tensions are creative ones, and as they collide and combine with each other over the next several years they could give rise to new forms for women's biographies. We may be about to see a new and exciting era of experimentation in the writing of female biography.

What are these tensions, and how do they relate to women's biographies? Let me begin with a general observation. Given the power of the traditional view of biography—a power still evident among critics and reviewers as well as readers—it is a perilous undertaking for a biographer to use any kind of feminist theory in an open, self-conscious way. She is then open to attack first for her feminism and second for committing the "unforgivable sin" of using theory openly. It is one thing for the feminist biographer to draw on Nancy

Chodorow's *The Reproduction of Mothering* and then assert, seemingly as if this were a naturally observed phenomenon, that her subject had an ambivalent relationship with her mother that was central to her life and art.[7] It is quite another thing to tell the reader that she is drawing on Chodorow and then make herself vulnerable to the charge of being reductive as well as feminist. The biographer's overt use of feminist theory explodes the possibility that she could be writing from a neutral, objective, uncontaminated stance. Like many others, I believe it is never possible to write from such a stance, but it is still the case that the biographer who admits her own historical and theoretical context defies dominant assumptions about the genre and so takes a considerable risk.

A feminist biographer who openly acknowledges, for example, her use of Nancy Chodorow's version of psychoanalytic theory also confronts possible displeasure from other feminist critics because of rifts and contradictions in feminist theory. The contradictions in feminist theory intensify depending on the extent to which the feminist critic embraces deconstruction. Deconstruction's questioning of the unitary, representable self and the fixed correspondence between signifier and signified leads to a questioning not only of the concept "identity" but also of the concept "woman." From the perspective of deconstruction, to posit a female voice or a woman writer's creation of identity is to confuse the social construction "woman" with an experiential reality; it is also to accept the patriarchal ideology of individualism. As Mary Poovey observes, from a deconstructionist viewpoint, "a feminism that bases its epistemology and practice on women's experience is simply another deluded humanism, complicit with the patriarchal institutions it claims to oppose."[8]

Yet the psychoanalytic and literary theory derived from the work of Nancy Chodorow (as well as the complementary work of Jane Flax and Carol Gilligan) is opposed to deconstruction's dismantling of the unified subject and the category "woman."[9] This strain of feminist theory (more popular in the United States than in Europe) seeks to disrupt the equivalence of the masculine with the universal by defining women's "different voice." These various formulations of the "different voice" have had an important influence on feminist thinking in the United States, in part, I think, because many American feminists resist abandoning the notion of the "real" or authentic self, even when they modify the definition of individualism in contending that the female self is more defined in relationship than in separation. Despite the importance of deconstruction to feminism, it may be easier for white men—whom Western ideology has allowed to possess the individual self (however fictive it is!)—to discard that self than for women. Certainly many women writers have found the narrative of self-creation or self-discovery empowering, a means to rescue the self from male definitions and to construct a female self. (Consider *The Awakening, The Song of the Lark, Their Eyes Were Watching God, The Color Purple.*) The notion of a female self grappling with or liberated from patriarchal constructions has important implications for biographies of women, of course, and it is likely that despite deconstruction this strain in feminist theory will influence the writing of biography for some time to come. My prediction is based on the compatibility between feminism's stress on the different voice and traditional biography's emphasis on the coherent and knowable self; and, as Carolyn Heilbrun says in *Writing a Woman's Life,* women need to use biography to narrate female lives.[10]

From the perspective of deconstruction, however, the influence on biography of the "different voice" theory of women's self and writing is problematic: this theory seems to promote the notion of the unified self and an essentialist definition of "woman." Thus, the emphasis on female difference obscures differences *among* women, differences connected with race, class, ethnicity, culture, or sexual identity. What seems to be the case at the moment is that feminist deconstructionists, not unsurprisingly, have not been attracted to biography as a genre, not even desiring to write feminist anti-biographies.

These tensions in feminist theory that affect biography are unfortunate, since I think we need more biographies of women. Women's lives have been erased, unrecorded, or represented by patriarchal stories, and biography can be a powerful means for reinscribing women in history. Biography can also contribute to the feminist/deconstructionist commitment to pluralism by offering us many female voices and stories, thus helping to deconstruct the monolithic category "woman" as well as giving us new ways of interrupting or rethinking theory. And biography can give us stories of other women's lives that can help us to invent or reinvent our own. Perhaps most important, by "our" here I mean both the feminist reader within the academy and Virginia Woolf's common reader: unlike academic essays such as this one, biography is a popular form read by many women. So biography is too essential a means of communication and connection for feminists to abandon, even if they are troubled by seeming incompatibilities among feminism, deconstruction, and biography.

Help is on the way. Mary Poovey's recent attempt to allow both feminism and deconstruction to interrupt each other, to establish common ground and points of contention, can give us ways to imagine new forms of female biography that would neither offer a falsely unified female self nor deny the importance of gender to female experience. Poovey observes, "The multiple positions real women occupy—the positions dictated by race, for example, or by class or sexual preference—should alert us to the inadequacy of binary logic and unitary selves without making us forget that this logic has dictated (and still does) some aspects of women's social treatment" (and, I would add, women's psychological and emotional experience).[11]

How would keeping in mind the inadequacy of "unitary selves" while at the same time attempting to speak of women's different "social treatment" or psychological experience affect the writing of literary biography from a feminist perspective? I would like to sketch in some possible models for literary biography that could avoid the falsely unified or essential self and unproblematic acceptance of female difference while at the same time preserving the benefits that biography can offer to feminism as well as to the narration of women's lives.

1. If the subject is living, the biographer could disrupt the traditional power relationship between biographer and subject (e.g., the biographer gets to define and represent the subject) as well as interrupt the unified, coherent narrative of the self. Deirdre Bair, author of the recently published biography of Simone de Beauvoir, had spoken to Beauvoir about the possibility of Beauvoir writing responses to Bair's analysis, which would then be included in the biography. The two women disagreed at times about interpretations of Beauvoir's life; including the subject's response, Bair thought, would allow for a dialogue rather than a monologue. Beauvoir died before this could be accomplished, but the idea of a double-voiced biography is an exciting one.[12]

If the subject is dead, it is obviously more difficult for the biographer to find ways of interrupting her own voice, but not impossible. One might interrupt the narrative or analysis with diaries, letters, or photographs that are not interpreted or that question the biographer's interpretation. (Of course, such evidence cannot be presented as the "real" or unmediated voice of the subject, and the biographer is still controlling the selection and omission of material.) It might also be possible for the biographer to incorporate into the text a record of the shifts and developments in her own construction of the subject. Most biographies are written over a long period of time, and the subject indeed has many "selves" for the biographer. What generally happens, though, is that the last "self" becomes the final one, the only represented one, and the former selves disappear, fading away in the biographer's memory as the first, second, and third drafts go into the wastebasket. Finding a way to incorporate this process into the biography (instead of just a sentence or two in the preface) could disrupt the illusion of the unified self as well as the illusion of biography as an objective, completed, unified narrative. A biography only freezes the biographer's story of the subject at one point in time, and the biographer could dramatize the contingent nature of the biographical narrative (for those biographies that stay in print) by writing a new preface. How, five or ten years later, might she tell her subject's story? Just as the earlier "selves" of the subject do not get represented in biography, so the later ones, the ones imagined after publication, remain invisible. This kind of belated preface could allow the reader to see that the seemingly stable narrative of a biography is in fact the meeting between two selves at a particular historical and personal moment.[13]

2. It would be an interesting experiment to have more biographies of living women writers, particularly those who are in midcareer. This suggestion runs completely counter to the academic grain, which is one reason I like it. Unlike biographers of actors, sports heroes, and politicians, academic biographers prefer dead to living writers for reasons feminists should challenge. First, academics like to wait for the canon to be established in order to be sure that the subject is important enough to warrant a biography. But feminists should be challenging the canon anyway, so why not take a chance and write biographies of Alice Walker or Bobbi Ann Mason? Second, academics distrust the writer's life that is in process: what if the next book should disrupt the biographer's paradigm or predictions? Far safer to wait until the writer is dead, the literary evidence in. But this act of waiting, of course, reinforces the biographer's tendency to create a unified, impermeable narrative. Writing the life of a writer in the process of living and writing would allow the biographer to develop more open-ended narrative structures.

3. By taking into account the possibility that the female subject may occupy many "subject positions" in a life—positions that vary according to class, race, sexual preference, family status, and age—the biographer can challenge the notion of the unified self without discarding a focus on gender. Considering these variations could also lead to new biographical forms, in particular disruptions of chronology and linearity. For example, when the issue of aging is considered along with the new forms female identity might take in the older woman's life, a biographer might decide to create different narrative structures for the early and later life rather than the typical march, chapter by chapter, from birth to death. It could be possible to offer such variations within the one-volume biography—a chronological first half, perhaps, and a

nonchronological second? If the biographer is writing a two-volume biography, the possibilities for narrative innovation are even greater. I am now thinking that if I write a second volume on Cather's later life, it will have a different vision of the self and thus a different narrative structure from the first volume (which was, by and large, a Bildungsroman). I think we should envision, then, two-volume biographies in which the second volume is not merely an extension of the first, but may collide with it in terms of form, structure, and theory.

4. Traditionally biographers have ended full-length biographies with the death of their subject. Descriptions of the gravesite or quotation of the epitaph are a favorite form of closure; R. W. B. Lewis ends his biography of Edith Wharton with "the Latin phrase she had selected: *Ave Crux Spes Unica,*" as if to leave us with the writer's last word.[14] This form of closure may be satisfying, but it is also another false ordering, implying that the biographer's text is coterminous with the life: who touches this book touches a woman.

Feminist biographers could think about going beyond the epitaph. We might want to ask whether struggles over possession of papers and manuscripts as well as representation and reputation constitute part of the "life story" stretching well beyond the writer's death. The case of Sylvia Plath is perhaps the most obvious one, since the efforts of Ted and Olwyn Hughes to control access to manuscripts and representations of Plath have been so dramatic, but there are many other instances. Whoever writes the biography of Pearl Buck, for example, should take into account the ways in which the Pearl Buck Foundation has sought to represent the author since her death. And if I do write the story of Cather's later life, I would want to write beyond the epitaph by taking into account the different ways in which Cather is used and interpreted by different groups, exploring the popular culture of Red Cloud, the Cather museum and tour of "Catherland," the literary pilgrimage to Nebraska, the ritual of annual Cather conferences, the Cather newsletter.

In an essay in the *New York Times Book Review,* Cynthia Ozick accounts for the continuing appeal of biography: "What we continue to prize in biography is the honest constancy of its narrative ripeness: the trustworthy satisfactions of a still-coherent form, the ancient name of which is Story."[15] While I think that feminist biographers should find ways to challenge the "still-coherent form" of biography, I do not think that we need to dispense with the pleasures of narrative or the power of storytelling. Storytelling itself is completely consistent with deconstruction—quite simply, we make everything up—and if we can find ways to tell the stories of women's lives without implying that these stories are inevitable, natural, transparent, objective renditions of other selves, we can retain the satisfactions of traditional biography without succumbing to the genre's troubling assumptions.

It would be foolish for feminist critics to ignore the appeal that biography has for readers. This is a form that can mediate between the academic and the general reader, and so—if we can deal creatively with the tensions in feminist and contemporary literary theory, experiment with the form, and rewrite its "ancient name" while still producing readable, accessible texts (what we used to call books)—we may be able to create a vibrant literary connection between academic and non-academic readers that can only enrich feminism as well as biography.

Notes

1. Leon Edel, "The Figure Under the Carpet," in *Telling Lives: The Biographer's Art,* ed. Marc Pachter (Washington, D.C.: New Republic Books/ National Portrait Gallery, 1979), 18.

2. Gordon S. Wood, "Star Spangled History," *The New York Review of Books,* 12 August 1982, 8.

3. Marc Pachter, "The Biographer Himself [sic]: An Introduction," in Pachter, ed., 7–8.

4. Walt Whitman, "So Long," in *Leaves of Grass,* ed. Harold W. Blodgett and Sculley Bradley (New York: Norton, 1965), 505.

5. Marc Pachter, "Half a Life: The Muse But Not the Spirit Lives," *The Washington Times Magazine,* 16 March 1987, 6M.

6. David Nye, *The Invented Self: An Anti-biography, From Documents of Thomas A. Edison* (Odense: Odense University Press, 1983).

7. Nancy Chodorow, *The Reproduction of Mothering: Psychoanalysis and the Sociology of Gender* (Berkeley and Los Angeles: University of California Press, 1978).

8. Mary Poovey, "Feminism and Deconstruction," *Feminist Studies* 14, no. 1 (Spring 1988): 52.

9. Jane Flax, "The Conflict Between Nurturance and Autonomy in Mother/Daughter Relationships and Within Feminism," *Feminist Studies* 4 (February 1978): 171–89; and Carol Gilligan, *In a Different Voice: Psychological Theory and Women's Development* (Cambridge, Mass.: Harvard University Press, 1982).

10. Carolyn Heilbrun, *Writing a Woman's Life* (New York: Norton, 1988).

11. Poovey, 62.

12. Carol Ascher, Louise DeSalvo, and Sara Ruddick, eds., *Between Women: Biographers, Novelists, Critics, Teachers, and Artists Write about*

Their Work on Women (Boston: Beacon, 1984) gives some examples of women biographers' relationships with their female subjects.

13. Jacqueleyn Dowd Hall has given such a retrospective look at her biography of Jessie Daniel Ames in an article ("Second Thoughts: On Writing a Feminist Biography," *Feminist Studies* 13, no. 1 [Spring 1987]: 19–37). Because her backward glance is published in a journal rather than in a second preface or author's note included with the biography, though, a reader of her biography might never encounter this second version, in which Dowd imagines how, at this later point, she might tell Ames's story.

14. R. W. B. Lewis, *Edith Wharton* (New York: Harper & Row), 532.

15. Cynthia Ozick, "Where Orphans Can Still Become Heiresses," *New York Times Book Review,* 8 March 1987, 13.

Valerie Ross

Too Close to Home
Repressing Biography, Instituting Authority

Isn't it strange how this castle changes as soon as one imagines that Hamlet lived here?
— Werner Heisenberg, *Physics and Beyond*

Whereas if we approach a poet without this prejudice we shall often find that not only the best, but the most individual parts of his work may be those in which the dead poets, his ancestors, assert their immortality most vigorously.
— T. S. Eliot, "Tradition and the Individual Talent"

While an undergraduate and graduate student of literature, I encountered one biography in a literature course. It was *The Life of John Milton,* by A. N. Wilson, and it was assigned as "optional" reading. I exercised the option. When, a few weeks into the semester, a female student criticized the sexual politics of *Paradise Lost* and met with some resistance from the professor, I eagerly contributed what I had inferred from Wilson's narrative: John Milton was a misogynist. He mistreated his wives (the first of whom, quite unconventionally, left him after only a few weeks of marriage) and, more to the point, he dictated *Paradise Lost* to his daughters in languages unfamiliar to them (they knew only English). Required to transcribe his words phonetically, they naturally enough made errors when he asked them to read aloud their transcriptions—for which they were severely berated. Milton was reported to have said that "one tongue was enough for a woman" and, while he made no effort to educate his own daughters, he went out of his way to secure the best education for his nephews, who were not themselves required to perform any tasks for their uncle.[1] Based upon such facts, I announced, John Milton was constitutionally

135

incapable of taking the feminist perspective that the professor seemed to find everywhere in *Paradise Lost.*

To my mortification, the professor was not only unimpressed that I had done the optional reading *and* applied it to the poem, he berated me for falling into the trap of the "intentional fallacy." I had no idea what that meant, but his intention was painfully clear.[2] For some time thereafter, I made no mention of authors' lives in literature classes (though I continued to read biographies) and would, with an immensely sophisticated air, dismiss similar faux pas by other students with the magical phrase, "intentional fallacy."

It was not until I entered graduate school that I actually read "The Intentional Fallacy," by W. K. Wimsatt, Jr., and M. C. Beardsley, in a course on literary theory. I had by then become familiar, as well, with Roland Barthes's "Death of the Author" and Michel Foucault's "What Is an Author?" which only served to reinforce my earlier hypothesis: professors of literature were averse to discussions of writers' lives, and New Critics and poststructuralists had their different reasons for this shared aversion. Yet, despite this rather unholy theoretical alliance, these same professors, almost without exception, would open or punctuate a discussion of literary text with a "bit of background" on the writer, often appending to this some dire warning about the naivete of "biographical readings." These free-floating biographical details were not the only discrepancy I encountered in the obliquitous space between theory and practice. I also began to notice that, if a professor of either allegiance was hard-pressed to substantiate a particular reading, s/he often enough resorted to biography—not as "truth," of course, but rather as supplementary evidence. The same reading, students were assured, could as easily have been performed by direct textual analysis. I did not try to sort out these contradictions. I only learned that I could dismiss discussions of authors' lives with a more dramatic and less phallocentric sounding phrase: the author, I'd say, is dead.

If in New-Critical and poststructuralist courses biographical readings were frowned upon, I came to find that, in some women's studies courses, they were practically requisite to participating in class discussions. This initially struck me as scandalous. Here not only were professors talking about the "authors" as if they were persons born at such and such a date, and thus having endured such-and-such conditions of oppression—*reflected* by their writings—but were also uninhibitedly speculating on relationships between the writers' personal and textual affairs: Was *Villette* really about Charlotte Brontë's love for her schoolmaster? I had been trained to view such discussions as, if not wrong, certainly misguided—humanist, essentialist, referential.

Yet, since I tended to find them more satisfying than some of the dryly theoretical and formal analyses taking place in other of my classes, I would, with schizophrenic, guilty pleasure, temporarily set aside death and intention and join in.

One last autobiographical note: When I began to focus upon literary biography as the topic of my dissertation, I was stunned to discover the number of professors, New-Critical and poststructuralist, who had read and continue to read biographies, despite the marked absence of these from their courses, recommended reading lists, and bibliographies. Those biographical details and bits of background, the stuff of literary classes and anthologies, had always seemed to me like the gossip one hears about a passing acquaintance—information that is simply in the air, its source or origin unknown and not especially relevant. Suddenly I felt as if I had bumbled into a literary cabal; professors, with demeanors of mingled authority and embarrassment, would suggest that I read this or that biography because, without doubt, it was the "best" treatment of X or the "best" example of biography.

With history making something of a comeback, it might have been supposed that biography, as the historiography of the individual subject, would have followed in its wake. Alternately, with a contemporary popular culture that thrives on biography—*People Magazine, Entertainment Tonight, Lifestyles of the Rich and Famous,* talk shows, bio-pics on television and film, best-selling biographies on criminals, politicians, and celebrities—one might suppose biography would be given a prominent generic or theoretical place in the recent turn to cultural studies. That it has not, despite what would appear to be its almost overdetermined condition of possibility, suggests, perhaps, the insular space of academic literary discourse, which has available to it, in Michel Foucault's terminology, only a certain number and repertoire of statements, concepts, and strategies, most of which seem to be theoretically unavailable, at this moment, to the biographical subject.

This essay is intended as an exploration of the repression of biography in literary studies. Focusing on the formation of departments of literature during the third quarter of the nineteenth century, I will argue that this repression is both generic and gendered, expressing a condensation of institutional anxieties about women, class, popular culture, affect, social and domestic existence, and other "outside" challenges to institutional literary authority. Arguing that the repression of biography is homologous with and constitutive of the formalization of academic literary authority, my aim is to problematize contemporary histories of the discipline and to revitalize a debate that has become something of a stalemate in contemporary literary theory—that of the "signature" or "author function" in textual and historical readings of literature—by implicating this debate in an institutional history. Being about the unruly "inside" that must be kept "outside" of institutional discourse, biography, I argue, facilitates and provokes the construction, consolidation, and reinforcement of professional identity and authority. Like an academic game of *fort/da,* the discipline of literature must continually confront and deny, elicit and repress this generically other in order to define and fortify its territory and mastery.[3] It may even be the case that "misrecognizing biography"—a phrase I am borrowing from William Epstein—is requisite to the maintenance of professional identity.[4]

I will not linger on the problem of historiography. This essay is no more than a story, personally, politically, and professionally motivated and implicated, making rather than "covering" history. My intention is to provide some notes toward a biography of the profession that can begin to address the private life and discourse of emotions that ripple through, for example, its repeated dismissals of biography, the feminine, and the popular—these three being nearly inextricable in nineteenth-century academic reception. The quarrel over biography, I will argue, has always been enmeshed in emotionally charged struggles for institutional identity and power—literary, social, political, economic, and sexual—and has always turned upon and metonymically entangled (mis)representations of gender and popular culture.

From Domestic Noise to White Noise: Institutional Distractions

For it is not the evils of organization life that puzzle him, but its very beneficence. He is imprisoned in brotherhood.
—William Whyte, *The Organization Man*

Historians of the discipline of literature, like historians in general, are inclined to a "public" story, rather than a "private" life, of the discipline. This public story takes place in the insular space of the academy and recounts the intellectually bloody battles of method fought by academic men. Gerald Graff's *Professing Literature,* for example, among the most compelling and enlightened full-length histories of the disciplines, details the wars between philologists and aestheticians and how these have recurred and been transformed over the years.[5] I do not wish to challenge Graff's model—my own is indebted to his—so much as trouble it by introducing some of the discipline's "private" life in its less dignified scuffles over the control of American literary culture.

My notion of the "private" should be clarified somewhat as the essay progresses; to dwell upon it would take me too far afield. For the time being, I hope it is sufficient to suggest that the "private life" of the academy is that which we, like our colleagues in business, are trained (and train our students) to "leave at home" or "leave at the door." It occurs "outside" the institutions' self-constituted public space; brought "inside," it provokes shame, embarassment, the taint of naivete and unsophistication. It must be suppressed, displaced, or sublimated into our work. Private life, within the academy, is held at bay by such literary-pedagogical cliches as "emotional baggage," a traveling metaphor in flight from the affectively feminine and concretely domestic. The profession of literature, bearing the burden of an object undeniably freighted by the social and the emotional—the "outside"—poses for the (masculine) academic subject a constant danger of feminization, for often merely to speak of such things as domestic life or the emotions is to seat oneself in a culturally shaped feminine position. Rather than to confront and become acclimated to its feminine furnishings, the academic male subject of the nineteenth century tried desperately to ignore, suppress, exorcise, or misrecognize and misrepresent it.

It is thus not surprising how seldom one confronts women in histories of the discipline; there will be few in this one, as well. Like biography, women have always been part of the profession; it is just that historically they have had problems being recognized.[6] Even when they were not there (such as in the front lines of the methodological battles), they have served well and are everywhere to be found in the charged and gender-imploded rhetoric of the disciplinary wars. Women's professional, material presence was even once confirmed at a nineteenth-century meeting of the Modern Language Association (MLA) by a male professor. Responding to a discussion of literary and pedagogical methods at the meeting in Philadelphia in December 1887, Paul F. Rohrbacher of Western University of Pennsylvania suddenly digressed:

> In speaking about cleverness and clever teachers, there is one fact to which I desire to call the attention of the Association, and it is that the clever teachers are not all confined to our own sex, but we find clever teachers in the other sex and some of them are in the midst of us and are members of our Association. I was at the meeting of the Association last year and I am here this year, but I have never seen one of these ladies placed on a committee or give her opinion on any question that came up.

"I must call the gentleman to order," the chairman responded, and a proper discussion of methods resumed ("Proceedings at Philadelphia," PMLA 3:xxxv).

Rohrbacher, obviously something of a troublemaker, later ruptured another discussion—this one about the teaching of the "mother tongue"—to insist that English was neither his nor his state's "mother tongue" and to inquire precisely when and by whom English had been elected to this eminent position. He was once again brushed aside (xxxv). Neither women nor tongues had anything to do with the business at hand.

Writing in 1906, Charles Thwing, president of Western Reserve University, which had a "women's affiliate," the College for Women of Western Reserve University, recounts the dread with which women students were first received and reassures his audience: "After more than a generation of the higher education of women, many questions which were asked at the beginning of the period have either been answered or have ceased to be asked. *Many of the perils which were prophesied have ceased to be dangerous, or time has proved that they were no perils at all*" (351, my emphasis). He recounts the many fears: that the physical health of women would suffer, that the fertility and marriage rates would decline (they did); and that the "great interests of the family" would be neglected or harmed.[7] He reassures his readers that all these concerns proved false and then supplements his reassurances with a report from the president of Smith College, written in 1904, that women who "are graduates are better qualified both for wifehood and for motherhood. They are as ready to wed as other women when the right man wooes them." Thwing seconds this, adding with only an apparent irrelevancy that women "cannot take the initiative and seek a husband," a comment that does little to illuminate the discussion but much to remind himself and his readers of masculine privilege (353).

The most telling of Thwing's reported perils is buried in his extended discussions and statistics about women's health, marriageability, and fecundity: "that the intellectual capacity of women would *depreciate scholarship*" (my emphasis). This peril succinctly expresses the anxiety of contamination and devaluation prompted by proximity to and affiliation with women and is not dissimilar to the literary discipline's anxieties about biography. Masculine identity, as the unmarked term, can only be arrived at by means of negation, a primitive mathematical calculation: castration, absence, subtraction, detraction: not phallus, not presence, not we men. "[I]t has been proved that, in the coeducational institutions, women maintain a scholastic rank slightly higher than that of men," Thwing continues, this time foregoing the attendant reassurances. "A higher moral standard, a greater diligence, the refusal to be absorbed in athletic sports, contribute to this result," he proclaims, remarking and detracting the "higher" achievements of women students as ideologically "lower," the obvious result of conventionally ascribed aspects of nineteenth-century femininity: morality, diligence, passivity. The apparent superiority of the female students only adds, in this inverted math of difference, to the prestige of the male students, naturalizing what would otherwise be a figurative inferiority: Boys will be boys. This, however, is not sufficient to Thwing's anxiety. He turns to his more prestigious British brethren for additional support: "The result in America of the relatively higher standing of women over men is similar to that proved by the class lists of the honor examinations of Oxford and Cambridge" (351). Boys are boys everywhere; lower achievement is good. It would seem that, when home gets too close, men would rather cross national borders than be caught working across gender lines.

I offer Rohrbacher and Thwing to suggest that, even though in the imaging and the rhetoric of the profession all students and colleagues are men, in reality many of those whom I will be discussing throughout this essay probably encountered and even taught or worked with women. Trapped in their masculine address, I hope to at least carry with me the objections of Rohrbacher and the perils of Thwing.

The first volume of the *Transactions of the Modern Language Association of America* (1884–85) opens with Franklin Carter's essay, "Richter's Correspondence with a Lady: Some Unpublished Letters." Carter, then president of Williams College, explores the difficulties Richter experienced as a writer who had to compose to the "music of the broom, the dish-pan, and the spinning-wheel," or what Carter terms the "domestic noises" made by a mother insufficiently sensitive to the needs of her prodigious son (1:3). Carter argues that Richter's correspondences with "attractive" women helped to transform "the dismal cottage that was his dwelling into an orchid-house, and in his thoughts hid the dingy walls behind fantastic, but brilliantly-colored blossoms of hope" (1:5). Carter's handling of Richter's correspondence produces a doubled homosocial exchange, one between Carter and Richter through the correspondence of attractive women, and another between Richter and himself, for all letters, in Carter's presentation, seem to be addressed to Richter, women remarkable only for their ability to stimulate his "capacity for higher music."[8] The mutual desire and recognition of Carter and Richter for the goods of women produce a masculine identity between scholar and writer.

Corresponding with this traffic in women is a second currency of homosocial exchange, one that entails the domestic, concrete, material, emotional, and social existence of women. By the time Carter writes, women's existence has been materially and ideologically constituted as the "feminine sphere" and thereby distinguished from the "masculine sphere" of public and intellectual life. The "feminine sphere," in turn, had been appropriated and reconstituted by intimate biography as the materials of the "private" life of men. Abstracting the concrete conditions of women's lives, the biographical production of a masculine "private" life functioned not only to deny women access to a "meaningful" private existence (a condition of nineteenth-century personhood); it also established a second currency of male homosocial exchange. Thus, using the figure of the nameless house-cleaning mother and her environment, Carter prepares the ground that both distinguishes Richter from mother/woman and produces Richter as transcending, by the sheer power of his imagination and genius, her dismal existence. Mother cleans the floors while Richter and Carter read and write (and while the women readers weep, as Carter notes) in a now abstracted, gender-differentiated, private life that has been launched with the aid of a dishpan and spinning wheel. By means of a few choice sociodomestic biographical details, Carter gives over the portrait of the artist as a man, able to transform dismal domestic noise into the "higher music" of abstraction and turn dingy walls into the brightly colored blossoms of a metaphor. Simultaneously depending upon, abstracting, privatizing, and devaluing the material realities of female domestic existence, Carter produces Richter not as someone who might have helped his mother scrub the walls but as a properly masculine artist: one who can ignore, exploit, and mask his "real life" in his writing (1:23).

The inaugural position of Carter's essay in the first volume of the *Transactions* was probably not arbitrary. Written some fifteen years after what is generally considered the formal organization and mobilization of American departments of modern literature, Carter's approach is something of a hybrid, embracing some aspects of philology—the study of the life and times of the author—and of the newer methodology of aesthetic appreciation. Both biographical and evaluative, it was perhaps a meliorist gesture, and, with its suggestion that the work of literary men was nothing like women's work, it offered a virtual wedding of the old, the new, and the borrowed.

Despite such advantages, Carter's approach did not, however, appear to catch on—it probably smacked too much of philology—though traces of it appear in the "personality" and "psychology" criticism that succeeded it, and which I will be discussing later in the essay. Suffice it to say that subsequent volumes of the *Transactions* (renamed in 1889 *Publications of the Modern Language Association of Ameri-*

ca), through the next few decades rarely contain anything resembling Carter's biographically based analysis. They are, however, rife with critiques of philology and the classics. As Gerald Graff has pointed out, those who were organizing departments of modern literature in the 1870s had initially appropriated the discourse of philology as a strategy of legitimation but very soon after, in a struggle first for institutional parity and then for institutional ascendancy, turned against philology and worked to differentiate their methods and philosophies from their self-constituted opposition.

This story of the philologists versus the aestheticians is compelling, especially in the way it helps to explain the ongoing rationalizations of departments of literature into a multitude of competing divisions and specialties. But it also betrays some of the circularity of autopoiesis. As Carter's essay hints, the appropriation of philology was not strictly an internal affair. It was also and perhaps more importantly used to distance and differentiate this newly organized discipline from the discourse and authority of popular literary culture—which included women writers, readers, and critics—flourishing at the time these departments of literature were forming.[9] Philology was, as well, part of the discipline's marketing strategy, an effort to create a demand for its product: what would motivate a student to enroll in courses on modern literature when, as far as he knew, he was already capable of reading and appreciating literature without the benefit of academic intervention? What, in other words, would distinguish the knowledge of a student from that of a professor when both were reading the same literature, reviews, and biographies?

Initially, the philological approach seemed the solution to such difficulties. Unlike popular literary study, philology was generally uninterested in questions of moral probity or aesthetic pleasure; evaluation was not its task. For philologists, blame or praise was naive—the stuff of untrained readers. Influenced by European historians such as Hippolyte Taine, philologists were devoted to the accumulation of information—detailed histories of languages, literatures, and authors. Evaluation a was a dream deferred, something that would be done when and if enough information was finally collected and categorized.

In marked contrast to the appreciative and judicial criticism that characterized popular literary study, philology initially appeared a distinct and hence attractive alternative—a truly scholarly approach to modern literature. The disadvantages of embracing philology wholesale, however, proved formidable. First, there were simple material constraints. As Bliss Perry, an influential figure in the academic development of aesthetic criticism—and, one might note, a biographer—pointed out, the lack of library resources and an adequate supply of modern literature affordable to faculty and students posed a nearly insurmountable obstacle to philological research and pedagogy. With scarce resources, faculty were placed in the unsavory position of making "second-hand" presentations of even the immediately canonized authors, Dante, Shakespeare, and Goethe. Such an approach not only threatened to tarnish the profession's scholarly image, it also made pedagogy a chore for teacher and student alike. Then, too, faculty were rather uncomfortable with the philological necessity of tracing the history of American letters rather than, like their popular-literary counterparts, merely declaring (and then setting out to define) a "tradition." Literary faculty were eager to participate—or more accurately, intervene upon and control—this nationalist project. The scholar of modern literature who elected to research a *history* of American literature would be obligated not only to locate and define such a tradition (none as yet having been agreed upon) but, more formidably, to negotiate the politically hazardous road that seemed inevitably to lead to Britain—the very tradition from which America always sought its literary independence.[10]

Modern literature faculty also began to realize that if their pedagogical aim—"mental discipline"—was no different from that of the classicists, the primary incentive for students to enroll in modern courses was that these were notably easier. Students were not compelled to negotiate the barrier of translating an ancient language, which comprised the greater part of classical pedagogy. This unpleasantly suggestive difference in appeal and rigor posed yet another threat to their professional identity. Finally, though not exhaustively, the philological approach produced so great a disjuncture between academic and popular critical approaches that faculty feared they would be shut out by what was becoming a priority: to fill, hegemonize, and institutionalize the contested space of popular literary authority. As Calvin Thomas complained, philology "puts critics out of business," leaving no way for the professor to "blame or praise . . . only to explain or describe" (303). James MacAlister was anxious about the potential lack of appeal this scholarly method would have for its target audience. He compared philology to the ancient schools of the Church, which, teaching nothing "but a little barbarous Latin and a great deal of scholastic philosophy," had been "deserted by the youth, eager to drink at the fountains of the new learning which had been unsealed" (9).

To beckon others to the academy's fountains of learning, the discipline surreptitiously grazed the literary marketplace, subtly appropriating and modifying its discourse. F. V. N. Painter, for example, argued that the study of the classics was fine for "mental discipline" but did not "represent the culture demanded at the present day, and especially in this country." The "educated man," he continued, makes the "past subservient to the present" (90). MacAlister, taking a slightly different tack, argued that the classics "cannot minister to our need for conduct, to our need for beauty, as do the poets and thinkers of the times in which the conscience and taste of men were moulded by influences to which the ancients were strangers" (14). He agreed with Matthew Arnold that the purpose of education was "to know ourselves and our world," and it was only the study of modern literature that would enable this knowledge (13). Even Carter, who obviously had some investment in philological scholarship, felt that as a *pedagogical* method (a distinction I will be discussing later in the essay) it was too arduous and mediated to facilitate a student's "influences quickening to breadth of vision and correct taste." It is "just here that the denunciation of Greek study has its standing ground" (2:16). These rallying cries of a new methodology were a barely masked reiteration of what were already the concerns, since the early nineteenth century, of American popular literary culture and its journalists, reviewers, presses, reading groups, lending libraries, and individual readers and writers. What is different here is the effort to revalue, abstract, and consolidate the culture's heterogenous discourse of literary reception. "Beauty," generally a secondary concern to popular literary studies and comprising anything from good grammar and sentence structure to spiritual soundness and use of allusions, becomes a privileged term and gradually displaces the primary concern of popular literary culture, issues of conduct and moral instructiveness.

A Home Away from Home

Perhaps the most influential figure and proponent of the new "aesthetic" approach was James Russell Lowell, referenced by nearly all who espoused this shift in methodology. Unlike many of his colleagues, Lowell was himself a well-known and widely published poet, essayist, and reviewer, the founding editor of *The Atlantic,* an editor of the *North American Review,* and a contributor and editor to several other publications. A member of the Saturday Club, Lowell associated with Emerson, Hawthorne, Longfellow, and Whittier, and was a prominent figure in many other of Boston's prestigious literary circles. His reputation in popular literary culture matched that which he came to attain in academic culture when he succeeded Longfellow as Smith Professor of Modern Languages and Literature at Harvard. His literary biculturism, his publishing career, and his fame appear to have made his views and his claims to literary authority quite persuasive.

Deploying the egalitarian rhetoric of popular literary culture, Lowell wrote of his "emancipation" from philology and the study of the classics, a discipline he dismissed as "the exclusive privilege of a class" making "an obstinate defence of its vested rights" (8). Comparing Latin to a pickle, he called for the "salt"—literature written in the "language in which a man writes" and which "really touched them [the readers] home" (6–7). He complained that for centuries "the languages which served men for all the occasions of private life were put under a ban" with literature its only "vent" and called for the "study of a living language" (6, 11). Lowell's conception of "private life" is formal—it is language that will "touch a man home"—without referring to his house. Like many other American (and British) male writers of the nineteenth century, Lowell could not put enough space between home and work, referentiality and transcension.[11]

Students of literature, he felt, should be taught to seek the "genius," the "style," the "truth to nature," the "shock" of a great book; they should be trained to look for that which "delights, inspires and surprises" (12). A book must be judged by its "total effect," both "moral and aesthetic"—but not be used "as courses of moral philosophy or metaphysics." Suggesting something of a return to the "old notion of literature as holiday," he lays the groundwork for a mystified aesthetic of appreciation—popular culture's "entertainment"—which required that the student be *trained* to enjoy a book:

> To give pleasure merely is one, and not the lowest, function of whatever deserves to be called literature. Culture, which means the opening and refining of the faculties, is an excellent thing, perhaps the best, but there are other things to be had of the Muses which are also good in their kind. Refined pleasure is refining pleasure too, and teaches something in her way, though she be no proper schooldame.

Entertainment thus becomes "refinement," and the "aesthetic and moral" are conjoined, laying the groundwork of the "genteel" and more openly classist aesthetic that would follow. To differ his mode of appreciation from that of the popular, Lowell reaches for "refinement," and this, particularly in combination with the moral, is potently feminine. Dancing over the border of this toxic sphere of nineteenth-century femininity, Lowell immediately purges through negation: the professor of literature is "no proper schooldame"—a phrase, it should be noted, perhaps the most frequently quoted by Lowell's colleagues ("schooldames" becoming "schoolmarms" as memories faded) in their own defenses and outlines of the new methodology. To further assure his readers of their masculinity (this project generally seeming to require two rounds of fire), Lowell later and quite royally proclaims: "And yet may we not without lese-majesty say of books what FERDINAND says of women"—which, in a gunshell, is that books and women, however attractive, are inevitably flawed. Here, as elsewhere, Lowell will ground his own claims exclusively by quotation of other authors, thereby implicitly forming a canon, exemplifying the new methodology, and establishing authors themselves as the central academic literary authority—a struggle for power that still haunts academic literary studies.

The place of the author in academic literary criticism is ambiguous in Lowell's approach; an author himself, he undoubtedly experiences something of an aporia concerning precisely how one should be received and treated by the academy. He variously presents literature as private, personal, and universal, alternately reflecting the capacities of the reader, the text, and the author. "It is always wise to eliminate the personal equation from our judgments of literature. But what is so subtle, so elusive [as this]? Are we to be suspicious of a book's good character," he asks, "in proportion as it appeals more vividly to our own private consciousness and experience? How are we to know to how many it may be making the same appeal?" (17). At the close of his essay, Lowell declares that literature "is the unconscious autobiography of mankind," the "record of Man's joys and sorrows, of his aspirations and failures, of his thought, his speculation and his dreams" (22). As an autobiography of mankind, it is no longer precisely a biography or personal production of its author. Yet, as "unconscious" autobiography, it is not quite public property, either, for only the great writer has the genius to tap into the collective unconscious; "mankind" could not have written it, though it reflects mankind's universal values and concerns. Lowell's notion of "genius," like that of language—which he distinguishes from philology's "linguistics"—is quite mobile and slippery, shifting from text to reader to author at critical points. "In literature [that which gives life] is what we call genius, in insoluble ingredient," he declares, employing the first person plural and presumably speaking as a fellow reader. Yet a few sentences later he seems to speak as author to reader as "other"; it is no longer literature, but "*men* of genius, like EMERSON, richly seminative for other minds; like BROWNING, full of wholesome ferment for other minds" (my emphasis). It is finally not clear precisely who bears this precious and mysterious essence; reader, writer, and text orbit in separate and perhaps unequal constellations of an aestheticized universe.

Ultimately, it would seem that genius rests in Lowell himself, who can inhabit all the positions he stakes out—author, critic, reader, scholar—and upon which he grounds, but does not foreground, his claims to authority. He bolsters his authority exclusively through quotation of other literary authors—another transformation of popular culture's use of quotation as illustration, sample, or example. Now authorized by Lowell, these texts are constituted as containing genius because of the genius of their writings—because Lowell says so. He defends neither his choices nor his authority; and they will not be challenged by his colleagues, who will instead quote him as a source of authority.[12] Lowell's method produces not only a dazzling circularity, guided by a single, containing question—does this work demonstrate genius?—but also helps to deflect the gaze of biographical scrutiny from author to reader: one must (like Lowell) have internalized aesthetic principles in order to grasp aesthetic genius. This seems a masterful renegotiation of the poetic principles of Samuel Taylor Coleridge's "public" principles, extremely influential in the development of American antibiographical poetic principles, such as those formulated by Edgar Allan Poe and later absorbed by the academy.[13] Where Coleridge only claimed poetic internalization as a natural talent and task of the poet, Lowell implies that such principles of genius must be internalized by the critic as well. Diffusing what Coleridge had called the "fugitive" (or biographically oriented) causes of a poem in a somewhat desperate attempt to deflect the biographical gaze, Lowell places the burden of proof on the critic/reader and text rather than author—providing the author with credit at zero biographical interest.[14] It is the *reader* who must be concerned with "personal fallacy's eartip," with what "is felt instinctively . . . a difference not of degree but of kind," and someone else's task to tell the reader whether his or her instincts are on the mark. Neatly deauthorizing the reader, Lowell also destabilizes the authority of the scholar. Lowell was sure that the student needed to be taught to "refine" such instincts and thereby to somewhat "neutralize" the effects and affects of the personal (17). But he was "not sure that this could be taught in any school" (13).

One can locate in Lowell's discourse the beginnings of what might be called the writer-scholar contract, the unwieldy distribution and transference of relations of power, authority, and credit between writers and academics, and one that, I will argue a bit later, is in part negotiated through the repression of biography to the benefit of both parties. As an author with an interest and authority "outside" the institution, and as a producer of the sole object of academic literary study, Lowell is loath to relinquish any authority to his disciplinary colleagues. As a member of the discipline, seeking its recognition and authority, however, he is equally loath to dismiss the academy out of hand. Perhaps this relation of power is peculiar to the arts, where producer and scholar of the privileged object of study often must compete within themselves and against each other for the same professional space and authority, however much it is rationalized into departments of "creative writing" and "literature." In any event, it is interesting to note how such phobically antibiographical writers as Poe, Henry James, and T. S. Eliot have not only been widely and consistently deployed as grounds of academic literary authority but have also been instrumental in the formulations of antibiographical academic critical methodology and a nearly century-long preference for the tale over the teller.

Like Lowell, who began his essay with an anecdote about a French dancing instructor, literary faculty were especially concerned with the popular assumption that "*any body* can teach" modern literature as if it "were accomplishments like dancing, fencing, or final touches to be put on ladies," the complaint of H. C. G. Brandt (61). Simultaneously expressing anxieties and producing distinctions between the masculine, academic environment and the feminine one of popular instruction and study, comparisons to ladies, schoolmarms, and French dancing instructors were abundantly employed by academic literary critics in their continuing efforts to define and consolidate their fragile professional identity. This production of otherness extended in various directions. Newspapers and the "lawless and inconstant public" were also passionately targeted. "Craving excitement at any price, journalized daily, neither knowing nor caring what should be the real aim and scope of the novel," Bliss Perry complained that the public "has the casting vote, after all, upon great books and little books alike." In contrast to other professions, Perry notes, the literary scholar has "no appeal" from the "public's Verdict" (84). In order for faculty to assume their rightful place as the high court of literature, journals and literary publications required delegitimization and thus feminization. Newspapers "prostitute the inventive aptitudes of our young men and women"—one of the few appearances of "women" in these essays—by publishing badly written literature, John Phelps Fruit declared.[15] Teachers of literature, he bravely argued, must take a stand against the "prodigious powers" of the "secular press" or risk becoming "mere drivellers in literature"—a metaphor perhaps best left unexplored (39). A. E. Spofford called upon the profession to "reject and discountenance the badly written books and the illegitimate words which tend to debauch our literature and degrade our language," once again underscoring the condensed and displaced relationships between the control of literary authority and that of female sexuality, language, and nation. We must, he declared, "recall attention from frivolous productions of the hour to study the great masters of thought and speech" (23). Like Lowell, Fruit and Spofford do not provide any grounds for their authority or outline their criteria for determining the "great" from the "little" productions; they simply claim it, often by quoting Lowell or other writers in their solidifying canon.[16]

Criticizing popular literary culture while appropriating its functions was effective in disabling the authority of journalists and audience alike, the latter, of course, including college students. Emphasizing and reversing another of popular culture's this time rather minor terms of valuation, faculty made contemporaneity an affliction and datedness a virtue, arguing that literature needed to be held up to the test of time. We must "accept nothing as orthodox literature on which the elder centuries have not laid their consecrating hands," solemnly declared Lowell (17). The duration of this laying on of hands was left rather open-ended; one can presume consecration took as much time as professors needed to select texts, study reviews and biographies, and mobilize arguments and approaches. This strategy of temporal delay also, like the proclamation of "great" versus "little" books, constituted faculty as ultimate arbiters in this newly temporalized determination of literary masterpieces as they culled the few from the many elected by their now at least imaginarily subordinated publishers, reviewers, readers, and students.

Students were further and more particularly undermined by constant metaphorical infantilization and feminization (they were incessantly labeled infant-school children, babes, growing boys). More importantly, in terms of this essay, they were subjected to and implicated in myriad dividing practices: student and professor, undergraduate and graduate student, higher and lower education, professor and "schooldame," university and college studies of literature, prepared and unprepared. The hope of the profession, Th. W. Hunt proclaimed, was that the nation's "literary development [be] made safe and reputable by being under collegiate guidance" (132). To enable such surveillance and control, faculty openly discussed the importance of building a "superstructure" that could envelop and dictate taste, refinement, and the literary tradition from nursery school to maturity.[17] As Raymond Williams, following Gramsci, argues, the project of a dominant class is to establish its authority by universalizing its values, appropriating the domain of morality, and convincing itself and those whom it has subordinated of the legitimacy of its views. A dominant class works to saturate the "whole process of living" and the "whole substance of lived identities and relationships" with its values and interests until these "seem to most of us the pressures and limits of simple experience and common sense" rather than a specific economic, social, and cultural agenda (110).

Contracting Authority, or the Fate of Small Beer

Caught in the midst of these debates and desires, biography, bearer of other livings and other lives, suffered a peculiar fate. First, it was dismissed from the undergraduate classroom as an encumbrance for already alienated, weary, and underprepared students, who should as much as possible be given an intimate and immediate relation to literary texts. Second, it was reconstituted as distinctively professional information. As Carter pointed out, it was a teacher's duty to have a "better knowledge of the author" than that held by the student (2:15). Prior to the installment of aesthetic criticism, biography had been a routine part of the undergraduate and graduate curricula of literary studies, unremarked in the lists of canonical poetry and prose. Its elimination from undergraduate curricula was justified essentially on class grounds—the presumably growing population of underprepared students who had enough to contend with without the burden of history. Edward S. Joynes, for example, argued that the "lower classes [by which he referred to undergraduates] not yet fully prepared for such study" should not prematurely be exposed to "such a mistaken study not of, but about them." Such studies, he felt, "should be made rather the privilege of the few than the task of the many:—for the higher classes only, in our collegiate work" (41).[18] Thus the pedagogical repression of biography served a valuable, "class-based" critical function; it both asserted and produced a clear differential in knowledge and thus relations of power between student and professor, graduate and undergraduate, "prepared" and "underprepared" undergraduate. As Hunt pointed out, *scholarly* work called for, among other things, the study of "the life and times of the author as related to his literary productions," and the professor, not the student, needed to be familiar with a "vast amount of English biography and history" (127).

The biographical work of the aesthetic scholar nonetheless had to be distinguished from the philological deployment of biography. Thus Hunt, like some of his colleagues, called for a "psychological study" rather than a philological one. This method confined the academic project to an evaluation of the "spirit" of the author, as well as a "history" and "biography" extrapolated solely from the literary text itself rather than from extraliterary historical and biographical sources (126). This proposed "spiritual" evaluation loosened the material and methodological grip of philology, but it also flirted with the kind of moral and character evaluations already being performed by the unruly "outside" readers and reviewers. The need to avoid such unfortunate conjunctures engendered an ingenious strategy: it was insinuated, or openly proclaimed, that *any* use of biography by either popular culture or philology was mere trafficking in gossip.[19] Echoing Woodrow Wilson, Albert Cook maintained that philologists "run their allusions—particularly female allusions—to cover" (186). Cook insinuated that philologists were no more than pernicious and persistent gossips, tracking down the trivial and lascivious details of romance from cover to cover, as it were. To wean students from their reliance on biography, biographer-scholar Perry argued that they must be "taught to look for the mark of personality, not in gossip about a novelist's hour of rising and favorite breakfast and favorite books, but rather in connection with the creative processes" (83). Marrying biography with the feminized spaces of sociodomestic relations and popular culture selectively delegitimated these forms and sources of knowledge, which were routed from and by the academy's masculine, scholarly purview.

Entangled in this dismissal of biography were the interests of academic scholars in the repression of authorial biography. Appropriating Lowell's notion of literature as mankind's unconscious autobiography, Fruit, for example, declared that it is "not the man in public life," but the *artist* that the professor of literature seeks—the author who "disindividualizes" himself and becomes "the vent of the absolute mind" (33). This "disindividualization" of the author was one of the most original contributions of academic aesthetic criticism; though its concepts and strategies can be traced to the discursive field of popular literary culture and individual authorial criticism, its effects and its subject positions are clearly transformed. Where Lowell had made a "vent" of literature, Fruit makes a "vent"—a veritable aeolian lyre—of the artist himself. This asserted, the study of literature logically demanded an expert mediator who could inhabit the position of ultimate authority, instructing reader and writer alike on where and how well the wind blew; disindividualized, the author could no longer lay claim to his text without jeopardizing his artistic identity. To doubly bind this contract of authority, Fruit insists that the mark of a *true* writer was that he recognized and agreed to this authorial disinvestment: the "artist does not feel himself to be the parent of his work" (33). The desire to drape a net of power relations over literary culture was expansive; departments of literature sought to bring not only literary reception and analysis but also the production of literature itself under academic surveillance. Like Fruit, Spofford felt that writers needed academic training in order to learn the "rudiments of literary art" (5). American literature *and* its critics, declared A. H. Smyth, will develop only by being academically guided through American literature (244). The tentacles of academic literary authority, at least in the imagination and ambition of these early faculty, would reach into the deepest recesses of American culture until all would be properly refined.

The academic version of the study of authorial "personality" or "spirit" or "psychology" had certain vague affinities with the principles of Coleridge, Poe, and Lowell in the hermeneutical circularity it proposed to resist the particularity, referentiality, and—from the scholar's point of view—authority of the individual author that could be produced and emphasized by historical and biographical readings. It differed from popular literary use of biography in that it was uninterested in evaluating the character and morality of the author; it strove to become one with him and his text in order to achieve the necessary degree of aesthetic appreciation. At the same time, it worked to displace and even devalue the significance of the author: "If it is scientific to care for the life-history of a bug or worm," declared Calvin Thomas, "why not for that of a man?" Thomas asserted that works and life were "indissolubly bound together," a knowledge of one leading to a knowledge of the other (312–13). He described the academic study of personality as "elusive" but "most instructive." One could study a man's life in detail, but never obtain the "certain amount of heat" necessary to comprehend the "heat of the creator." This elusive heat, facilitated by but not attainable through historical or biographical information, could be experienced and transmitted only by training one's *imagination*—thus neatly appropriating and transferring the Romantic aesthetic of the artist to the scholar—until one could "look at Luther's world through Luther's eyes" (311). Thomas's "imagination" was not available through some mystified notion of internalized poetic instinct or genius, but rather through a mystified *training*—the domain of the academy.

Like Thomas, a few academics attempted to produce similar versions of biographical criticism, but most simply crowded biography, along with history and philology in general, into a contained space; all of these were valuable as scholarly background, but none was particularly illuminating for the primary project of the scholar—aesthetic analysis. Spofford, for example, argued that "so vast a literature of criticism has grown up about Shakespeare's personal, poetical, and metaphysical characteristics" that "we've failed to do entire justice to his style." Style was as mysterious as personality, often tautologically defined. Spofford offered as his catalogue of stylistic qualities such items as the mastery of style, force of passion, simplicity, organic structure, condensation, elevation of thought, and reach of imagination (11–12).

Needless to say, and a century later, there remains a paucity of detail on Shakespeare relative to his "personal characteristics." Yet, despite its various academic deformations and evictions, biography continued to inhabit the profession in a most peculiar way. In the formative years of the discipline, the professor of literature, free to choose from and having at least rhetorically appropriated and colonized any number of subject positions and identifications—from reader, critic, and student to republican, judge, and parent—generally chose, like Thomas, to identify with authors. Their rightful claim to this position was based upon a primarily affective identification, the effect of their "intimate relation" with and "training" in the authors and texts they studied. They would see through Luther's eyes, for they had no eyes, professionally and psychoanalytically speaking, to call their own and no emotions that they wanted to identify as theirs alone. Hart, upon Lowell's death, had asked: "Have we no personality worth imparting?" and called for teachers to be more like Lowell and to "infuse" their pedagogy with their personalities "and—shall I say it—make ourselves personally interesting and objects of imitation" so that students would learn to read for pleasure—something they had once been capable of doing without the charms of academic assistance (7:28–29). Professors such as Lowell were widely admired and emulated; the most "personable" were those, like him, able to read texts aloud with the enthusiasm, grit, and verve imagined to be identical to that of its author, thus turning the classroom into a literary theatre and imbuing the students with the learned pleasure of a text—another invention of the academy.[20]

In return for this acoustical-affective identification with and incorporation of the author and his authority, the aesthetic approach promised writers that scholars would keep their noses out of the author's private life, directing, containing, and ostensibly even halting biographical scrutiny. This was hardly a sacrifice on the part of the literary faculty; among other things, to overparticularize the author would only jeopardize one's impersonation and feminize one's discourse. Biography would become academically private reading; only the most facilitative biographical details would be freed in the classroom or in the work of criticism, details that enabled the sought-after appreciation and, perhaps, that suggested a personality type compatible with that of the professor. Young men, Perry said, "most need to be taught the fallibility of the [market value] standard" of assessing literature, which "tempts [them] to mistake literary gossip for literary culture." Perry continues:

> The English historian's famous sneer, upon the proposition to introduce courses in English literature at the universities, was that the study of Shelley would end in men being coached in "the Harriet problem." But

the Harriet problem is innocent and edifying material for the classroom, compared with the themes of some of the most widely-read English novels of the past five years. If these books are to be discussed at
all, they should be discussed frankly, but the teacher's desk gains nothing in dignity by being turned into a clinic one day and a pulpit the next.
If a man thinks he can teach literature, then, for his pupils' sake, as
well as his own, he should stick to his trade.[21]

The "Harriet problem" is what biography brings to the academy. Trail-
ing in its wake such volatile issues as gender, nation, sexuality, and the
very purpose of literary studies, biography threatened to undermine
professional authority and the fragile identity upon which such authority had only recently been constituted. To discuss the "themes of
the most widely-read novels," much less provide "gossip" or biography
of the writers who produced them, could blur the boundaries of professional identity beyond recognition. The "Harriet problem" could
lower the profession a notch in relation to the more prestigious work
and nation of the sneering British colleague, feminize and contaminate
it simply by being in the air or placing the professor in the unsavory
position of speaking from a conventionally feminine voice and site of
authority—the social, domestic, and specifically affective. It could tear
the delicate fabric upon which institutional authority grounded itself—
neither clinician nor minister, what is my area of expertise?—until it
was indistinguishable from that of the common reader; and solicit endless and difficult questions about the object of study and what the
professor, the author, and the text finally had to say about morality,
gender, class, sexuality, and other unsavory "themes." Last, though
not exhaustively, biography could potentially devalue or demystify the
professor's identifications with and claim to the text, rupturing his fantasy of autonomy and control. To address literature on any but the
profession's deliberately antibiographical terms might be to call into
question its identity, claims to authority—even its function. Thus it is
indeed for his own sake, as well as that of his students, that Perry, his
rhetoric bulging with metaphorical masculinity (one would have to be
"coached" in the Harriet problem) aligns himself with working-class
men and declares that a professor had better "stick to his trade," keeping the Harriet problem, and all that it entailed, at bay.

Even biographically oriented professors such as Perry and
Thomas vowed to avoid such a Harriet problem. They promised that
neither would they, like philologists, hunt down biographical allusions
nor, like journalists, popular biographers, and students, pry into a writer's "dinner-bills and freight-bills, the record of his goings and com-
ings, the gossip of his friends and enemies, his chronicles of small
beer" (Thomas, 313). They would, instead, map out the difference

between literary history and literary gossip, and, credited with the authority of aesthetic and identificatory subject and "parent" of the text, they would freely acknowledge the prodigality and the privacy of their child, producing and managing only such biographical notes and details as necessary to a proper presentation. They would even, over time, take upon themselves the task of "authorizing" biographies by "outsiders"—continuing, of course, to exclude these from their courses on literature.

It would be peremptory, if not mistaken, to presume that the academic repression of biography in literary studies has strictly functioned as a conservative and oppressive strategy. The use of biography in the popular literary culture of the nineteenth century to condemn and delegitimate the work of nineteenth-century women writers suggests its destructive potential. I would argue, however, that biography (like history) must have its uses as well as abuses. What these are remains to be seen: theorists and scholars of both history and literature have generally been so shy—or more accurately, ignorant—of biography that we scarcely can make claims about its potential advantages and disadvantages. What is clear is that biography, as private reading and public scourge, has since the formalization of departments of literature been granted no legitimate place in academic literary discourse; I hope to have shown that this lack of place suggests something of a displacement of institutional anxieties about such issues as gender, identity, and popular culture. The dismissal of biography was, in the nineteenth century, part of an elaborate strategy of defense and consolidation against real and imagined challenges to professional authority by "outside" forces, generated as much by feelings of uncertainty, inferiority, and superfluity as by more aggressive impulses and motives. Feelings of discomfort may, for the male subject, be indigenous to the study of literature in a patriarchal culture; the work is by its nature "derivative," its "origins" always elsewhere and its concerns and conventions—affect, sociodomestic existence and relations, conduct—historically more "feminine" than "masculine."

Along with more apparently politically and intellectually motivated agendas, a discourse of uneasy emotions perhaps helped to fuel the "war of methods" between the New Critics and the social and political critics of the 1930s and 1940s in their contest for literary authority. In their return to history and biography, the social critics had once again dragged in the "outside," and the New Critics, with the aid of such craftsmen-authorities as Eliot, evicted them. The intentional fallacy, the antibiographical rallying cry from the 1940s onward, had by the 1960s become something of an academic mantra, a white noise used to drown out any notes of domesticity and writer—or reader—particularity. A reactivated effort to rout biography was enacted during the 1970s and 1980s, a response in part to the noisy challenges of feminists, African-Americans, gays and lesbians, the working class, and other "outsiders," who had brought in and begun to unpack their emotional baggage, bringing outside sources indoors and openly challenging professional identity, authority, and function. Structuralists and poststructuralists (at least some of them) often returned fire with the best of intentions, littering the discursive filed with fragmented, functionalized, and dead authors, and once again contaminating biography as the domain of the naive, essential, humanist unsophisticate, which, in the 1990s, certainly must be worse than being "feminine": we've come a long way.[22]

It might be worthwhile to ask, in light of our discipline's many dismissals of biography or biographically oriented work—as "gossip" (Calvin Thomas and others of the nineteenth century; Wimsatt and Beardsley in the twentieth), as reductive or tyrannical (Roland Barthes), as "cosmetic humanism" (Peggy Kamuf, following Michel Foucault)—what it is we are talking about when we talk about biography.[23] Barthes and Foucault are today as entrenched and internalized in our discourse as the intentional fallacy and gossip that preceded them; without question, they have been the most invaluable anti-biographical imports of American theory; yet both were involved with biographical productions, a fact that might give at least a pause. Barthes, along with an autobiography, authored *Michelet,* and Foucault edited and wrote the introduction for *Herculin Barbin: Being the Recently Published Memoirs of a Nineteenth-Century Hermaphrodite.* Both of these authors—at least as academic gossip would have it—were gay, and perhaps it is not too speculative to suggest that both probably had, considering the climate and time in which they produced their influential essays, a personal interest in repressing, dismantling, or "overthrowing" the biographical-authorial subject. "I am no doubt not the only one who writes in order to have no face," Foucault rather plaintively noted in his otherwise terribly sober *The Archeology of Knowledge* (17).

In the dysfunctional family of academic literary studies, the code of silence these renowned authors seem to have promulgated might be regarded as enabling—an act of survival in a field of few choices that, as both men acquired continued professional prestige and recognition, they began to reconsider and renegotiate. In *The Use of Pleasure,* Foucault observed that it was not until writing this, one of his last works, that it occurred to him to consider "those intentional and voluntary actions by which men not only set themselves rules of conduct, but also seek to transform themselves, to change themselves in their singular being"(10). He called for a new kind of history, one that would take into account the different realities that are covered by the term. This history, he wrote, would "study the extent to which actions of certain individuals or groups are consistent with the rules and values that are prescribed for them by various agencies" (29). I imagine this discursive shift to be as well a personal one for Foucault; and I cannot help but think it a gesture toward biography, for what he describes has been one of biography's longstanding, if seldom well-realized, aims.

With the proliferation of academic commitments to such issues as difference and particularity, it may be time to at least consider why our particular interests continue to be drawn to broad, discursive histories that we call "local" or "genealogical," and in which we "situate" individual texts, a situation typically entangled with our professional, political, and pedagogical agendas. By overlooking biography, we are likely to avoid a confrontation with the ways in which the specific constellation of individuals and agencies involved in the production of a text in its historical moment complicate, dispute, and alter discursive history. I do not wish to fly in the face of the substantive critiques that have been made of the humanist individual and the ideologically saturated burden of responsibility placed upon her by liberal humanism, but I think antihumanist critiques can err, as well, by pessimistically mystifying relations of power even as they strive to demarcate and subvert them. What seems to me to be at stake in the many debates about the author—*within* the institution in which our professional discourse is implicated—is not so much the status of the individual but rather the production, management, and maintenance of our professional authority. In that light, debates about whether or not it is "sound" or "humanist" to take an individual subject as the object of study—which continues to be the most prevalent theoretical strategy deployed to repress and delegitimate biographical inquiry—may be something of a philosophical distraction or, unwittingly, an essentially conservative gesture that keeps our circles small and our discourse elevated.

In any event, what "historiographies of the individual subject"— a phrase I here proffer as a way of making biography sound a bit more theoretically sophisticated and palatable—do seem to promise, particularly in relation to the prodigious, monstrous, deviant, or marginalized subject, is a path to the ways in which these "othered" subjects negotiated, embraced, rejected, created, and transformed the rules and behaviors prescribed for them and us, and the way in which biography, in its serial focuses on a figure and as a reflection of the contemporary consciousness of its biographer and reader, constitutes and evaluates such subjects. In this way, biography could help to locate and complicate other avenues of thought and action, resistance and complicity, affects and interests—the slender inroads and veins of history that must necessarily be bypassed by the historiographer, whose task, equally but not more important, is to map the major throughways and the general order of things.

Notes

I would like to thank Gregory Jay, Herbert Blau, Kathleen Woodward, Patrice Petro, and William Epstein, without whose critical insights and generosity this essay would not have been possible.

   1. Wilson is more ambivalent than I was at the time; he argues that "Milton was not utterly misogynistic" and receives as gossip the reports by his daughters of their mistreatment. "It is hard to accept any of their memories of their father without scepticism," Wilson declares, for "one sees the distorting power of domestic irritation at work" in their accounts (218).

   2. It is an unhappy irony that I single out this professor—a brilliant, kind, and engaging teacher—precisely because of his exceptional willingness to entertain both the chaos of formal biography and the issue of feminism in his classes.

   3. The notion of the "outside" of a discipline and its tendency to avoid analyzing its own problems is indebted to Michel de Certeau's "Psychoanalysis and Its History," *Heterologies: Discourse on the Other,* Theory and History of Literature vol. 17, trans. Brian Massumi (Minneapolis: University of Minnesota Press, 1986), 3–16; I am grateful to Connie Balides for calling this text to my attention.

   Fort/da is the term Freud used to describe the sado-masochistic dialectic as well as the way in which a child learns to constitute his identity by mastering the unpleasure of renouncing his attachment to his mother. Freud's theory was derived from observing his grandson tossing and retrieving a toy while muttering "Fort. Da" (here, gone), and viewed it as symptomatic of the way we need to repeat experiences that inspire trauma, in this way learning to take pleasure in them and, for the male subject, to take on the masterly role which disengagement from the mother promises. *The Standard Edition of the Complete Psychological Works of Sigmund Freud,* trans. James Strachey (London: Hogarth Press, 1958), 5:451f, 18:14–17.

   4. I am here more generally referring to (and inverting) one of Epstein's definitions of biographical recognition as "an enabling act accompanying the transfer of authority," suggesting that biographical misrecognition, within the academy, effectively disables and preserves certain types of literary authority (10). Epstein's formulation of recognition and misrecognition is far more complex than I am here presenting it. See *Recognizing Biography,* especially chapters 5 and 7.

5. Along with Graff's, some of the more useful histories of the profession include those by Lawrence Veysey, *The Emergence of the American University* (Chicago, Ill.: University of Chicago Press, 1965); Burton J. Bledstein, *The Culture of Professionalism: The Middle Class and the Development of Higher Education in America* (New York: W.W. Norton & Co., 1976); and Frederick Rudolph, *The American College and University: A History* (New York: Vintage, 1962).

6. And, like a few works by women writers, a few biographies (for example, James Boswell's *Life of Samuel Johnson,* Lytton Strachey's *Eminent Victorians,* and Leon Edel's *Henry James*) have achieved canonical status. Constituted as exceptions and innoculations, these few are embraced precisely because of their ability to transcend generic (or gendered) criteria that is used to rationalize the exclusion of "others" of their kind.

7. For histories of women's colleges and discussions of the relationship between higher education and women's rates of marriage and child-bearing, see for example Helen L. Horowitz, *Alma Mater: Design and Experience in Women's Colleges from Their Nineteenth Century Beginnings to the 1930s* (New York: Alfred A. Knopf, 1984); Lynn D. Gordon, "The Gibson Girl Goes to College: Popular Culture and Women's Higher Education in the Progressive Era, 1890–1920," *American Quarterly* 39:2 (Summer 1987) 211–30; Mabel Newcomer, *A Century of Higher Education for American Women* (New York: Harper, 1959); and Thomas Woody, *A History of Women's Education in the United State,* 2 vols. (New York: Science Press, 1929).

8. Gregory Jay, following Eve Sedgwick, writes that woman can be put into circulation by men "even as a letter (or *l'être*) sent by Man to Himself to confirm his correspondence to the image of his own desired identity," (*America the Scrivener: Deconstruction and the Subject of Literary History* [Ithaca, N.Y.: Cornell University Press, 1990], 172). For discussions of the homosocial exchange, see Luce Irigary, *This Sex Which Is Not One,* trans. Catherine Porter (Ithaca, N.Y.: Cornell University Press, 1985) especially pages 170–97. Also see Eve Kosofsky Sedgwick, *Between Men: English Literature and Male Homosocial Desire* (New York: Columbia University Press, 1985). My formulation of a biographical homosocial exchange has also been informed by William Epstein's "(Post)modern Lives: Abducting Biography." (Paper delivered at New Approaches to Biography: Challenges from Critical Theory: First Annual Conference, University of Southern California, Los Angeles, 18 October 1990).

9. For discussions of American popular literary culture of the nineteenth century, see, for example, Cathy Davidson, *Revolution and the Word: The Rise of the Novel in America* (Oxford: Oxford University Press, 1986); Nina Baym, *Novels, Readers, and Reviewers: Responses to Fiction in Antebellum America* (Ithaca, N.Y.: Cornell University Press, 1984) as well as her *Women's Fiction: A Guide to Novels by and about Women in America, 1820–1870* (Ithaca, N.Y.: Cornell University Press, 1978); Michael T. Gilmore, *American Romanticism and the Literary Marketplace* (Chicago, Ill.: University of Chicago Press, 1985); Mary Kelley, *Private Woman, Public Stage:*

Literary Domesticity in Nineteenth-Century America (New York: Oxford University Press, 1984); and Carolyn Karcher, *Shadow Over the Promised Land: Slavery, Race, and Violence in Melville's America* (Baton Rouge: Louisiana State University Press, 1980).

10. A. H. Smyth, for example, arguing for scholarly biographical studies of such figures as Henry David Thoreau and Walt Whitman as a means of forming an American literary canon, pointed out that the British scholars "have, of late, labored mightily to account for the personality of EMERSON, and to fasten upon him a critical label." He urged that "the guardianship and direction of the noble American literature that is to be, must rest mainly with American critics educated in our own schools" rather than with the British or those trained by the British ("American Literature in the Class-room," *Transactions of the Modern Language Association of America* 3 [1887]: 244).

11. The belated American emergence of Romanticism may be an effect of male writers' desire to distance themselves from what might be called the biographical realism of their female contemporaries—"tales of truth" that often took as their titles, like biographies, the names of individuals and promised their readers that the stories were based on real people or incidents. In contrast, writers like Nathaniel Hawthorne (notorious for his anxiety about women writers) would produce obvious (auto)biographies and then insist that these had a "suitable remoteness" from "every-day Probability," however they might be haunted by some "faint . . . shadowing." In his preface to *The Blithedale Romance,* Hawthorne continues this justification of what he correctly anticipated his contemporary readers would recognize as a barely masked account of Brook Farm and Margaret Fuller by insisting that he had used this setting as a "theatre, a little removed from the highway of ordinary travel, where the creatures of his brain may play their phantasmagorical antics" (New York: Penguin Books, 1986), 1. It would take the academic repression of biography for Hawthorne to be constituted as an artist able to transcend the earthly matter of his life.

12. In his eulogy for Lowell, James Morgan Hart does somewhat contest "one element" of Lowell's authority—his flat dismissal of Goethe. Hart believed that Lowell "never quite mastered the great German, that he never bestowed upon him the patient loving devotion" he had on Dante, Cervantes, and Molière ("James Russell Lowell," 30).

13. Nina Baym argues in *Novels, Readers, and Reviewers* that American critics and journalists were generally not interested in the private lives of male writers. While I would more or less agree with her, I would want to question the boundaries of the private in this formulation, but more importantly would wish to note that not just women, but more specifically any subversive or deviant writers, tended to endure intensive biographical scrutiny. Thus Catharine Sedgwick was less the object of biographical investigation than Margaret Fuller, who was treading on masculine ground with her essays, reviews, and feminist treatises, or Walt Whitman, who was labeled a "monster" by several contemporary reviewers. For examples of Whitman's contemporary reception, see *Critical Essays on Walt Whitman,* ed. James Woodress (Boston: G. K. Hall, 1983).

For some examples of the *biographobia* of male writers, see Coleridge's "A Prefatory Observation on Modern Biography," excerpted in *Biography as an Art,* ed. James L. Clifford (London: Oxford University Press, 1962), 57–59. For Coleridge's poetic principles, see *Biographia Literaria or Biographical Sketches of My Literary Life and Opinions,* ed. James Engell and W. Jackson Bate, 2 vols. (Princeton, N.J.: Princeton University Press, 1983). For Poe's, see "The Poetic Principle," *Edgar Allan Poe: Essays and Reviews,* ed. G. R. Thompson (New York: Library of America, 1984), 71–94. Of Poe, Baym observes that his was the only review of the two thousand she studied that specifically discounted, as Poe wrote, "reference to any supposed moral or immoral tendencies (things with which the critic has nothing to do)." Poe's aversion to biographical reference and the moral intention and character of a work helps to explain his later usefulness to the academy (quoted by Baym, 183).

14. For a discussion of the economy of biographical debits and credits, see William Epstein, *Recognizing Biography,* chapters 5 and 6.

15. It perhaps need not be underscored that women appear to have been the major consumers of literature in the nineteenth century. Also, while newspaper ownership and reviewing was male-oriented, Nina Baym suggests that the proportion of women reviewers in antebellum American letters may have been as high as 20 percent. *Novels, Readers, and Reviewers,* 21.

16. Unlike the far more heterogenous literary marketplace, where a broad range of writers were nominated (and debated) as representatives of an "American" literature—including Margaret Fuller, Eliza Leslie, Catherine Sedgwick, and Frederick Douglass—the academy's rapidly hardening canon of American literature was exclusively white male: Emerson, Thoreau, Irving, Franklin, Whittier, Longfellow, and other figures familiar to late twentieth-century students of American literature.

17. For a feminist version of the history of the discipline in its interrelationship with public schools and canon formation, see Nina Baym, "Early Histories of American Literature: A Chapter in the Institution of New England," *American Literary History* 1, no. 3 (Fall 1989): 459–88.

18. Whether or not there was an influx of "underprepared" students or any general change in student population continues to be disputed. Thomas Miller, for example, argues that colleges "with the closest ties to the Dissenters and Scots, colleges like those at Princeton and Philadelphia" historically had broader student populations than did such elite universities as Harvard and Yale. "Where Did College English Studies Come From?" *Rhetoric Review* 9, no. 1 (Fall 1990): 51.

19. The labeling of biography as gossip served a double purpose. Popular publications of the time often featured columns entitled "literary gossip," which would variously discuss such things as new books by or the literary and social lives of writers. The *OED* notes that gossip's earliest reference was to the witnessing of baptisms by either gender; by the sixteenth century, it had come to refer to information about persons and social incidents and had acquired some of its gender inflection. In the early nineteenth century, concomitant with the emergence and popularity of intimate biography, gossip first became used as a verb to describe *written* or oral discourse about persons and social incidents and had acquired a distinctly pejorative, gender-specific connotation. With its simultaneously popular and feminine affiliations, "gossip" thus served to produce, contaminate, and silence discussions of individuals or the "social" that were not academically transfigured.

20. For discussions of this identificatory teaching method, see, for example, Wendell Barrett, "Mr. Lowell as a Teacher," *Stelligeri and Other Essays Concerning America* (New York: Charles Scribner and Son, 1893), and Fred Lewis Pattee, "The Old Professor of English: An Autopsy," *Tradition and Jazz* (New York: Century, 1925).

21. Perry, 80–81. While the British professor is probably referring to the scandal surrounding Harriet Shelley's life (and death), the "Harriet problem" probably had a distinctly American currency, as well, due to Harriet Beecher Stowe's internationally notorious biographical essay on Lord Byron, which exposed his alleged incentuous relationship with his half-sister and nearly ruined Stowe's career and reputation. Byron, of course, became a canonical figure in American academic literary studies.

22. It is interesting to note that, faced with this new challenge to academic authority, the discipline abruptly shifted its identification and basis of authority from author to reader, resulting in a proliferation of theories of reception and reader response. By appropriating and colonizing the position of reader, the theorist is able to contain and even recuperate the threat that a diverse and authorized reading population poses to institutional authority. As with the quest to define "American" literature, reader response theory is often eager to claim, define, and discipline "the reader," while the basis of institutional claims to and upon this often suspiciously universalized notion of "reader" remains free of interrogation. Theories of reader response can thus serve to reinscribe the academic as ultimate arbiter in the high court of literature and reproduce the unequal relations of power that had characterized those between academic and author. For a feminist critique of the power relations of reader-response theory, see Patrocinio P. Schweickart, "Reading Ourselves: Toward a Feminist Theory of Reading," *Gender and Reading: Essays on Readers, Texts, and Contexts,* ed. Elizabeth A. Flynn and Patrocinio Schweickart (Baltimore, Md.: The Johns Hopkins University Press, 1986), 31–62. For a critique of tendencies to theorize from an imaginary reader, see Janice Radway, *Reading the Romance: Women, Patriarchy, and Popular Literature* (Chapel Hill: University of North Carolina Press, 1984).

23. Peggy Kamuf's critique of signature-oriented textual analysis appears in "Replacing Feminist Criticism," *Diacritics* 12 (Summer 1983): 42–47.

Works Cited

Barthes, Roland. "The Death of the Author." *Image Music Text.* Translated by Stephen Heath, 142–8. New York: Hill & Wang, 1977.

Baym, Nina. *Novels, Readers, and Reviewers: Responses to Fiction in Antebellum America* (Ithaca, N.Y.: Cornell University Press, 1984).

Brandt, H. C. G. "How Far Should Our Teaching and Text-books Have a Scientific Basis?" *PMLA* 1 (1884–85): 57–63.

Carter, Franklin. "Richter's Correspondence with a Lady. Some Unpublished Letters." *Transactions of the Modern Language Association of America* 1 (1884–85): 3–24.

————. "Study of Modern Languages in Our Higher Institutions." *Transactions of the Modern Language Association of America* 2 (1886): 1–21.

Cook, Albert S. "The Province of English Philology." *PMLA* 13 (n.s. 6) (1898): 185–204.

Eliot, T. S. "Tradition and the Individual Talent" (1917). *Selected Essays, 1917–1932.* New York: Harcourt Brace, 1932.

Epstein, William H. *Recognizing Biography.* Philadelphia: University of Pennsylvania Press, 1987.

Foucault, Michel. "What Is an Author?" (1979). *Textual Strategies: Perspectives in Post-Structuralist Criticism.* Edited and translated by Josué Harari, 141–60. Ithaca, N.Y.: Cornell University Press, 1979.

————. *The Archeology of Knowledge and the Discourse on Language.* Translated by A. M. Sheridan Smith. New York: Pantheon, 1972.

————. *The Use of Pleasure: The History of Sexuality. Volume Two.* Translated by Robert Hurley. New York: Vintage Books, 1986.

Fruit, John Phelps. "A Plea for the Study of Literature from the Aesthetic Standpoint." *PMLA* 6 (1891): 29–40.

Graff, Gerald. *Professing Literature: An Institutional History.* Chicago, Ill.: University of Chicago Press, 1987.

Hart, James Morgan. "The College Course in English Literature, How It May Be Improved." *Transactions of the Modern Language Association of America* 1 (1884–85): 84–95.

————. "James Russell Lowell." *PMLA* 7 (1892): 25–31.

Heisenberg, Werner. *Physics and Beyond.* New York: Harper, 1971.

Hunt, Th. W. "The Place of English in the College Curriculum." *Transactions of the Modern Language Association of America* 1 (1884–85): 118–32.

Joynes, Edward S. "Reading in Modern Language Study." *PMLA* 5, no. 2 (1890): 33–46.

Lowell, James Russell. "Address." *PMLA* 5, no. 1 (1890): 5–22.

MacAlister, James. "The Study of Modern Literature in the Education of Our Time." *Transactions of the Modern Language Association of America* 3 (1887): 8–16.

Painter, F. V. N. "Recent Educational Movements in Their Relation to Language Study." *Transactions of the Modern Language Association of America* 2 (1886): 83–91.

Perry, Bliss. "Fiction as a College Study." *PMLA* 12 (1896): 76–84.

"Proceedings at Philadelphia, December 28, 29, 30, 1887." *Transactions of the Modern Language Association of America* 3 (1888): i–lix.

Smyth, A. H. "American Literature in the Classroom." *Transactions of the Modern Language Association of America* 3 (1887): 238–44.

Spofford, A. R. "The Characteristics of Style." *PMLA* 7 (1892): 5–23.

Thomas, Calvin. "Literature and Personality." *PMLA* 12 (1897): 299–317.

Thwing, Charles F. *A History of Higher Education in America.* New York: D. Appleton & Co., 1906.

Whyte, William H. *The Organization Man.* New York: Simon & Schuster, 1956.

Williams, Raymond. *Marxism and Literature.* Oxford: Oxford University Press, 1977.

Wilson, A. N. *The Life of John Milton.* Oxford: Oxford University Press, 1984.

Wimsatt, W. K., Jr., and M. C. Beardsley. *Verbal Icon: Studies in the Meaning of Poetry.* Lexington: University of Kentucky Press, 1954.

Rob Wilson

Producing
American Selves
The Form of American Biography

. . . for biography contracts to deliver a self.
—James Clifford

As postmodern ethnography increasingly defamiliarizes the genre of
life-writing into a voracious apparatus of textualized selfhood, the underlying cultural function of biography, at least as a *Western* genre,
can be seen to insinuate and extend what James Clifford has called
"the myth of coherent personality."[1] That is, by means of a massive
life-writing consuming and producing selves from George Washington
to Cary Grant and Alice James, the primary function of biography is
to disseminate a plethora of *selves* who might instantiate this integrity
of selfhood as achieved against a more or less recessive social background, what Lévi-Strauss, Lacan, and Althusser have theorized (less
blithely) as the overdeterminations of mythic structures, libidinal
codes, and economic base. Hence, in contracting to document and
amass the thematics of such a particularized self, the biographer enters
the terms of a genre in which he/she contracts to deliver the individual
as a tormented journey toward coherent unity, striking personality, and
expressive selfhood.

A corresponding assumption of this omnipresent labor is that,
through narrative tactics of subjectivized perspective staunchly tied to
Victorian realism, the biographer will render the cultural codes tra-
versing this quest for autonomy as so much factitious background the
well-rounded self can encounter, negotiate, and overcome. Even the
strong self of the biographer (say, Leon Edel), amassing and giving
shape to an infinite of social data (Henry James), renews another

instance of this agonistic struggle to achieve representative ego-mastery in which the individual can rise above his/her time and society. It seems fair to assume that biography, feeding upon the subjectivity effect of earlier genres of interiority, such as the diary, examination, letter, and confession, has functioned since the Renaissance as a supreme technology of Western selfhood wherein, as Foucault has claimed of this Greco-Roman tradition, "the self is something to write about, a theme or object (subject) of writing activity."[2]

Yet, granting this Western emphasis upon the written production of individuality, it still needs to be emphasized that the enframing origination of this "self" within the consensus-shaping rhetoric of American culture dominantly eventuates in and affirms an all-too-representative shape of subjected verbalization. The self the biographer produces can be seen to ratify ideological messages and enact forms of discursive practice prior to and beyond the language of self-invention. By "representative" I mean that the "coherent personality" overcoming everyday circumstances that the American biographer, like a second-level autobiographer of America, is called upon to reproduce and inhabit through the genre of life-writing would implicitly take on the shape of a "representative American self." The latent, if not politically preconscious, mission of the biographer becomes the representation of another personality who can strikingly act out the liberal project of American culture as a consensual adventure toward ratifying states of freedom and risk within a globally regenerative plot of self-invention. As in other genres and prior codes, criticism and celebration of "America" as a sublime trope deferring and awaiting fulfillment in history are conjoined to enforce the shape and status of a personally reexperienced jeremiad—to invoke the well-known cultural analysis of Sacvan Bercovitch—as individual Americans decline from yet imaginatively reaffirm this obdurate idealism and self-mystifying metaphor in various historical contexts.

One implication of diverse projects in postmodern American studies is that the archetypal American biographer is not James Boswell—as might be, and has been, professionally assumed—but Cotton Mather, that omnivorous minister of colonial Boston whose typological predisposition turned his New England subjects into so many messianic types on an "errand in the [Massachusetts] wilderness" to redeem the social collective as well as to sanctify the labor of the private self. Drawing upon biblical *figura* and typological parallels to allegorize the individual life into communal shape and representative value, such an American biography would conjoin the vocation of the writing/written self and the project of the community into one hermeneutic adventure: the production of another American *Johannes in Eremo* (John in the [social] wilderness) who can act out and legitimate a "rhetoric of consensus," no matter how contradicted by the counterevidence of history, reality, or fact.[3] If American biography arguably emerges within the didactic matrix of such generic origins, as I will claim, I would also urge that it need not stay locked within such a rhetoric of social accommodation and sublime subjection. Yet, as Werner Sollors summarizes the hold of this belief-laden discourse of upward mobility and political entitlement as a master code able to socialize, encode, and subjectify multiethnic selves far dispersed in American time and space from Mather's Puritan ethos, "[t]ypological rhetoric may indicate the Americanization of people who use it."[4]

The emerging post–cold war attitude toward the reenactment of this deep-rhetorical consensus, however, is not to propagate liberal piety toward the exceptionality of American culture but to take a stance of more radical skepticism toward the banality and totalizing closure of any such undeconstructed nationalism.[5] The inner workings and cultural dynamics of biography as a social form have to be scrutinized and laid bare in terms that challenge this grand empiricism and representative individuation. Although the claim is often adduced of American biography that *pathography*—the digging up of glamorous dirt on every citizen from Jean Stafford to Elvis Presley rather than searching for signs of moral election as in Cotton Mather's portrayal of John Winthrop as a "Nehemias Americanus"—has replaced *hagiography* as the biographer's generic task within the literary marketplace, still, the one mythology that refuses to be dismantled is the grand production of American selves whose lives can assume the stigmata and blessings of an exemplary political system that is worth all the lies and pains.

In many respects, these confessional extremes of pathography and hagiography remain locked within a master narrative affirming the very hold of self-Americanization. The self is still the site and ground of affirmative socialization, and biography conspires in this task. Just as biography now threatens to become what Justin Kaplan (biographer of Whitman and Lincoln Steffens) calls "the highest form of gossip," it goes on producing an expanded array of "significant lives" for the American tribe.[6] Indeed, this all-intrusive probing and confessing of subjectivity to society is framed within a generic technology of selfhood whereby inner and outer, sinning and sainthood, self and the struggle for capital, can represent, challenge, and yet affirm opposite sides of this same problematic of Americanized self-engendering. Perhaps Paul Mariani captures this liberal technology of Americanized self-engendering when he describes his own biography of William Carlos Williams, *William Carlos Williams: A New World*

Naked, in the following terms of liberal representation: "In my own version of the metapoetics of the biography, I would inundate the reader with the river of facts surrounding Williams even as the reader should become aware that, if Willliams' was a representative life, a life shared on many accounts by many Americans in his roles of father, husband, lover, physician, citizen, and artist, it had somehow managed to move along another, original axis as well."[7]

Taking a pragmatic stance toward these collective practices and commonplace themes, as William James urged the self to take toward affirmatively American ideas and beliefs (like "health," "wealth," "God," and "truth"), it can be said that the mytheme of *America* functions not only as a trope enjoining *belief* in self-invention upon the self, but also that this pragmatic fiction of social mobility is still disseminated—like consensual glue—throughout a tradition-thin and nervously pluralizing culture. Any immigrant soon learns that "America" comprises exactly such a set of "'cash-value' ideas" that the self is enjoined to interiorize and, believing in, enact into a circular, self-fulfilling prophecy of liberal modernity in which the success-failure of this individual is metaphorically equated with the success-failure of "America" itself. Despite a heterogeneity of little narratives of alternative selfhoods, this master narrative of "Americanization" drones on in the blinding light of everyday practice. One need only invoke President Ronald Reagan's farewell address to his populace in 1989—with its jeremaic invocation of America as a by-now global "City on the Hill" once again threatened by an eroding "American spirit," its sense of history as upbeat progress toward democratic benefits liberally dispersed to country and globe, its evocation of a boundless future in which any "pilgrim" self can still thrive in an America "more prosperous, more secure and happier than it was eight years ago"—to suggest the currency (and somnambulent hold) of this starry-eyed rhetoric on the ideology of the American self.[8] In many respects, the postmodernist Reagan represents the catastrophic collapse of such performative rhetoric of mastery into its simulacrous reiteration.[9]

Oddly enough, nonetheless, this prophecy of a sublime "America"—enjoining a new form of liberty upon a regenerated self, an inventing upward through practices and technologies of self-empowering belief—at some deep-rhetorical level (as Reagan's outrageously Puritan metaphors recycle) would encode the identity of any American selfhood into much the same plot, from William Bradford and Ben Franklin to Yashiko Uchida (in *Desert Exile*) or Richard Rodriquez, who "clearly considers himself representative [in *Hunger of Memory* (1982)]—representative not of the Mexican-American but of the

[American] middle-class."[10] Or consider the case of Samuel Goldwyn, whose life, as his biographer A. Scott Berg proclaimed on National Public Radio, "was such a perfect metaphor of the American Dream," proving again that immigrant glovemakers and furriers could become the stuff of Hollywood gods.[11] Granting ongoing modifications within ethnic and feminist counternarratives that would challenge and de-create this code of an ebullient American selfhood, can such national piety and latter-day myth making long withstand the onslaught (in-creasingly stimulated from France and Germany) of deconstruction and cultural critique?

Even the "hyperpoliticized" reading of biography as an Ameri-can genre of self-socialization presented in Michael Shapiro's *The Poli-tics of Representation* (1988) comports with Bercovitch's more expressly Puritan genealogy of such cultural forms in *The American Jeremiad* (1978); both explain that "the self" the American biographer feels conjoined, by discursive convention, to reproduce is typically a "representative self" (playing upon Emerson's trope of the American will's *Representative Men*) incarnating American social codes and norms and thereby affirming the power of liberal ideology to sacralize its own goals.[12] No matter how lowly or ethnic or seemingly outside such codes, the humblest self is still burdened with the larger, typical, latently typological mission of America in the spirit becoming America in fact. Diverse subjects (no matter how ethnic or foreign) can experience typological conversion to such a mainstream rhetoric, ul-timately affirming, if at times castigating, the virtues, freedoms, and goals of this American Way. The self-made man in 1991 still embodies not so much a fortune but a metaphysics of collective redemption as the self becomes the site of social redemption and/or private disaster.

Whether in Ben Franklin's rags-to-riches *Autobiography,* Booker T. Washington's "gospel of Work and Money" in *Up From Slavery,* or Schmuel Gelbfisz's penniless conversion into "Samuel Goldwyn," the self narrated his/her semitormented journey as a plight of agency insinuating what Shapiro calls a "sacral emblem" of national oppor-tunity and, implicitly, the success or failure of the American political system. Like Walt Whitman's omnivorous performance of political identification in "Song of Myself," the representative American writer enacts a discourse enjoining the self with *"representing America"* in a double yet hardly ironic social sense: (a) depicting (*imaginatively representing*) contemporary social processes; and (b) standing in for (*politically representing*) its deepest values, as the more politically de-bunking Thoreau realized in his first encounter with Whitman in 1856: "I did not get very far in conversation with him,—two more being present,—and among the few things I chanced to say, I remember that one was, in answer to him as representing America, that I did not think much of America or of politics, and so on, which may have been somewhat of a damper to him" (letter to H. G. O. Blake, 7 December 1856). Though Thoreau may not have thought much of America or its expansionist politics of manifest destiny, as he makes clear in "Resistance to Civil Government" and his scathing John Brown eulogy, *Walden* (1854) has come to be read as an autobiographical fable of exactly such an entrepreneurial selfhood preaching rebirth to the fallen citizens of Concord through agrarian labors and market-transcending symbols drawn from the counterdiscourse of nature. In other words, the agency of Thoreau can be said to perform the representative enactment of an all-too-American trope or "life-myth" of world regeneration.[13]

Latently Puritan in value structure as well as palpably capitalist in social behavior, the exodus of this Americanized agent into such New-World spaces of self-invention (as at Walden Pond, along the open road, or at Pilgrim Creek) helped to reenact the socializing hold of postbiblical typology on the imagination of the lone writer. Both biography and autobiography have conspired in this self-Americanizing dissemination. Although "biography has been an admissable subject in literary studies quite a lot longer than autobiography," as James Olney has observed, American autobiography nevertheless has been much more relentlessly theorized as a distinctive cultural form reflecting upon, if not finally enacting, the Americanization of such a self through democratic structures of mimetic rivalry.[14] Not surprisingly, the reason why I have invoked autobiography as much as biography to illuminate the dynamics of these interacting genres, as does Michael Shapiro, is that this cultural rhetoric of American selfhood has been mapped in countless studies of American autobiography as a "metaphorical" or "prophetic" form of exemplary selfhood subsuming the agent as typical or "typological" of larger codes and roles. But such a genealogy has not been imposed upon the practice of American biography, which claims to be grounded (often less self-reflexively) in more universal (or at least more broadly Western) assumptions of selfhood as a conflicted drama of individuation. Robert F. Sayre summarizes this focus upon native selfhood that has proliferated since his *The Examined Self* (1964) charted the metaphoric dynamics of this genre in Franklin, Adams, and Henry James: "Autobiography may be the preeminent kind of American expression."[15]

Sayre establishes a democratic archive capaciously running from Puritan diaries to ethnic-identity narratives and enlisting selves as disparate as John Woolman and Maxine Hong Kingston whereby, in any typically American autobiography, the self resists a lurking sense of impermanence and social anonymity by being narrated to serve a "didactic national purpose" (158). I would go beyond Sayre's consensual analysis to claim that this genre of autobiography has become so widely practiced in America as the land of pluralized selfhood and infinite me's struggling for recognition because both self and country are metaphorically conjoined in the quest for economic and cultural capital. So that, in effect, the production of self *in* America gets identified *with* the production of America as that space in which such exemplary selfhood is maximally possible. Caught up in the myths and contagious structures of mimetic rivalry under capital, that is, the American self becomes both model and rival to itself as competition becomes so thoroughly interiorized and normalized that the democratic self not only competes with "his neighbor as the model/rival" but even competes with himself.[16]

American autobiography proliferates, then, as that generic enclave of privacy in which the model/rival self can narrate his/her eternal selving in relation to other model/rival selves seeking to express and totalize the "only true America." (How much less enchanted is Peter Handke's deconstructive aside to his political countrymen in *The Weight of the World:* "About Austria: I never identify the people I love best there with the country!"[17]) Rather, as Jean Baudrillard claims of the self-advertising American gaze pervading the malls, freeways, technoscapes, and theme parks of postmodern America, "This is a society that is endlessly concerned to vindicate itself, perpetually seeking to justify its own existence. Everything has to be made public, what you earn, how you live." In this national hermeneutic of everyday life, as Baudrillard registers, even the self is enlisted to serve the hegemonic trademark and disseminate this good brand name: "It is simply the label of the finest successful international enterprise, the US."[18]

In such a social arena of infinite selfhood and utopic experimentation, where, as Emerson urged in his journal (touring Europe in 1833), "wherever we go, whatever we do, self is the sole subject we study and learn," each self potentially is that representative success story; each American *is* America both as object and subject, exception and rule, deviation and norm, in self-textualizing ways that "make interchangeable the modes of biography and autobiography."[19] In Romantic America, for example, two forms of this biographical project to install representative selfhood occur in their nineteenth-century origins: Melville's trenchantly democratic sense that the marginalized and silenced Bartlebys and Israel Potters of the society—"I believe that no materials exist for a full and satisfactory biography of this man ["Bartleby, the Scrivener"]"—constitute material for a national biography; and Emerson's more transcendentalist sense that the self forms itself only through the emulation of great souls, completed wills who can dominate history and compel national institutions.[20]

High and low classes would demand equal narration in such a democratic polity, however, as American selves struggle to find a shape and outlet within appropriately American forms of subjection. This can make for a plethora and elasticity of emerging forms, as the poetry of Whitman, Dickinson, Poe, and even Longfellow attest. But have the forms that biographers use matched their American subjects' own struggles with the recalcitrance of inherited literary forms to change? Is democracy, as a social system leveling and equalizing the self, conducive to stranger forms of aggrandizement, inquiry, and cultural differentiation? If for Leon Edel, amassing the "life-myth" of Henry James or Edmund Wilson, the biographer must intuit and match some unique sense of biographical form to this narrative subject, does this mean that, in America, an American self (like Whitman) would demand a distinctly *American* form from the imagination of the biographer?[21] Or should the life-writer not *distance* this American rhetoric that gave shape to, indeed narrated, the very self of his subject? In producing a self, would the American biographer have to produce an American self, hence enact (on another narrative level) the very hold of this American rhetoric? In short, can the American biographer resist *Americanizing* his subject, with all the distortions and legitimations that this ideology of form implies?

My claim has been that even the most textually scrupulous literary biographies, wary of entrenched language and dead metaphors, risk enacting an American "rhetoric of consensus" and thereby end up affirming liberal values and moral symbols within the closures of fallen history. The American biographer's task, in short, is to deliver another densely particularized self that can emerge kicking into a "new world naked." The "hyperpoliticization" and deconstruction of form now called for in the 1980s and 1990s can fail to occur in American biographies, then, which more or less subtly enact a liberal rhetoric of Puritan/democratic idealism and contract to produce self-made, profoundly Americanized selves. I want to illustrate *and* challenge this Americanizing rhetoric at work in the biographical construction of identity/selfhood in four American poets of liberal modernity: William Carlos Williams, Wallace Stevens, Langston Hughes, and Emily Dickinson. Presumably, such poets (and biographers working on these poets) can resist the allure and narrative entrenchment of metaphor and symbol, their stock-in-trade. Finally, I will theorize an emerging mode of biographical "dissensus" that would better challenge this consensual rhetoric of American selfhood through the invention of postmodern forms that would more critically enact "heteroglossia" and register voices and codes from the margins, regions, or frontiers of a decentered polity.

In Paul Mariani's 874-page biography of the modernist poet, *William Carlos Williams: A New World Naked* (1981), one of the themes organizing this highly particularized narration of poetic genesis is that Williams, as "extraordinary revolutionary" of his era, labored to freshen language in the increasingly polluted environment of northern New Jersey ("the filthy Passaic") and to deliver, redemptively, "a new world naked" in a dumping place.[22] Supporting Mariani's vision of the poet as a stylistic, yet thoroughly middle-class, *revolutionary* of such new worlds naked is that throughout his life Dr. Williams had to do battle against the Anglophilic establishment of English professors and bookish critics who took their codes and cues from T. S. Eliot's *The Waste Land.* Such Eurocentric movements opposed the remythologizing of place ("Kore in a New World Hell" [9]) that Williams (and Mariani, admittedly a latter-day, Williams-like poet himself) sought to disseminate.

In other words, through an interweaving and literalizing of Williams's own highly *Americanist* metaphors and thematics of sublime exceptionality, as enacted in works such as *In the American Grain* and *Spring and All,* Mariani advocates and "Americanizes" his exemplary subject, Williams, into a modernist utopian of aesthetic revisioning who could deliver (doctor-poet that he was) *"a new world naked."* Williams did this, in effect, by displacing the seemingly New-World possibilities of democracy and perpetual revolution into his style and language. This took place increasingly in defiance of Paterson's ecological and social counterfactuality. The transference of identity between Americans, early (fathers) and late (sons), is crucial and complete: the poetic language of Williams's poem "Spring and All" (199) gives Mariani his structuring title, if not his overarching language and total vision, as the later poet-scholar (himself born in New Jersey) mimics, recycles, and riffs on the mythology of Williams throughout his life history in a compelling (yet pietistically American) way.

Mariani reenacts the liberal assumption that the America of spirit and imagination must redeem the America of fallen fact and materialist reification. Despite Shapiro's deconstructive pleas for more discursive self-surveillance and political resistance within the genre, the "hyperpoliticization" of this literary biography, miming its American subject, does not fully challenge the workings of entrenched authority nor the myths of self-empowerment circulating through the American polity. Or, it only does so in an idealized, thoroughly affirmative way that we could call nonthreateningly democratic, showing poets and scholars living on foundational myths and reaccenting ideals and symbolic utopias that would redeem the falls and damages of twentieth-century history.

Yet as Bercovitch (speaking then as a Canadian "outsider") warned about the mimetic contagion of such "American" rhetoric in its Americanizing power to interpellate selfhood along consensual lines of upward mobility, social regeneration, and affirmative self-making, "Virtually every one of the hundreds of mid-nineteenth-century biographers of great Americans insisted that his subject was not someone unique, but the emblem of American enterprise."[23] Such writers, high or low, "found a common framework in the concept of representative selfhood," Bercovitch claims, and took refuge in a "rhetoric of consensus," linking the rise of a rags-to-riches self (now, perhaps, it would be rags-to-riches-to-rags, as in Jay McInerney's *Bright Lights, Big City* [1984] or in the life of Texas Governor John Connally) to the imperial mission of a country to validate its own deepest beliefs, myths, and figures of assent. Criticism of America is recuperated into the projection and displacement of an "America" ever beginning, ever about to be what its mythology proclaims. Is Mariani's revolutionary Williams any less representative of this American rhetoric of a self capable of generating a "new world naked" even in a fallen world, which another New Jersey poet, Allen Ginsberg, more caustically portrayed in the Vietnam era as *The Fall of America?*

Even Arnold Rampersad's well-wrought *Life of Langston Hughes* (1988), with its tellingly utopian subtitle affirming unflagging American idealism, *I Dream a World: 1941–1967,* fails to resist the frame of Americanizing narratives that would situate this heteroglossic African American "folk poet" within the liberal mainstream of private entrepreneurship: (a) Rampersad employs a survivor narrative that stresses the power of Hughes's resilient ego to overcome the indignities of Jim Crow and anticommunist phobias that threatened to depoliticize his poetry in the early 1940s; and (b) he uses an entrepreneurial narrative that articulates Hughes's career as a jockeying for literary position and for capitalist worth as the poet tries everything from war jingles and newspaper polemics to radio dramas "to capitalize" his own worth.[24] Rampersad summarizes Hughes's social and literary positioning in 1944 Harlem, using tones and verbs that would mimic the poet's own sense of his American life-world: "The big break, the windfall that would give him financial security as he moved steadily into his mid-forties, still eluded him. But he had carefully restored himself and was ready to capitalize on such opportunities as peace would bring" (107).

However radical Hughes's use of semiliterate voices, blues forms, and the propagandizing of black masses during World War II (62), Rampersad's Hughes persists in a quest for literary and economic capital that is hardly distinguishable from a mainstream careerist positioning of the American self: retreating from leftist politics after the ideological phobias awakened by "Goodbye Christ" in 1941, Hughes's career is portrayed by Rampersad as "a massive campaign of consolidation" (17) and as a centrist rhetoric affirming the power of self-making and gradual social change. Hughes's poem "Freedom's Plow" (1943) captures the mythology of such an Americanized self as both poor black and white are called upon to affirm a shared ideology of self-making and to embrace a perpetually deferred utopian politics of freedom and dream:

> When a man starts out with nothing,
> When a man starts out with his hands
> Empty, but clean,
> When a man starts out to build a world,
> He starts first with himself
> And the faith that is in his heart—...
>
> . . . .
> America is a dream.
> The poet says it was promises.
> The people say it *is* promises—that will come true.

Despite the segregation and Jim Crow treatment afforded black soldiers during the war, the poet goes on to affirm this idealist sense of American covenant ("promise"), powered by shared faith, communal imagination, and social dream (*the* dream of self-invention, spreading from farm to city to world): "America! / Land created in common, / Dream nourished in common, / Keep your hand on the plow! Hold on!" Though this is "hardly great art," as Rampersad admits (58), it is a foundational rhetoric affirming the myth of oneness and lure of liberal progress and reiterating the power of American selfhood to dream of change, to rise in the world, to bless the ground of one's own poverty and symbolic domination. Rampersad's subtitle, *I Dream a World,* and metaphoric tactics advocate more than critique this primal mythology of America and the American self's power of liberal self-making.

In Milton J. Bates's *Wallace Stevens: A Mythology of Self* (1985), the author's goal as stated at the outset is not so much to articulate empirical biography as it is to convey the inner dynamics of literary biography. Bates would establish "a mythology of self," showing "how one poet transcended biography" (ix) through the production of contradictory personae and imaginal selves that allowed Stevens to carry on in the actuarial world of Hartford business (as his lawyer father had wanted) yet to transcend or at least transfigure this marketplace through ideal imaginings (as his mother, a teacher, had tried).[25] Success took shape in the mind of father and son alike as "the myth of the self-made man" (4), Bates affirms, who can rise from nothing to accrue corporate (or literary) grandeur. The result for the mature Stevens would be an ambidexterous self that was "half Emerson, half Franklin," trying to live the life of the ideal imagination (as did the poet-philosophers Emerson and Santayana) within a pragmatic culture devoted to money making (as did the businessmen Garrett Stevens and Franklin). The father enjoined an American regime of self-development that the younger Stevens was drawn to reenact like "his fellow Pennsylvanian Ben Franklin" (31), without surrendering altogether to that "ladylike activity," poetry. Highly attuned to the Romantic myths and compensatory metaphors shaping the inner/outer self of Stevens, Bates finely illuminates the lifelong hold of this virtually schizoid American rhetoric upon Stevens, who is enjoined to live in the marketplace but not of it. Poetry becomes the site of sublime and often obfuscatory subjection where the transcendence of materialist norms that Stevens found exhilarating and repugnant could take place.

Both middle-class burgher of reality and aristocratic dandy of dream, Stevens achieves balance and accommodation to the economic reification that so distressed him in New York City, in Bates's reading, by conjugating a biography-transcending literary "mythology" of selfhood. This mythology of polity and place remains fully Emersonian in its grand bipolarity of inner self and outer society: that is, it remains pietistically American to the core. Literature becomes the site wherein social contradictions of the American system can play themselves out in ironies, evasions, and comical masks. This bifurcation of imagination and reality in Stevens is shown to be a feat of character, however, more than a function of social subjection. Bates rounds up the data for a critique of American subjection that is never made, finally, as a portrait of the liberal imagination transfiguring the marketplace emerges fully textured and fully toned. Again, transcendental idealism and liberal selfhood have found a way to live within American alienation as such by propagating what Stevens called "a mythology of place" compounded of ludic metaphors and fictive masks that live otherwise and elsewhere. (Later, I will invoke Frank Lentricchia's more critically charged counterreading of much the same biographical data.)

As our most deconstructive poet avant la lettre, Emily Dickinson must stand immune to any such idealist recuperation by mainstream American ideology. As David Porter characterizes her idiom of "terminal modernism" Dickinson produces privatized lyrics that create a space of linguistic solipsism blasting the hymnal form free of church, state, and history:

> Dickinson's withdrawal of language was perfectly, even predictably, consistent with her life. When she went into reclusion in her father's house in Amherst, she took her language with her. That is why words like "circumference" or "wife" have no ties to reality. They are language talking to itself, not negotiating with the outside world. In this separated state, Dickinson's idiom existed not as representative, but rather in its exclusive state only as literature.[26]

In Cynthia Griffin Wolff's biography, *Emily Dickinson* (1986), the poet who created such posthumous language is portrayed not only as a "genius" of Romantic imagination but also as a socially contextualized woman caught up in the affections and daily intrigues of genteel Amherst. The narrative effect is one of multiplying selves in furtive privacy if not one of soap opera. Nothing unusual about that, especially for biography. But, beyond such Romantic notions of singular selfhood, Wolff's Dickinson is fleshed out (as in Richard B. Sewall's *The Life of Emily Dickinson* [1974], which documents an entire volume of ancestral background before Emily is even born) through evoking a mode of "hagiographic hermeneutics" that is not so much immune to the social conditions in which art gets produced but which sediments this lyric subjectivity in a "lineage model" of Protestant ancestors and relatives that can finally "justify and legitimate the established order" of Amherst culture.[27] Filial piety and middle-class custom infect the inmost tone and shape of such a life-text.

Not surprisingly, the literary genealogy Wolff situates Dickinson within is that of the Protestant Sublime, but this traditional grandeur of the American sublime is now wrested from God-the-father into a woman's voice and mode:

> Like Melville, Dickinson was an anachronism. Writing rebelliously, but writing nonetheless within the great tradition of latter-day Puritanism, Emily Dickinson was a time traveler from an earlier epoch. She was determined to construe writing as an heroic undertaking. . . . [Thomas] Higginson had explicitly denied the practical possibility of this way of construing poetry: "If, therefore, duty and opportunity call," he admonished, "count it a privilege to obtain your share in the new career . . . but *never fancy for a moment that you have discovered any*

> *grander or manlier life than you would be leading every day at home"* (255).

Rejecting ordinary wifehood, yet seeking this self-empowering sublimity of voice through a competitive struggle with male model/rivals, Dickinson (in Wolff's Harold Bloom-like reading of the American struggle to accrue "symbolic capital," that is, to become a voice of "countersublimity") ends up fighting with Higginson, Emerson, and God to become *America's representative voice* of synoptic selfhood and cultural sway: "However, it was grandeur, only grandeur—and Power—that Dickinson wanted. She wanted to be America's Representative Voice, and she wanted that Voice to challenge God Himself and wrestle for dominion." In other words, Dickinson wanted to beat the American males and their half-Protestant, half-capitalist selves seeking cultural "Power" at their own language game of eternal competition. Her career, however solipsistic it seemed, would conjoin private grandeur and public significance. The ideology of liberal individualism has found, in Wolff's biography of Dickinson, another massively particularized defense. No matter how cuttingly and nihilistically Dickinson's metaphors appear to sever historical continuity or estrange the ego from normative community (as in Porter's more critical reading), her biographer has labored to produce the self into another "Representative American."

Working within the revisionary terrain of American studies in the 1980s and 1990s, the Americanist production and celebration of exceptional qualities and characteristics has given way to counter hegemonic lament, distancing, internal exile, and a sense that these ideological and discursive practices must be shifted from "consensual" belief in any shared myths and codes (incarnated by the self-relying Emersonian as another "representative sublime hero") toward a more genuinely "dissensual" suspicioning of this centrist language.[28] The "American Adam" of cold war myth-studies—once proud of self-origination and a stance of sublime transcendence toward politics and the marketplace—has given way to a poststructural "American Jeremiah" infiltrated by capitalist materiality and ruses of Emersonian ambiguity that nonetheless tries to transform or abandon this "rhetoric of consensus" as so much nationalist chatter able to reabsorb opposition into the romance of a future "America." As Bercovitch argues the case for this revamped American model of liberal dissensus in his preface to *Reconstructing American Literary History,* "It will be the task of the present generation to reconstruct American literary history by making a virtue of dissensus."[29] Similarly, Gerald Graff provides a genealogical analysis of "chronic dilemmas" and conflicted models of vocation/selfhood informing English and American studies departments in the United States and posits a more dissensus-driven model foregrounding dialogue, theory debate, a wholesale deconstruction of the foundations by which the study of literature has been constituted around some hegemony-creating "myth of consensus" that never in fact did exist.[30]

Yet the professional danger remains that, as Donald Pease has argued, even such a vision of American dissent and opposition will, through well-worn tactics of liberal pluralism refuting and absorbing subversive energies and movements, merely continue "the cold war consensus by taking opposition to a point of powerless dissensus."[31] This could happen because of the very function of Americanist discourse, which, no matter how critical it gets of existing society, only is granted professional legitimacy and social currency if it can evoke "an affirmative relation to 'America' as the process of national self-affirmation and international self-assertion."[32] Yet the hegemonic self-representations of America and the discourse of the Americanist do seem threatened by the revisionist forays into liberal canons and scholarly genres now underway. Even the staid language of the Harvard Divinity School is challenged by "heteroglossia," contentious dialogue, and voices from the margins and frontiers of Americanist scholarship.[33]

Is biography, as an American genre reflective of its culture's deepest plots, myths, and themes of national identity, somehow immune to this larger social transformation of discursive practices and forms that would better challenge, distance, and defamiliarize the Americanized rhetoric of selfhood? With the ground of Americanist discourse so shaken and visibly contested, can the biographer again produce American life-histories and emplotments of selfhood in any "business-as-usual" fashion? Must biography, as a form, remain tied to modes, norms, and perspectives of Victorian realism?

By more fully activating dissensus and critique, the goal of demystifying such American (auto)biography in which the American self is subjected and reproduced would be analogous to Michel Foucault's in historiography: that is, "to make the cultural unconscious apparent," or, by "excavating our own culture," in effect, "to open a free space for innovation and creativity." This kind of genealogy of form would reveal the production of the "self" as a multidisciplinary construct of "subjectification" configuring power and knowledge in arbitrary ways that bespeak deformation, normalization, and domination by liberal codes.[34] The generic goal would be to excavate the Americanizing of the self in sedimented ways that bespeak and challenge the ideology of the (biographical) form, hence make the fate of being an "American" more available to contention and critique, more open to empowering what Myra Jehlen terms "alternative Americas" to the ideology of liberal individualism that enframes works such as *William Carlos Williams: A New World Naked* or *Goldwyn: A Biography.*[35]

In sum, there remains a need for the nuts-and-bolts biographer not only to challenge the ideological content of his/her life-study but also to resist the latent "ideology of the form" itself as potentially another cultural apparatus by which the self is reproduced ("interpellated") and reaffirmed as redemptively ("piously") American.[36] The transitive verb *Americanize* would suggest the active role the biographer plays, or fails to play, and hence suggests the possibility for formal contestation and challenge, as in fictional life-studies that more impiously expose their American subjects through counterlanguages and counterforms that better exemplify the so-called facts (as in works by Norman Mailer, John Wideman, E. L. Doctorow, Don DeLillo, Lyn Hejinian, and Peter Handke). I would also invoke, as an emerging counterexample, the inventive use of biographical and historical contexts by scholars such as Frank Lentricchia and Susan Gillman, who would recover and expose the sexual and economic contexts that molest the self-production and literary careers of American authors like Wallace Stevens, Mark Twain, and Don DeLillo.[37] Focusing on the dynamics of "econo-machismo" in the emergence of Stevens as a modernist poet, for example, Lentricchia puts forth the critique of American subjection that Bates declined to make in showing how torn and tormented the young Stevens actually was, as father and worker, to vindicate the imagination in a culture of moneymaking. As Lentricchia summarizes the antagonism of duty and happiness within the career of Stevens, the schizophrenia of his rhetoric was more a function of social necessity than of moral character:

> A brilliant success in two areas, Stevens' bifurcated career perfectly realizes the hegemonic aims of his capitalist socialization. Assiduously "masculine" in his pursuit of economic fulfillment—Stevens worked well beyond retirement age because he had no intention of ever retiring—in his aesthetic life he cultivated the self-abnegating virtues that his society relegated to the "feminine" sphere: in other words, he cultivated "culture" itself in the sense that capitalism shaped for that term. (147)

Sensitive to poetic models, gender dynamics, economic factors, and social contradictions, Lentricchia situates the biographical emergence of Stevens within the larger sway of American capitalist contradictions and thereby subjects American society to a hard-hitting critique in which the ruses of poetry are themselves implicated.

In disrupting the "signifying order" of biography as a consensual narrative managing and containing the production of an Americanized self, the goal can be the more affirmatively deconstructive one mapped by Jean-François Lyotard: "The function of the [postmodern] artist, from then on, is no longer to produce *good* forms, new good forms, but on the contrary to *deconstruct* them systematically and to accelerate their obsolescence [within the marketplace ruled by commodity-exchange]."[38] As in Mailer's *The Executioner's Song* (1979) or Lyn Hejinian's *My Life* (1980), it is time for the biographer of the postmodern condition to go beyond the entrenched Puritan/liberal rhetoric of American selfhood and to insinuate counterlanguages and counterforms more critical of inherited subjects and narrative modes. It is time for American authors to invent biographical forms that resist legitimating competition, domination, and an ethos of self-absorption that timelessly equates success with the (symbolic) achievement of high capital. In pursuing such desublimated forms, dissensus would be activated not only in content but as style and form, releasing an avant-garde invention that refuses more pious legitimations of the social bond by transforming the "language game" (genre) of biography itself: "Is legitimacy [of the social bond through master narratives] to be found in consensus obtained through discussion, as Jürgen Habermas thinks? Such consensus does violence to the heterogeneity of language games. And invention is always born of dissension."[39]

Beyond confessing and protesting a unique self with the savor of massive American particularity, this call for more inventive forms of life-study comports with Leon Edel's hard-won credo as a biographer: "The only imagination allowed a biographer (I said this long ago) is the imagination of form."[40] If any biographer is bound, like Jack Webb, to the telling of facts as much as the reshaping of history, the written form of this life-project remains open. It is time, then, to reimagine and contest the available forms of American (or British, or Japanese) biography in ways that challenge the life-myth of being that globally blessed creature, "that new man, the American." Dissensus need not degenerate into another simulacrum of dissent but can emerge from and express forces and movements that threaten the hegemonic self-representation of "America" to itself and to the world. Calling for the reimagining of biography in inventive forms and pluralized modes, admittedly I run the risk of calling for an expanded market of textual production, for the production of emergent forms and selves, but I will end on this pragmatic, all-too-American note.[41]

Rob Wilson

Notes

This essay appears in a slightly changed form in *boundary 2: An International Journal of Literature and Culture* 18 (Fall, 1991) published by Duke University Press.

1. James Clifford, "'Hanging Up Looking Glasses at Odd Corners': Ethnobiographical Prospects," in *Studies in Biography,* ed. Daniel Aaron (Cambridge, Mass.: Harvard University Press, 1978), 44. Clifford urges Western biographers—such as his father—to use modernist and cross-cultural models that might enact self-doubling, discontinuity, flux, social decentering. For an ethnographic analysis of the way "the self" is culturally constituted within arbitrary meaning-systems and discursive regimes, also see James Clifford, "On Ethnographic Self-Fashioning: Conrad and Malinowski" and other essays in *Reconstructing Individualism: Autonomy, Individuality, and the Self in Western Thought,* ed. Thomas Heller, Morton Sosna, and David Wellbery (Stanford, Calif.: Stanford University Press, 1986), 140–62; and Robert Sullivan, "Marxism and the 'Subject' of Anthropology," in *Modernist Anthropology: From Fieldwork To Text,* ed. Marc Manganaro (Princeton, N.J.: Princeton University Press, 1990), 243–65. On the polyvocal encoding of American selfhood as an ethnically split or self-doubled construct resulting in "a textured sense of being American" that my own analysis will often elide, see Michael M. J. Fischer's study of autobiography, "Ethnicity and the Post-Modern Arts of Memory," *Writing Culture: The Poetics and Politics of Ethnography,* ed. James Clifford and George E. Marcus (Berkeley and Los Angeles: University of California Press, 1986), 194–233.

2. Michel Foucault, "Technologies of the Self," in *Technologies of the Self: A Seminar with Michel Foucault,* ed. Luther H. Martin, Huck Gutman, and Patrick H. Hutton (Amherst: University of Massachusetts Press, 1988), 27. In this University of Vermont seminar of 1982, Foucault is not speaking of biography as such but of any discursive technology of selfhood "linked to constant writing activity" that "is not a modern trait born of the Reformation or of romanticism; it is one of the most ancient Western traditions" (27). It seems fair to treat (auto)biography, however, as exactly one of those "technologies of the self which permit individuals to effect by their own means or with the help of others a certain number of operations on their own bodies and souls, thought, conduct, and way of being, so as to transform themselves in order to attain a certain state of happiness, purity, wisdom, perfection, or immortality" (18). So conceived, the communal function of American biography becomes the inscription and thereby attainment of the status of an immensely Americanized self. In "Opponents, Audiences, Constituencies and Community," Edward W. Said describes the function of Anglo-American biography in the following terms: "The current interest in producing enormous biographies of consecrated great authors is one aspect of this priestifying [literary profession]. By isolating and elevating the subject beyond his or her time and society, an exaggerated respect for single individuals is produced along with, naturally enough, awe for the biographer's craft," *The Anti-Aesthetic:*

Essays on Postmodern Culture, ed. Hal Foster (Port Townsend, Washington: Bay Press, 1983), 150.

3. For a Puritan genealogy of this "rhetoric of consensus," see Sacvan Bercovitch, "The Rites of Assent: Rhetoric, Ritual, and the Ideology of American Consensus," in *The American Self: Myth, Ideology, and Popular Culture,* ed. Sam B. Girgus (Albuquerque: University of New Mexico Press, 1981), 5–42; "How the Puritans Won the American Revolution," *Massachusetts Review* 17 (1976): 597–630; and *The Puritan Origins of the American Self* (New Haven, Conn.: Yale University Press, 1975). In this sweeping analysis of Puritan forms as belief structures enforcing consent through modes of community scolding and community building, the generic prototype compelling such an Americanized version of Christian selfhood becomes Cotton Mather's *Magnalia Christi Americana; or, The Ecclesiastical History of New England, from its First Planting in the Year 1620, unto the Year of Our Lord 1698* (1702). Also see Ursula Brumm, "'What Went You Out in the Wilderness to See?': Nonconformity and Wilderness in Cotton Mather's *Magnalia Christi Americana,*" *Prospects: An Annual of Americal Cultural Studies* 6 (1981): 1–17; and Mason Lowance, "Biography and Autobiography," in *Columbia Literary History of the United States,* ed. Emory Elliott (New York: Columbia University Press, 1988), 67–82, on the colonial prototypes of American life-writing. The case for James Boswell as generic precursor of any modern English-language biographer is commonplace: see William C. Dowling, "Boswell and the Problem of Biography," in *Studies in Biography,* 73–93.

4. Werner Sollors, *Beyond Ethnicity: Consent and Descent in American Culture* (New York: Oxford University Press, 1986), 49. Sollors describes the way a myth of "chosen peoplehood" is used to create cultural coherence even for African-American minorities in W. E. B. Du Bois's *The Souls of Black Folk* (1903) and Booker T. Washington's *Up From Slavery* (1901). Analyzing this deep rhetoric of cultural consent, however, Sollors himself (like Bercovitch, one of the methodological heirs to Perry Miller) cannot be immune to the charge that he himself is enacting the self-conscious production of this very American typology as a German immigrant professionalized/Americanized into the "Harvard" method. On "ethnic autobiography," see also the special issue of *MELUS* 14 (1987); and Arnold Rampersad, "Biography, Autobiography, and Afro-American Culture," *The Yale Review* 73 (1982): 1–16.

5. Two exemplary critiques of disciplinary subjection into Americanist rhetoric that would resist the closure of cold-war consensus as well as the accommodated allure of pluralist "dissensus" are Donald Pease, "New Americanists: Revisionist Interventions into the Canon," *boundary 2* 17 (1990): 1–37; and Paul Bové, "Notes Towards a Politics of 'American' Criticism," forthcoming in *In the Wake of Theory* (Middletown, Conn.: Wesleyan University Press). The latter provides a vigilant critique of any self-enclosed Americanist rhetoric, especially as this informs the consensus/dissensus model of Sacvan Bercovitch. See also William H. Epstein, "Counter-Intelligence: Cold-War Criticism and Eighteenth-Century Studies," *ELH* 57 (1990): 63–99, on the cold-war connection of the "biographical fallacy" and the seemingly innocuous cognitive and research tactics of Yale New Critics whose biographical methods were used by the CIA and the OSS.

6. Attributing the genealogy of American "pathography" to Freud and not to Joyce Carol Oates, who scapegoated David Roberts's *Jean Stafford: A Biography* as such a work (see "Adventures in Abandonment," *New York Times Book Review,* 28 August 1988), Justin Kaplan defined the cultural function of biography as "a tribal ritual" and "the highest form of gossip" at a University of Massachusetts at Amherst conference on "The Subject and the Subject: Biography and Memoir," April 7, 1989; see Jim Hillas, "Writers: Line Dividing Fact, Fiction Blurring," *Daily Hampshire Gazette* 8 April 1989), p. 1. In her analysis, Oates aptly terms pathography "hagiography's diminished and often prurient twin." Akin to hagiography as another biographical form of hero worship, Tom Wolfe now uses the term "plutography" to capture the American fascination with "lifestyles of the rich and famous," wherein it is no longer necessary in the 1980s (as in William Dean Howells's *The Rise of Silas Lapham* [1885]) to have both spiritual and material blessings because wealth alone can create this exemplary selfhood; see Robert F. Sayre, *The Examined Self: Benjamin Franklin, Henry Adams, Henry James* (Madison: University of Wisconsin Press, 1988), xi.

7. Paul Mariani discusses the assumptions of his Williams biography, which my own analysis will return to, in "William Carlos Williams," in *The Craft of Literary Biography,* ed. Jeffrey Meyers, (New York: Schocken, 1985), 152.

8. On "truth's cash-value in experiential terms" generating psychological and behavioral benefits measured solely by the self and enacting beliefs and ideas as instruments of American practice, see William James, "Pragmatism's Conception of Truth," in *The Writings of William James,* ed. John J. McDermott (Chicago, Ill.: University of Chicago Press, 1977), 430–36. President Reagan's farewell address stressing "why the Pilgrims came here, [and] who Jimmy Doolittle was" (a kind of history-as-myth, in which great Americans perform ideal deeds of courage and moral conviction, rather than downbeat facts) is reprinted in *The New York Times,* 12 January 1989, B8.

9. On the postmodern sign-tactics of Reagan's presidency, see Robert Merrill, "Simulations: Politics, TV, and History in the Reagan Era," *Ethics/ Aesthetics: Post-Modern Positions,* ed. Robert Merrill, (Washington, D.C.: Maisonneuve Press, 1988), 141–68. Similarly, Jean Baudrillard claims of such nostalgic simulacra of America's Puritan and frontier origins, "What we see here is the success of Reagan's illusionist effort to resurrect the American primal scene," *America,* trans. Chris Turner (London and New York: Verso, 1988), 108.

10. For critiques of these Americanizing dynamics in *Hunger of Memory,* see Shirley K. Rose, "Metaphors and Myths of Cross-Cultural Literacy: Autobiographical Narratives by Maxine Hong Kingston, Richard Rodriguez and Malcolm X," *MELUS* 14 (1987): 11, and Ramón Saldívar, *Chicano Narrative: The Dialectics of Difference* (Madison: University of Wisconsin Press, 1990), 155–70. On the dynamics of "the ethnic autobiographer's con-

version to America" in Japanese-American authors such as Yashiko Uchida and Mine Okubo, see Ann Rayson, "Beneath the Mask: Autobiographies of Japanese-American Women," *MELUS* 14 (1987): 43–57.

11. Claiming that he was drawn to write Goldwyn's biography because "[h]is life was such a perfect metaphor of the American Dream," in which Goldwyn deeply believed (interview on National Public Radio, 10 April 1989), A. Scott Berg narrates an immigrant's saga of inventing the self imperially upward in *Goldwyn: A Biography* (New York: Knopf, 1989); as Berg explains in *The New York Times Book Review* (26 March 1989), "The most interesting part of the book has nothing to do with the movies. It has to do with the teen-age runaway, the alien, the immigrant who came to this country without knowing a soul. . . . They were all glovemakers and furriers who became gods" (24). As "self-made man" with "self-made name," Goldwyn's life embodied capital and symbolic capital and represented not only a fortune but an "ideologeme" of the American Dream (social metaphysics) that his movies came to reflect.

12. See Sacvan Bercovitch, *The American Jeremiad* (Madison: University of Wisconsin Press, 1978); and Michael Shapiro, *The Politics of Representation: Writing Practices in Biography, Photography, and Policy Analysis* (Madison: University of Wisconsin Press, 1988), chap. 2.

13. On the troubled relationship of Thoreau and the accrual of economic/cultural capital, see Michael T. Gilmore, "*Walden* and the 'Curse of Trade,'" in *Ideology and Classic American Literature,* ed. Sacvan Bercovitch and Myra Jehlen (Cambridge: Cambridge University Press, 1986), 293–310. On the personal and cultural defensiveness of Thoreau's "life-myth," see Leon Edel, "The Figure Under the Carpet," in *Telling Lives: The Biographer's Art,* ed. Marc Pachter (Philadelphia: University of Pennsylvania Press, 1981), 27–29: "The biography [of Thoreau as "New England narcissus"] would have to be written not in a debunking spirit but in compassion and with the realization that this man who felt he had lost so much was able to transcend his losses and create an American myth and the work of art known as *Walden*" (29). Yet Bercovitch argues of Emerson's disavowals of actual America (much the same could be said of Thoreau's idealist critiques and life-myths): "But his criticisms were couched in terms that reaffirmed the structures and beliefs of his society" ("The Rites of Assent: Rhetoric, Ritual, and the Ideology of American Consensus," 31). In some respects, the ideological closure of such a Foucault-like Americanist model informs the economic analysis of Emerson's subject-centered claims to transcend marketplace discourse in Wai-Chee Dimock, "Scarcity, Subjectivity, and Emerson," *boundary 2* 17 (1990): 83–99.

14. James Olney, ed., *Autobiography: Essays Theoretical and Critical* (Princeton, N.J.: Princeton University Press, 1980), 19–20.

15. Robert F. Sayre, "Autobiography and the Making of America," in *Autobiography: Essays Theoretical and Critical,* ed. James Olney, 147. For increasingly incongruous, deconstructive and/or dissensual connections of genre and culture, see also Albert E. Stone, "Autobiography and American Culture," *American Studies: An International Newsletter* 11 (1972): 22–36; Robert F. Sayre, "The Proper Study—Autobiographies in American Studies,"

Rob Wilson

American Quarterly 29 (1977): 241–62; Mutlu Konuk Blasing, *The Art of Life: Studies in American Autobiographical Literature* (Austin: University of Texas Press, 1977); G. Thomas Couser, *American Autobiography: The Prophetic Mode* (Amherst: University of Massachusetts Press, 1979); Joseph Krupat, *For Those Who Came After: A Study of Native American Autobiography* (Berkeley and Los Angeles: University of California Press, 1985); Shari Benstock, ed., *The Private Self: Theory and Practice of Women's Autobiographical Writings* (Chapel Hill: University of North Carolina Press, 1988); and James Olney, "The Autobiography of America," *American Literary History* 3 (1991): 376–95.

16. See Asada Akira, "Infantile Capitalism and Japan's Postmodernism: A Fairy Tale," *South Atlantic Quarterly* 87 (1988): 630: "Through this new stage of mutual competition in which everyone competes with his neighbor as the model/rival, a strange kind of *shutai* [subject-position or selfhood] emerges. This is the *shutai* [in American adult capitalism] which, having internalized the model/rival, has begun to compete with himself." Consider as an example the competitive plight of John Steinbeck, who underwent the following self-torments while composing *The Grapes of Wrath* (published 1939): "My work is no good, I think—I'm desperately upset about it. . . . I'm slipping. I've been slipping all my life." And when a young writer approaches Steinbeck as model/rival of literary "greatness," he opines: "Young man wants to talk, wants to be a writer. What could I tell him? Not a writer myself yet." See William Kennedy, "'My Work Is No Good,'" *New York Times Book Review* (9 April 1989), 1.

17. Peter Handke, *The Weight of the World,* trans. Ralph Manheim (London: Secker & Warburg, 1984), 40.

18. Jean Baudrillard, *America,* 85–86.

19. See Sacvan Bercovitch on *Walden, Democratic Vistas,* and Mather's biographical mode of conflated selfhood, "'Nehemias Americanus': Cotton Mather and the Concept of the Representative American," *Early American Literature* 8 (1974): 234–35.

20. For differing versions of producing symbolic selfhood in American biography, see Kenneth Marc Harris, "Transcendental Biography: Carlyle and Emerson," *Studies in Biography,* 95–112; Michael T. Gilmore, "Eulogy as Symbolic Biography: The Iconography of Revolutionary Leadership, 1776–1826," *Studies in Biography,* 131–57; and William E. Cain, "Violence, Revolution, and the Cost of Freedom: John Brown and W. E. B. Du Bois," *boundary 2* 17 (1990): 305–30, on Du Bois's appropriation of Brown's biography to serve a civil-rights agenda. For Melville's novelistic reworking of biographical form, see "Bartleby the Scrivener," *Herman Melville: Selected Tales and Poems,* ed. Richard Chase (New York: Holt, 1968), 92.

21. Leon Edel's theory of biographical form, derived from working on Henry and William James, Virginia Woolf, Edmund Wilson, and related inventors of perspectival modernism, is that "every life takes its own form and a biographer must find the ideal and unique form that will express it." This is quoted and discussed, against competing practioners of such life-forms, in

188

David Novarr, *The Lines of Life: Theories of Biography, 1880–1970* (West Lafayette, Ind.: Purdue University Press, 1986), 117–125, 165. This essentializing claim is in keeping with Novarr's overall sense that biographical form should maintain that "'protestant' quality quintessential to good biography" (162); in other words, that biographers should produce individuals who protest their own uniqueness and distinction. This assumes a fully Americanized notion of self and form befitting a post-Protestant country in which Emerson could claim of Thoreau, "He was a born protestant" and again "a protestant *à outrance* ("Thoreau," *Selections from Ralph Waldo Emerson,* ed. Stephen E. Whicher (Boston: Houghton, 1960), 380). For related claims, also see *Essaying Biography: A Celebration For Leon Edel,* ed. Gloria G. Fromm (Honolulu: University of Hawaii Press, 1986); and Shoichi Saeki's Japanese (yet oddly Jungian) case against the biographer's forever reproducing and protesting the case for "pure individualism" in "The Curious Relationship Between Biography and Autobiography in Japan," *New Directions in Biography,* ed. Anthony M. Friedson (Honolulu: University of Hawaii Press, 1981), 81.

22. Paul Mariani, *William Carlos Williams: A New World Naked* (New York: McGraw-Hill, 1981), x. Henceforth page references will occur parenthetically.

23. Sacvan Bercovitch, "The Rites of Assent: Rhetoric, Ritual, and the Ideology of American Consensus," *The American Self,* 20. On such public uses of biography, see also Edward H. O'Neill, *A History of American Biography, 1800–1935* (New York: A. S. Barnes, 1961).

24. Arnold Rampersad, *The Life of Langston Hughes,* 2 vols. (New York: Oxford University Press, 1988). Henceforth parenthetical references will be to volume 2. Rampersad is well aware that biographers can be agents who legitimate forces and symbols that dominate their subjects, as he points out in reading Alex Haley's complicitous role in composing *The Autobiography of Malcolm X;* see "Biography, Autobiography, and Afro-American Culture," 15.

25. Milton J. Bates, *Wallace Stevens: A Mythology of Self* (Berkeley and Los Angeles: University of California Press, 1985). Henceforth references will occur parenthetically.

26. David Porter, *Dickinson: The Modern Idiom* (Cambridge, Mass.: Harvard University Press, 1981), 116. My only quarrel with Porter's portrayal of Dickinson's "terminal modernism" (as it is transmitted to linguistically playful poets such as James Tate and John Ashbery) is that such poetic "modernism" is not so much cause as effect of large-scale "modernization" processes that fragment, privatize, and disengage the subject from more public modes of discourse and community. For a counterpart to Porter, see Susan Howe, *My Emily Dickinson* (Berkeley, Calif.: North Atlantic Books, 1985), who reads her as a politicized poet.

27. Cynthia Griffin Wolff, *Emily Dickinson* (New York: Knopf, 1986), part 1, "My Father's House," 1–136. The "functions of genealogies and *genealogists*" as a mode of discursive practice that legitimates the dominant class through communal "misrecognition" of underlying interests and all but unspoken doctrines of symbolic power ("doxa") are discussed in Pierre

Bourdieu, *Outline of a Theory of Practice,* trans. Richard Nice (Cambridge: Cambridge University Press, 1977), 19. Also see Bourdieu's analysis of the accrual of "social capital" (names, relatives, awards, degrees, prizes, tastes, styles, manners, the disinterested idolatry of "art" and so on) as a rarefied mode of domination produced through symbolic-economic differentiation (171–97).

28. I provide a critique of the Americanist and State-Department professing of this Emersonianism in "Literary Vocation as Occupational Idealism: The Example of Emerson's 'American Scholar,'" *Cultural Critique* 15 (1990): 83–114. On the American implementation of the literary scholar as "representative sublime hero," see the disciplinary critique of Paul A. Bové, *Intellectuals in Power: A Genealogy of Critical Humanism* (New York: Columbia University Press, 1986), especially on the synoptic function of European scholars such as Erich Auerbach.

29. Sacvan Bercovitch, ed., *Reconstructing American Literary History* (Cambridge, Mass.: Harvard University Press, 1986), viii.

30. For a well-documented case against the conservative myth that "the academic humanities up to recently were based on a coherent consensus on fundamental goals" that collapsed in the radical 1960s, see Gerald Graff and Michael Warner, eds., *The Origins of Literary Studies in America* (New York: Routledge, 1989) and Gerald Graff, *Professing Literature: An Institutional History* (Chicago, Ill.: University of Chicago Press, 1987).

31. Donald Pease, "New Americanists: Revisionist Interventions into the Canon," 29. Ramón Saldívar has trenchantly objected to the "dissensus" model of American subjection used in Bercovitch and Sollors in the following terms: "The crucial factor here is that, often, these terms refer to consensus and dissent among the ruling groups alone [at Harvard] and to their legitimacy as members of the ruling elite state apparatus" *Chicano Narrative: The Dialectics of Difference,* 216.

32. Paul Bové, "Notes Towards a Politics of 'American Criticism,'" 15.

33. See Elisabeth Schussler Fiorenza's dialogical, postfeminist approach to "doing theology" in a postmodern key, "Commitment and Critical Inquiry" [Convocation Address, 28 September 1988], *Harvard Divinity Bulletin* (Winter, 1989): 8–10.

34. Foucault's work demonstrates that any society produces and circulates discourses and genres that set the syntax and problematic of "truth" in arbitrary, shifting ways (for example, in "confession" or psychoanalysis as a form), so that the subject must not only speak truth but, more exactly, be "inside the truth" (*dans le vrai*) in order to be heard as such. A cultural genealogist, then, should map the historical originations and domineering effects of this self-infiltrated "truth," hence "make the cultural unconscious apparent" as it subjects and disciplines the self with peculiar forms of power/knowledge; see Michel Foucault, *Foucault Live (Interviews, 1966–1984),* trans. John Johnston (New York: Semiotext(e) Foreign Agents Series, 1989), 71 ("Rituals of Exclusion") and 139 ("End of the Monarchy of Sex"). Given the power of discourse to entrap any subject's encoding of "truth" in a syntax of capture and release, there can be no easy egress from ideology through self-reflection or linguistic bracketing of the natural and normal. Foucault's goal remained projective, nonetheless, as carrying out "the necessity of excavating our own culture in order to open a free space for innovation and creativity" ("Afterword," *Technologies of the Self,* 163).

35. The hegemony of possessive individualism as an American construct is challenged in Myra Jehlen, *American Incarnation: The Individual, the Nation, and the Continent* (Cambridge, Mass.: Harvard University Press, 1986).

36. On the "ideology of form" embedded in narrative genres such as romance and historiography, see Fredric Jameson, *The Political Unconscious: Narrative as a Socially Symbolic Act* (Ithaca, N.Y.: Cornell University Press, 1981), I also draw upon Louis Althusser's analysis of ideology's "interpellation" of the political subject as "subject" ("Ideology and the Ideological State Apparatuses," in *Lenin and Philosophy,* trans. Ben Brewster [New York: Monthly Review Press, 1971]).

37. See the historicized strategies for recoding and refiguring American biography at work in Frank Lentricchia, *Ariel and the Police: Michel Foucault, William James, Wallace Stevens* (Madison: University of Wisconsin Press, 1988), especially "Patriarchy against Itself—The Young Manhood of Wallace Stevens"; Frank Lentricchia, "*Libra* as Postmodern Critique," *South Atlantic Quarterly* 89 (1990): 431–53; and Susan Gillman, *Dark Twins: Imposture and Identity in Mark Twain's America* (Chicago, Ill.: University of Chicago Press, 1989). As a postmodern experiment, I also call attention to Hillary Clark's analysis of Lyn Hejinian's deconstructive autobiography of the American self, "The Mnemonics of Autobiography: Lyn Hejinian's *My Life,*" essay forthcoming in *Biography* 14 (Fall 1991).

38. Jean-François Lyotard, "On Theory," in *Driftworks,* trans. Roger McKeon (New York: Semiotext(e), 1984), 26–29. I applaud the postmodern stance toward refiguring the life-study form ("altering the life-text") taken in William H. Epstein, *Recognizing Biography* (Philadelphia: University of Pennsylvanie Press, 1987). Epstein, while bypassing the history of American biography as a coherent field (4), usefully defends the deconstructive claim that "biographical recognition has been, and, for the most part, still is reluctant to abandon the 'natural attitude' [toward "life-text"], for, here as elsewhere, we discover that epistemological naivete is a distinctive feature of biographical recognition" (38). Epstein would ground the history of English biography in four intertextual dynamics: (a) the quasi-hagiographics of conversion narrative in Isaac Walton's *Life of Donne;* (b) the admission of thoroughly secular subjects and techniques in Samuel Johnson's *Life of Savage;* (c) most crucially, the modernist accruing of economic/symbolic "credit" to legitimate authority for the biographer within the liberal marketplace of ideas in Boswell's *Life of Johnson;* and (d) the corrosive counternarratives of Victorian impiety in Lytton Strachey's *Eminent Victorians.* In this latter regard, Epstein shows how Strachey partly undermines James Anthony Froude's classic claim in "Representative Men" (1850) not to represent the national or self-relying will (as does Emerson) in biography but to typify the middle-class professions of lawyer, merchant, landlord, and so on (143–44).

39. Jean-François Lyotard, *The Postmodern Condition: A Report on Knowledge,* trans. Geoff Bennington and Brian Massumi (Minneapolis: University of Minnesota Press, 1986), xxv. Counterlanguages and counterlogics to the elision of cultural/political differences under capital (as well as under Marxist totalizing) are also called for in Paul A. Bové, "The Ineluctability of Difference: Scientific Pluralism and the Critical Intelligence," *Postmodernism and Politics,* ed. Jonathan Arac (Minneapolis: University of Minnesota Press, 1986), 3–25. *Differences* (of class, gender, race, nation, culture) must not be universally—or imperially—elided in an era of multinational corporations and mega-media games when U.S. representations impinge upon the narratives and self-representations of other cultures; see Masao Miyoshi, *Off Center: Power and Cultural Relations Between Japan and the U.S.* (Cambridge, Mass.: Harvard University Press, 1991).

40. Leon Edel, *Bloomsbury: A House of Lions* (New York: Avon, 1980), ix.

41. I would like to thank Mari Hoashi, Marc Pachter, George Simson, Masao Miyoshi, Peter Lee, Michael Stephens, Brook Thomas, Amy Kaplan, William H. Epstein, Kim U-chang, and the editors of *boundary 2* for help in theorizing the relationship between biography and cultural form in generous and insightful ways they may not have been possessively aware of.

Steven Weiland

Becoming a Biographer
Erikson, Luther and
the Problem of Professional Identity

A completed identity is only one crisis won.

The Reformation is continuing in many lands, in the form of manifold revolutions, and in the personalities of protestants of varied vocations.
—Erik H. Erikson, *Young Man Luther* (1958)

Biographers study motivation and, of course, have motives of their own. This essay addresses the question, Why did Erik Erikson become a biographer? Though a complete answer would reveal the reason to be overdetermined, the Freudian term for multiple causes, one explanation is that Erikson underwent a kind of protracted midlife vocational "crisis," his term for a turning point. He says at the outset of *Young Man Luther* that work is the great neglected theme of psychoanalysis. Hence I will stress that book's meaning for its author's professional identity. During the 1950s, in his attention to the career of Freud and to the life of Luther, Erikson sought to reassert a form of professional identity then in danger of being submerged in the medical hegemony of orthodox psychoanalysis.

The Professions of Psychoanalysis

By the time of the 1956 centenary celebration of Freud's birth, psychoanalysis was a secure and prosperous profession. It was established enough to earn a congratulatory telegram from President Eisenhower, who reassured members of the American Psychoanalytic Association (APA) gathered in Chicago that "their deliberations . . . will advance and improve our knowledge and methods and our skills for the betterment of the nation's mental health."[1] Such generic presidential greetings confirmed the optimism and public acceptance of the psychoanalytic community. Psychoanalysts interested themselves in the symbols of postwar prosperity while they specialized in the period's peculiar anxieties. One analyst found the popular convertible to be an automotive dream symbol used by his patients to represent bisexuality and verbal "plasticity."[2]

Yet there were signs in the mid and late 1950s of a serious professional dispute. Some of its consequences are observable today in this paradox: even as the clinical foundations of psychoanalysis are experiencing their most sophisticated challenge, psychoanalytic methods and ideas are flourishing in the disciplines of the humanities and the social sciences.[3]

For those who followed him, Freud left in his last writing the example of his original struggle for a durable vocation. Shortly before he died, he termed psychoanalysis an "impossible profession" ("Analysis Terminable and Interminable" [1937]),[4] having in mind chiefly the uncertainty of its results, the chance that patients would not benefit. By the time that Janet Malcolm used the phrase as the title for her widely admired book on contemporary psychoanalysis, its other, more ironic meaning was also plain. The anonymous analyst who dominates *The Impossible Profession* (1981) has few doubts about his technique; he favors Freud's suggestion that psychoanalysis is like surgery, with the same need for detachment and precision and the potential for permanence in its results. He is one of the "soldiers of Freud," according to Malcolm, whose own ambivalence about the professional ethos of orthodox psychoanalysis only hints at how its historical development has prompted many styles relying on different aspects of Freud's example. In other recent accounts of the psychoanalytic vocation, the meaning of Freud's career survives as a professional problem. As F. Robert Rodman—a disciple of D. W. Winnicott—puts it, "[T]hroughout his career the therapist stands between the objectivity of science and the inwardness of poetry. In confronting the resulting tensions, he fashions himself."[5]

Of course, many of today's scholars in the humanities and social sciences have well-cultivated habits of contemplating how they construct, and are constructed by, their disciplinary and professional traditions. Some post–World War II psychoanalysts—Erikson among them—did likewise. But most were confident about the structure and future of their profession. In the vocabulary of ego psychology, just then becoming an influential clinical theory, psychoanalysts found a convenient defense against professional doubts in the consolidation of theory and clinical technique and in the manifest public admiration for their work.

The psychoanalysts saluted by Eisenhower in 1956 had a few years earlier celebrated the fifteenth anniversary of their national association with justifiable pride—the number of American psychoanalysts had doubled each decade since 1932. The American Psychoanalytic Association had 485 members by the early 1950s but nearly double that number in training at fourteen institutes across the country. It was, according to a retrospective account, "the central aspiration and the central activity that brought so many of the brightest and best into the psychiatric ranks."[6] And in the years just after World War II, the Association had successfully asserted its independence within the International Psychoanalytic Association, especially with regard to the matter of training and the exclusion of lay analysts (those not trained as physicians) from clinical work. Indeed, such was the organizational success of psychoanalysis that the APA president was criticized in 1955 for offering a presidential address that sounded like "the Board of Directors' report on some sprawling industrial combine."[7]

The masthead roster of editors in the first issue of the *Journal of the American Psychoanalytic Association* (1952) shows only Erikson without an M.D. after his name. Still, Robert Knight, APA president for that year, at that time also a sponsor of Erikson's work at a New England clinic, spoke for psychoanalytic pluralism and historical recognition of the place of innovation in an artfully phrased review of professional essentials. For him, psychoanalysis "is not set once and for all by its original form, but . . . forever evolves as the intuition, resourcefulness, and artistry of treatment today are reduced to the scientific techniques of tomorrow."[8] "Reduced" is a chemical metaphor he might better have withdrawn, suggesting as it does precisely the hierarchy of relations between humanistic and scientific (or medicalized) psychoanalysis that Knight was seeking to loosen. Still, other psychoanalytic and psychiatric leaders (four out of five American psychoanalysts were also psychiatrists) were noticeably less hospitable to broad intellectual applications of psychoanalysis at the putative expense of its pragmatic and urgent medical intentions.[9]

Just five years after the centenary celebration, a widely read essay by Robert Coles carried the rueful title "A Young Psychiatrist Looks at His Profession." Displaying what came to be his characteristic gloom about the American professions generally, Coles asked that his colleagues reassert the intellectual eccentricity and social rebelliousness of their forebears and regain interest in "the entire range of human activity." The inspiration he found in the career of Anna Freud (she had trained Erikson in Vienna) was threatened by the bureaucratization of psychoanalysis, its "Organization Men," and its uneven assimilation into psychiatry, itself a medical specialty lacking in Coles's view suitable moral and social ideals. "Once there were the curious and bold," he says, "now there are the carefully well-adjusted and certified."[10]

By the mid-1960s, psychoanalysis no longer held its dominant position among psychotherapies, and soon after it became a common target of criticism for its apparent complacency.[11] Erikson's anticipation of this trend, his efforts to fortify his profession with clinical and theoretical innovations (including biography) and to adapt its historical momentum to the social and political ethos of the 1960s later earned him the epithet "prophet" in a review of his reputation in the mid-1970s.[12] During World War II he did government-sponsored psychological studies of soldiers, and in the years after the war he participated in an ambitious program of cross-cultural inquiry organized by Margaret Mead and others. An analyst with a firm reputation in the multidisciplinary intellectual community represented by Mead, Erikson had not yet achieved a consolidated psychoanalytic identity that would represent his unique background (including training as a Montessori teacher), wide intellectual and historical interests, and innovative life-cycle theory. So, too, would he need a suitable format for his clinical stance and distinctive prose voice.

Childhood and Society (1950; 1963), the book that made Erikson's reputation, displays technical achievements in child and adolescent psychoanalysis in "a program of studies," as Erikson described it in *Young Man Luther,* "which might account for the dovetailing of the stages of individual life and of basic human institutions."[13] Still, while significant parts of the book were composed during the late 1930s and early 1940s, it is also a document of the first years of the cold war. It was first published in the same year that Erikson left the University of California after refusing to sign a loyalty oath. His academic position at Berkeley was the most formal of the posts he had had in America, but his decision to leave it reflected his interest in a more durable professional commitment.

With his statement of refusal, he affirmed his dedication to academic values but noted the particular features of his vocation: "Mine is a highly specialized place in an area of knowledge still considered rather marginal to true science." Accordingly, he must vigorously protest "empty gestures" to "ban evil in some magic way." Above all, the signing of the oath would signify a breakdown in the relations between the scholarly generations. "Older people like ourselves can laugh this off; in younger people, however—and especially in these most important students who are motivated to go into teaching—a dangerous rift may well occur between the 'official truth' and those deep and often radical doubts which are the necessary condition for the development of thought."[14]

Erikson's cold-war experience strengthened his convictions about conviction itself, about the psychology of protest, and about the historical antecedents (in and beyond psychoanalysis) of his own moderate but rebellious temperament. The scientific component of religion was to become his subject in *Young Man Luther,* just as the ethics of science was a preoccupation as he completed *Childhood and Society,* where Robert Oppenheimer and the moral dilemma of the atomic physicists hover over the last part as Freud dominates the first. "There is a point," Erikson notes, "where the scientific ethos and armament races do not live well together in one identity, and on being forced to merge endanger the very spirit of inquiry."[15] The problem of holding together a new professional identity was one that made psychoanalysis a uniquely self-conscious enterprise.

Medical Temperament and Lay Analysis

The question of professional descent in the history of psychoanalysis, a field barely half a century old when Erikson matured in it, was a crucial one for him as it was for other analysts. He confronted the problems of tradition and authority in the making of his academic and clinical vocation directly through a series of essays on Freud in the mid-1950s and then indirectly in his studies of Luther and Gandhi. Erikson identified with the Freud who had advocated the expansion of psychoanalytic interests and the adaptation of training procedures to accommodate nonmedical candidates.

Erikson, born in 1902 in Denmark, was raised in Germany as the adopted son of a prominent Jewish pediatrician who expected him also to enter medicine. He pursued art instead after graduation from the gymnasium, but his career was, in effect, the result of a medical controversy. Freud's *The Question of Lay Analysis* (1927) was prompted by its author's wish to defend Wilhelm Reik from charges of "quackery." But it also represents an episode in the institutional development of psychoanalysis. As his polemical text made plain, Freud had a long-standing resentment of the medical establishment for its indifference or hostility to psychoanalysis. He took some pride in noting that "[a]fter forty-one years of medical activity, my self-knowledge tells me that I have never really been a doctor in the proper sense. I became a doctor through being compelled to deviate from my original purpose; and the triumph of my life lies in my having, after a long and roundabout journey, found my way back to my earliest path."[16] It was scientific inquiry that defined Freud's first vocation and then, of course, his broadly humanistic interests, an application of scientific psychoanalysis in the same sense he insisted that its medical uses were. Modern partisans of the "physicianly attitude" as indispensible to psychoanalytic practice must account for Freud's admission (however shaded by his polemical purposes) that he had not when young had any "craving . . . to help suffering humanity." But he adds, "I scarcely think . . . that my lack of a genuine medical temperament has done much damage to my patients."[17]

Shortly after the publication of *The Question of Lay Analysis,* Freud said that opposition to lay analysis was "the last mask of the resistance against psychoanalysis, and the most dangerous of all."[18] The psychoanalytic community was divided on the question. As Kurt Eissler has noted, "the idea of lay analysis was a stillbirth, the first complex idea of Freud's to be disregarded by the majority of his own followers."[19] Even highly regarded lay analysts like the distinguished art historian Ernst Kris spoke for the importance of medical training, his own having been discontinued at Freud's urging in order that he might become the editor of a new psychoanalytic journal (and later, of course, an influential clinician and theorist). Ernest Jones, whose authoritative, if hagiographic, biography of Freud appeared in the mid-1950s, proposes that lay analysis was the feature of the psychoanalytic movement that "most keenly engaged Freud's interest, and indeed emotions," during his late years.[20] A physician himself, Jones, too, found in lay analysis one of the few themes on which he disagreed with Freud.

As an exposition of theory, *The Question of Lay Analysis* reflects the evolution of the psychoanalytic vocation during the 1920s. Just a few months after World War I ended, Freud encouraged his colleagues to consider the "widening scope" of their science.[21] *The Question of Lay Analysis* is an example of ways in which the ego, the mind in society, came to occupy a greater place in Freud's work. And it appeared to him that it was work by lay analysts, including his daughter, which offered perhaps the most promise for the evolution of the new psychoanalytic theory and its application in novel settings. Near the end of *The Question of Lay Analysis,* he expresses special admiration for those who are "not ashamed to concern themselves with the affairs in a child's world, and who understand how to find their way into a child's mental life."[22] In endorsing the work of his daughter, Anna, he authorized, too, the training of the first generation of child analysts, few of whom were physicians and most of whom succeeded in demonstrating the fruitfulness of new psychoanalytic applications.

Freud closed his book with the hopeful assertion that "the things that really matter—the possibilities in psychoanalysis for *internal* development—can never be affected by regulations and prohibitions."[23] Inevitably, lay analysis remained a "question" in succeeding decades as the national psychoanalytic societies established standards for training and practice. The Americans earned a reputation for steadfast orthodoxy in the matter of medical preparation. And even within the famous psychoanalytic schisms of the 1940s, medical credentials divided otherwise unified opponents of the APA. Erich Fromm, for example, was denied clinical privileges as a training analyst by medically prepared colleagues in the fledgling American Institute for Psychoanalysis.[24] The result, underscored today by interest in the search for "common ground" in clinical approaches, was pressure on psychoanalysis to develop along complementary but still divergent paths, one of which was marked out by Erikson's theory of the human life cycle and its applications in history and biography.[25]

Erikson's Freud

During Erikson's first decade in America, Freud's example was obscured by affiliations with empirically oriented research programs at Harvard, Yale, and Berkeley. Erikson found there fruitful research and clinical formats for his novel ideas about children's play and the structure of the life cycle. Freud had only an ambivalent reception in American academic psychology. Harvard's personality theorist Henry Murray (he called his approach "personology") was an early member of the Boston Psychoanalytic Society, which Erickson joined when he emigrated to the United State in 1933, the year the Society was founded. But Murray, who had been trained in medicine, later left it over his displeasure with the narrow interests of his colleagues.

Just as Erikson was able to work productively with behaviorist-oriented academic psychologists—like those at Yale's Institute for Human Relations—and to fit his psychoanalytic interests to the longitudinal studies underway at Berkeley, he was a loyal member of the American psychoanalytic community despite lacking its primary credential. In a confrontation indirectly related to the problem faced by Fromm, Erikson sided firmly with his APA colleagues.[26] He was one of the handful of European lay analysts granted automatic membership in the Association prior to the installation of strict educational requirements.

The success of *Childhood and Society,* first published in 1950, made Erikson impossible to ignore. He was recognized with editorial responsibilities in the new Association journal, publication in it of two long landmark essays, and then with the prized role of representing American psychoanalysts at the Freud centenary celebration in Frankfurt. In his inventive study of an important section of *The Interpretation of Dreams,* which appeared in the *Journal of the American Psychoanalytic Association* in 1954, Erikson proposed viewing Freud's Irma dream as "an event reflecting a critical stage of the dreamer's life cycle." He found evidence for "a crisis in the life of a creative man of middle age"—according to Erikson's scheme, the crisis of "generativity"—here noted for its "plasticity" because it includes works of science and scholarship intended for their effects on succeeding generations. Thinking of Freud's habits of intellectual restlessness, Erikson interprets his dream to show that "the creative mind seems to face repeatedly what most men, once and for all, settle in late adolescence."[27]

And while that stage was the subject of Erikson's next major contribution to developmental theory (in the *JAPA* in 1956), he found it necessary to pass beyond ego-identity formation to its "derivatives" in later adult stages. The example he chose was his own field, proposing that his colleagues ponder how their work reflects a "particular configuration of drives, defenses, capabilities, and opportunities." The clinical and theoretical significance of psychoanalysis represents also the historical contingencies of its development as a profession:

> I am not denying here the necessity, in a suddenly expanding and unexpectedly popular field, to define the original sources of its inspiration and the fundamentals of its specific morality. Yet, psychoanalysis, in its young history, has offered rich opportunities for a variety of identities: it gave new function and scope to such divergent endeavors as natural philosophy and Talmudic argument; medical tradition and missionary teaching; literary demonstration and the building of theory; social reform and the making of money.[28]

By finding room for many traditions and motives, Erikson no doubt was justifying his own unusual background and, in effect, inviting legitimacy for psychoanalytic interests across the disciplines of the humanities and social sciences. His influence in these domains reflects admiration for his theory and his "psycho-historical" (a term he dislikes) biographies.

Still, the variety of such vocational images is also, in his view, a sign that in order to interact with others in advancing a field, individuals must make "a total orientation out of a given stage of partial knowledge." The give-and-take of analytic development derives, in turn, from allegiance among Freud's followers to different elements of his work or to different stages of his career. At their best, such identities fortify innovations and inventive applications. But "such identities easily find elaboration in ideological schools and in irreversible systematizations which do not permit of argument and change." To break the professional deadlock, Erikson urges an inclusive orientation in which psychoanalytic teaching (and historical inquiry) illuminates "the ideological background of principal differences in what is felt to be most practical, most true, and most right at various stages of this developing field."[29] With *Young Man Luther* just ahead, the feasibility of such projects was more apparent than perhaps even Erikson realized.

At the Freud centenary in Frankfurt, Erikson delivered an eloquent synthesis of his views, including now the significance of Freud's formative relationship with Wilhelm Fliess.[30] Whatever he believed about the flexibility of the post-Freudian psychoanalytic vocation, Erikson shares, inevitably, in the image of Freud being elaborated in Jones's influential biography, whose third and last volume was about to appear. Accordingly, Erikson's Freud carries out a "lonely discovery" on behalf of motives like Darwin's and other intellectual pioneers. But in Erikson's view, Freud was a man of great "inner contradictions," and these may have misled his followers and biographers into finding a decisive motive or method. "Any exclusive emphasis . . . on the infantile or the great, the neurotic or the creative, the emotional or the intellectual, the medical or the psychological aspects of a creative crisis sacrifices essential components."[31] Freud's genius was many-sided, but its activation depended on the fittedness of his temperament and rhetorical gifts to particular historical circumstances. Hence Erikson ignores the success of psychoanalysis as a theory and method of scientific inquiry in favor of the need to recognize that "an innovator's achievement can be seen most dramatically in that moment when he, alone against historical adversity and inner doubts, and armed only with the means of persuasion, gives a new direction to human awareness—new in focus, new in its method, and new in its inescapable responsibility."[32]

Erikson chose to emphasize novelty in psychoanalytic method (with diversity in professional orientation and plasticity in generative intentions) at just the time when psychoanalysis was seeking to consolidate its organizational gains and to stabilize its clinical practices on behalf of medical tradition. Near the close of his tribute, he speaks directly to his professional colleagues, warning them that "wide recognition and vast organization" may actually endanger essential

Freudian professional values. Psychoanalysts must stay close to the contract with the patient and must "relinquish the security of seemingly more 'objective' methods . . . , pursue continuous conceptual redefinition . . . ," and put "self-observant vigilance above the satisfaction of seeming professional competence."[33] Freud's was not only an achievement in science, Erikson argues, but one in "scientific conscience," a distinction drawn from a vocabulary he employed (with Coles) more comfortably than most of his American colleagues. Freud himself, granting the possibility that there would be gaps in the backgrounds of potential lay analysts, had asked that if they won the approval of the medical profession and the opportunity of cooperation, "might they not have some interest in raising their own ethical and intellectual life?"[34] For Erikson (and Coles in writing about Anna Freud, for example), the history of psychoanalysis had, conversely, demonstrated precisely these advantages for many of the products of medical training.

Time, Place, and Stage

Even as Erikson was reasserting a particular historical Freud, he was modifying his own method for commentary on the founder's career and on psychoanalytic history. Erikson's clinical authority, as is evident from the last few pages of his Frankfurt address, derives from the blessing Freud gave to child psychoanalysis and not from the unqualified stature of such work (in the 1950s at least) within the psychoanalytic community.[35] The years between his departure from California and his appointment at Harvard in 1960 were spent at the Austen Riggs Center in Stockbridge, Massachusetts, and the Western Psychiatric Institute in Pittsburgh. Paradoxically, the freedom to concentrate on clinical work led to his scholarly study of Luther, meant originally to be simply a historical sketch illustrating his maturing theory of ego identity. By now, Erikson's innovations included the discursive form in which he could consolidate his historical, social, and developmental interests. He had called *Childhood and Society* an "itinerary." But it had more structured elements of narrative and biography as well, some represented indirectly, of course, in the biological processes of epigenesis, others in psychohistorical experiments meant to demonstrate applications of the theory in world affairs.

Young Man Luther shares with *Childhood and Society* the psychological atmosphere of the cold war and fear of communism, both elements in Erikson's distinctive professional and public voice. Like Arthur Miller, who found contemporary dramatic meaning in the Salem witchcraft trials, Erikson notes historical continuities in the origins and uses of superstition.[36] But he asserts, too, a liberal psychology of totalitarianism that is more hopeful than realistic, even though it includes skepticism about Western democracy (a point ignored by those finding Erikson an uncritical patriot in the 1950s).[37] Attempting as he is to extend the political boundaries of psychoanalytic insight—like Freud in his anthropological and historical inquiries—Erikson at times is *too* inclined to an inclusive vocation. His weakness was national character, the subject of two long psychobiographical essays in *Childhood and Society.* These portraits of Hitler and Gorky (the first appeared in an earlier version during World War II) demonstrate how serious Erikson was about making the "outer world" a developmental theme and how psychoanalysis could help guide the nation—through insight into the enemy—toward a more peaceful future. They were the first signs of Erikson's willingness to follow the logic of his epigenetic theory into biography with concentration on stage-specific crises for understanding life-cycle trends.

The organization of *Childhood and Society,* with its developmental theory placed in the middle of the text as a summary of the clinical and empirical first half and as a prelude to the biographical and historical second half, might be seen as a sign of the direction of Erikson's career. The impulse behind *Young Man Luther* can be traced to the sketches of Hitler and Gorky but the full-scale biography displays its timeliness, too, in Erikson's acknowledgment that the problem of youthful rebellion—or "juvenile delinquency," as it was called by some in the 1950s—is one that binds his historical interests with his clinical ones.[38]

Young Man Luther also strives to be a contemporary book in its attention to the problems of psychoanalysis, especially the fate of Freudian tradition in the paradoxically prosperous and threatening postwar environment. Like its successor, *Gandhi's Truth* (1969), it presents the psychoanalytic movement through analogies with religious and political reform; and it explores the psychoanalytic vocation by identifying techniques of introspection and inquiry that it shares with the methods of great spiritual innovators. Though *Young Man Luther* is a book about the psychology of religion, the intense international debate over its historical accuracy and methods has obscured Erikson's allied intention: to present a portrait of the psychoanalytic vocation in terms of the monastic, spiritual, and scholarly one of the late Middle Ages and early Renaissance.[39]

Luther (like Gandhi) turns out to be a figure resembling Freud, an unlikely lesson for contemporary practitioners in the secular profession that they had inherited from the antireligious Freud. Erikson's effort to smuggle a bit of midcentury liberal Protestantism into the nation's most popular psychotherapy reflects his intellectual (at least) affiliations with other lay analysts such as Fromm, whose book on *Psychoanalysis and Religion* (1950) found a large audience. But Erikson made his case from within mainstream psychoanalysis (he was never a neo-Freudian), giving it, whatever its other virtues, unusual interest in the history of psychoanalysis as an institution. And in light of his subsequent work, *Young Man Luther* was a plain sign of his intention to transform his stage theory into a format for unifying psychology and religion generally.[40]

A Psychoanalytic Reformation

Young Man Luther begins where the centenary address "The First Psychoanalyst," ends, with a worried review of the fate of institutionalized psychoanalysis, or as Erikson calls it, "psychoanalysisism." He complains, with unintentional irony considering complaints by others about the impact of Erikson's own work, about the careless application of ideas revealed in treatment to the general human condition: "This is the reason why the fragments of case histories or psychoanalytic interpretations which flutter around in increasing numbers in our newspapers and magazines seem lost like bats in the daytime."[41] Psychoanalysts themselves are also accountable for undue emphasis on "originology," a coinage Erikson presents, aware both of its awkwardness and utility, in suggesting the reductive habit of locating in every human situation an analogy with an earlier one until an origin or infantile precursor is found.

Having alerted his readers and colleagues that he sees how they share in the stereotyping of psychoanalytic ideas, Erikson in the rest of his often dense but eloquent text turns to the themes that express how he gained the confidence of his differences from other psychoanalysts. There is first the matter of orthodoxy in psychoanalytic technique and theorizing, which have, in Erikson's view, elements of the "meditative descent" Luther made as a monk "into the inner shafts of mental existence, from which the aspirant emerges with the gold of faith or with gems of wisdom" (109). But "descent" counts, too—in a connection I hope does not appear forced—in the matter of what will happen in midcentury America to Freud's discovery. For the "greatest advances in human consciousness are made by people who demand too much, and thus invite a situation in which their overstrained followers inevitably end up either compromisers or dogmatists" (143). What is needed in contemporary psychoanalysis is the habit of "reformulation," not merely of the conceptual framework (including the controversial metapsychology) but of what Erikson himself calls the "work ideology." This is a point easy to make, of course, in a biography of Luther, where the failure of the Church to maintain "perpetual communal revival" made it ripe for progressive intentions on behalf of intellectual honesty and public accountability.

Erikson chose also to stress Luther's rhetorical achievements, an important historical theme in psychoanalysis. He had closed his Frankfurt address with a reminder that Freud had been especially proud of the Goethe Prize he had been awarded (in Frankfurt, too) for his literary achievements. Indeed, Freud's prose has the admiration of scholars and teachers in many fields, and of most psychoanalysts as well, whose hopes for fidelity to this element of tradition, however, often cannot be reconciled with their scientific ambitions. So when Erikson notes that it was in his rhetorical skills that Luther "gained the courage of his conflicted personality" (196), he also means to call attention to the matter of "craftsmanship in communication." Hence Luther is an example, too, in making "the verbal work of his whole profession more genuine in the face of a tradition of scholastic virtuosity" (220). Erikson's strong personal identification with Luther—and his ambivalence (like Coles's) about the midcentury discourses of psychoanalysis and psychiatry—relies on this neglected theme.

There is now a large literature on the form of psychological biography, for which *Young Man Luther* is a pioneering text.[42] But Erikson expressed his interest in narrative in a remarkably simple form when, explaining his admiration for Ingmar Bergman's film *Wild Strawberries,* he said that "a good story does not need a chart to come alive and . . . a chart [like the familiar one illustrating his eight-stage theory] can use a good story."[43] Accordingly, the outline of his theory and its stage-by-stage application to Luther's life—is postponed until the epilogue of *Young Man Luther.* The historical psychologizing is distributed throughout the narrative within the unfolding of Luther's career. But Erikson is not diffident about the premises of psychoanalytic narrative, about what must be taken from the consulting room and the clinical case history to the construction of biography.

The opening chapters of *Young Man Luther* include the reasons he found previous biographers wanting, including the naive assumption of some that a biographer can write without a developmental point of view: "There is always an implicit psychology behind the explicit antipsychology" (36). No one, he asserts, could present Luther's life in quite the way that Freudian technique permits the astute biographer to produce a convincing historical reconstruction based on a paucity of facts. "If any determining insight had to be drawn from this material alone, it would be better not to begin. But a clinician's training permits, and in fact forces, him to recognize major trends even where the facts are not all available; at any point in a treatment he can and must be able to make meaningful predictions as to what will prove to have happened" (50). And, even as Erikson finds the structure in Luther's life within the history of Christianity and then modern intellectual and scientific history, he suggests themes in his own career within the history of psychoanalysis. The double (or fourfold) narrative belies the limits suggested by the "young man" of the title, just as his epigenetic theory is misunderstood to explain independent products of stage-specific developmental crises in a straightforward linear progression.

Apart from its intention to predict the past in reconstructing Luther's life, the plainest anticipation of postmodern theorizing is, of course, Erikson's effort to cross the boundary between biographer and subject. While he is not as self-conscious about the psychoanalytic countertransference in *Young Man Luther* as he was to be in *Gandhi's Truth* (where he addresses Gandhi directly), the earlier biography aligns Luther with Freud in order to underline his relationship, too, with Freud's followers. Erikson stresses what can be determined of the "logic" of Luther's development (35) as if to certify the science of psychoanalysis—including its affiliations with medicine—in the service of biography. But his relations with his subject are anything but scientific (or objective) except within the special definition of the introspective Freudian science as it is practiced in biography. "It would seem," he proposes more tentatively than he actually believed, "that even the best-trained historical mind could not 'live in the historical process' without underscoring and erasing, professing and denying, even loving and hating, and this without trying to know himself as so living and so knowing."[44] Erikson put positively what Freud had stated negatively: "[N]o psychoanalyst goes further than his own complexes and internal resistances permit."[45] He progressed in self-consciousness of the countertransference with his next biography, but his study of Luther gave suitably complex form to his midcareer review of professional problems and opportunities.

It is the historical actuality of Luther's career as a particular kind of thinker and his capacities as a reformer that structure the interactive biographical-autobiographical drama. With the form the biography gives (as it must) to matters of individual conscience, Erikson directs attention to the professional struggles of psychoanalysis, for which Luther's generativity stands as a remote and timely example of institutional rejuvenation. But so, too, does Erikson's mid-1950s preoccupation with Freud and his career stand as a prelude to the psychohistorical experiment of *Young Man Luther.* He believed in the universal meaning of Luther's career, a man whose life promises "to solve for all what he could not solve for himself alone." Hence Luther's circumstances in middle age are summarized in these terms: "The *crisis of generativity* occurs when a man looks at what he has generated, or helped to generate, and finds it good or wanting, when his life work as part of the productivity of his time gives him some sense of being on the side of a few angels or makes him feel stagnant" (243).

Erikson does not appear to have had manifest public reasons to doubt his own achievements, but he would not need to have them in order to move through middle age, according to his own theory. Besides, as he suggested in his essay on ego identity, the psychoanalyst's psychology is a cornerstone of the choice and renewal of his vocation. In his only directly autobiographical statement, Erikson is exceedingly tactful on the question of medical orthodoxy, hoping that the "quiet contributions" of (presumably) well-qualified analysts like himself would prevent the field from complete subordination to medicine. He notes there, as well, the importance to his professional identity of Freud's phenomenological and literary approach. While he is coy, I think, about being "inept" on theoretical issues and their scientific vocabularies, he is perfectly direct in asserting that his biographies were attempts to "objectify" his identification with Freud's "freedom and enjoyment of inquiry."[46] Luther, too, is presented as a teacher and scholar whose gifts of verbal "craftsmanship" reflect developmental coordinates derived jointly from Freud and Erikson: "We are able to manage and creatively utilize our drives only to the extent to which we can acknowledge their power by enjoyment, by awareness, and through the activity of work" (218).

The Borderline

Surely the most heterodoxical sign in *Young Man Luther* of Erikson's differences with the medical psychoanalytic community is his proposals for an alliance of psychoanalysis with religion, part of a larger aspiration to make it more socially and morally self-conscious. The question of Freud (cleverly termed a "devout skeptic" by Erikson) and faith has, of course, been thoroughly documented and debated, usually from the side of his declarations of contempt, based as they were on his enlightenment disposition and his archaeological and historical inquiries.[47] Erikson appears to reestablish the religious instinct with this aside in his discussion of Luther's psychological and biological (and sexual) realism: "We can often actively assert our mastery over a major aspect of life only after we have fully realized our complete dependence on it" (162). And Luther overcame the "dogmatic permanence" of the Church with the installation of a continuing "living reformulation of faith." His example is no less urgent now than Freud's because of the "common undercurrent of existential anxiety" prompting the search for new meanings in individual experience. And it does not obscure a critical vocational paradox. For while Luther welcomed the cognitive consequences of monasticism as Erikson stated them ("It opens the individual wide to the contradictory voices within him" [131]), he is a reminder now of questions that might be asked of worldly intellectual life. "As Luther said," Erikson reports with approval, "a man without spirituality becomes his own exterior" (135).

But Erikson is a man of his time, too (to deepen the paradox or signify the durability of "contradictory voices"), in restating this theme with the religiosity modified enough to satisfy the liberal secular community in his audience. Hence to "the great human question" posed at the end of *Young Man Luther*—to what moral uses will early child training be put?—he proposes: "The answer lies in man's capacity to create order which will give his children a disciplined as well as a tolerant conscience, and a world within which to act affirmatively" (263). Church historian Martin Marty has noted how clear it is now that the "secular theology" movement of the 1950s and 1960s was "wide of the mark." But he grants that it is important to ask why such ideas were plausible at the time.[48] One answer is in the history of psychoanalysis, where professional self-consciousness, for some analysts at least and for fellow travelers in the humanities and social sciences, prompted new formats for intellectual reconciliation or attention to old ones.

The conciliatory metaphor that Erikson favored is one he borrowed from his Harvard colleague and theologian Paul Tillich: the borderline. It represents the point of overlap where undiscovered or rediscovered relations between traditions and ideas can be found. But it represents an autobiographical theme as well. When he cited Tillich's description of his own life as one "on the boundaries," Erikson added that "throughout my career I worked in institutional contexts for which I did not have the usual credentials."[49] His own "improvised profession" had, perhaps inevitably, featured a dialectical theory of human development with its sequenced pairs giving form to definitions of personality. Tillich favored "existential contradictions" as the sign of the borderline "not as conflicts to be 'cured' by adjustments and conformity, but as opposites to be bridged and thus transformed into creative polarities."[50]

Young Man Luther offered the borderline of psychoanalysis and religion as more than a place for inquiry into the meaning of the second from the point of view of the first.[51] For more was at stake, as the increasing spirituality of Erikson's work has shown. He came to define his sense of being an outsider initially as a matter of credentials but then also as a matter of beliefs, about the nature and goals of his profession, and about belief itself. On this most delicate of issues, Erikson had to reassure his psychoanalytic colleagues that a return to religiosity was not, as Freud would have it, a hopeless regression and abandonment of enlightened modernism. In doing so, he incorporated the meaning of Luther's life into a contemporary psychological justification (to use an essential term from Lutheranism) of faith: "At their creative best, religions retrace our earliest inner experiences, giving tangible form to vague evils, and reaching back to the earliest individual sources of trust; at the same time, they keep alive the common symbols of integrity distilled by the generations. If this is partial regression, it is a regression which, in retracing firmly established pathways, returns to the present amplified and clarified" (264).

Conclusion: On a Mirador

The Jesuit and lay analyst Oskar Pfister was Freud's good friend but could not convince him to recognize belief as anything but a delusion. Indeed, shortly after the publication of *The Question of Lay Analysis* (which, of course, had the effect too of justifying Pfister's analytic activities), he wrote to the clergyman: "I do not know whether you have guessed the secret tie between my [book on] lay analysis and my [*Future of an*] *Illusion*. In the first I want to protect analysis from the doctors, in the latter from the priests."[52] Erikson had entered the psychoanalytic community at precisely that time as an art teacher in the private school run by Anna Freud and Dorothy Burlingham for the children of analytic patients (mainly Americans). His career in psychoanalysis began a few years later when Anna Freud convinced him that he was well qualified for it by virtue of his artistic talent and intellectual temperament.

In Erikson's lifetime, the specialty of psychoanalytic work with children gradually came to authorize the expansion of analytic interests more generally, a process he urged with confidence in the results of applications of clinical work to biography and other fields of scholarship. These will not, like psychoanalysis itself, have instant legitimacy, but their progress will carry important implications for the source of their innovation. "Considering the revolutionary ingredients of such [work], it should not be surprising that it will take generations to find proper forms of verification as well as the range and limits of application, which, in turn, will lead to transformations in the professional identity of the psychoanalyst."[53]

Erikson wrote *Young Man Luther* in the most unlikely of places, a small fishing village in Mexico. In the meditative closing paragraphs, he presents himself sitting on a "mirador," that is, a balcony commanding an extensive view, where he speculates on the local political events and their roots in Western history. Hence my second headnote: "The Reformation is continuing in many lands, in the form of manifold revolutions, and in the personalities of protestants of varied vocations." This is certainly an allusion to Erikson's own psychoanalytic "reformation," his effort to make out of his extensive view a new clinical and scholarly vocation.

The large and varied audience for Erikson's work of the 1950s, especially for the pathmaking *Young Man Luther,* attests to the potential for such a role, even if he has been ignored in recent accounts of the model public intellectuals we no longer have.[54] But his was a private pursuit as well. He might have said with Luther, who, of course, named "theology" as the object of his learning in this declaration: "I did not learn my [psychology] all at once, but I had to search deeper for it, where my temptations took me" (251).

Notes

1. "The Freud Centenary Celebration of the American Psychoanalytic Association," *Journal of the American Psychoanalytic Association* 4 (1956): 591–92.

2. Alexander Grinstein, "The Convertible as a Symbol in Dreams," *Journal of the American Psychoanalytic Association* 2 (1954): 466–72.

3. For the most influential criticism, see Adolf Grünbaum, *The Foundations of Psychoanalysis* (Berkeley and Los Angeles: University of California Press, 1984) and "The Role of the Case Study Method in the Foundations of Psychoanalysis," *Canadian Journal of Philosophy* 18 (1988): 623–58. A response to Grünbaum's most recent arguments can be found in Richard Miller, "A Clinical Science," *Canadian Journal of Philosophy* 18 (1988): 659–80. For other responses, see those gathered for an elaborate symposium on Grünbaum's views, which he himself summarizes for the purposes of his allies and critics: "Precis of *The Foundations of Psychoanalysis: A Philosophical Critique,*" *Behavioral and Brain Sciences* 9 (1986): 217–84. Other essential statements are Robert Wallerstein, "Psychoanalysis as a Science: A Response to the New Challenges," *Psychoanalytic Quarterly* 55 (1986): 414–51; and "Psychoanalysis, Psychoanalytic Science, and Psychoanalytic Research— 1986," *Journal of the American Psychoanalytic Association* 26 (1988): 3–30; Marshall Edelson, *Psychoanalysis: A Theory in Crisis* (Chicago, Ill.: University of Chicago Press, 1988); and Peter Gay, *Freud: A Life for Our Time* (New York: Norton, 1988). Gay's book is itself a comprehensive illustration of the relations between psychoanalysis and the humanities, and his extensive bibliographic essay demonstrates the range of writing about and related to Freud, now, he says, "almost out of control."

4. Sigmund Freud, *The Standard Edition of the Complete Psychological Works of Sigmund Freud,* trans. James Strachey (London: Hogarth Press, 1955), 23:248.

5. F. Robert Rodman, *Keeping Hope Alive: On Becoming a Psychotherapist* (New York: Harper and Row Perennial Library, 1987), 12.

6. Robert S. Wallerstein, "The Psychoanalyst's Life: Expectations, Vicissitudes, and Reflections," *International Review of Psychoanalysis* 8 (1981): 292. The less happy features of such enthusiasm—the inability of the profession to meet the benevolent ambitions of its new members—are explored by Allen Wheelis in "The Vocational Hazards of Psychoanalysis," *International Journal of Psychoanalysis* 37 (1956): 171–84.

7. Kurt R. Eissler, *Medical Orthodoxy and the Future of Psychoanalysis* (New York: International Universities Press, 1965), 93.

8. Robert P. Knight, "The Present Status of Organized Psychoanalysis in the United States," *Journal of the American Psychoanalytic Association* 1 (1953): 211. Erikson noted in 1972 Knight's combination of European and American psychoanalytic traits, "the *width* of activities which [he] was able to pervade with his style, reconciling not only divergent personalities, but such warring methods and theories as have characterized the history of psychoanalysis" ("Robert P. Knight: By Way of a Memoir," *A Way of Looking at Things: Selected Papers from 1930 to 1980,* ed. Stephen Schlein [New York: Norton, 1987] 735–36.)

9. See, for example, Maxwell Gitelson, "Psychoanalyst, U.S.A., 1955," *American Journal of Psychiatry* 112 (1956): 700–705. Gitelson's is one of a group of papers on psychoanalysis presented at the 1955 annual meeting of the American Psychiatric Association. Gregory Zilboorg spoke more favorably of "Psychoanalytic Borderlines" (706–10), a metaphor that appeals to Erikson also, as I suggest later.

10. Robert Coles, "A Young Psychiatrist Looks at His Profession," *The Mind's Fate: Ways of Seeing Psychiatry and Psychoanalysis* (Boston: Little, Brown, 1975), 5–12. The essay was first published in 1961 in the *Atlantic*.

11. Here is how it appeared to an influential psychoanalyst at the end of the 1970s: "We are very widely seen as members of a self-serving guild, set self-contentedly within the heart of the conservative social and political establishment, and incidentally not just for our espoused positions or rather our failures of espousal, but abetted as well by the very accurate perception of our material well-being as psychoanalytic practitioners, members economically of the most advantaged segments of society and partaking of all the fruits of that position" (Wallerstein, "The Psychoanalyst's Life," 295).

12. Frederic Crews, "American Prophet," *New York Review of Books* (16 October 1975): 9–14. In this judicious summary, Crews stresses Erikson's efforts to find a position in relation to Freud's that is both loyal and post-Freudian. He finds, however, some strains of political opportunism, as does

Paul Roazen in his account of Erikson in *Encountering Freud* (New Brunswick, N.J.: Transaction, 1990), 139–61. Similarly, Roazen believes that Erikson's purpose in *Young Man Luther* was to "propagandize only a partial aspect of Luther" on behalf of mythologizing him (*Erik H. Erikson: The Power and Limits of Vision* [New York: Free Press, 1976], 78–85). Robert Coles, in his biographical profile and close readings of the key texts (*Erik H. Erikson: The Growth of His Work* [Boston: Little, Brown, 1970]), is certainly less skeptical than Crews and Roazen, the former of whom claims that Coles perhaps mythologizes Erikson. Coles proposes that when Erikson's thinking and writing in *Young Man Luther* become "exceptionally luminous," they reflect the fact that "the emergence . . . of an enormous and powerful talent in a great man could only demand of the biographer a fitting and comparable effort of his own" (239).

13. Erik H. Erikson, *Young Man Luther: A Study in Psychoanalysis and History* (New York: Norton, 1958), 254.

14. Erik H. Erikson, "Statement to the Committee on Privilege and Tenure of the University of California Concerning the California Loyalty Oath," *A Way of Looking at Things,* 619–20. The statement was published originally in 1951 in *Psychiatry.*

15. Erik H. Erikson, *Childhood and Society* (New York: Norton, 1963), 415.

16. Freud, *Standard Edition,* 20:253.

17. Freud, *Standard Edition,* 20:253–54. A forceful statement of the value of the "physicianly attitude" can be found in Wallerstein, "The Psychoanalyst's Life" (287). He cites the durability, in history and in individual careers, of the Hippocratic oath "that even the most jaded of us tend to treasure as one of our life's most unambivalently offered emotional expressions." The "physicianly attitude" is defined as "that blend of compassion, concern, responsibility, and zeal to cure that seems to come so naturally to most of those who choose medicine." The phrase is borrowed from Leo Stone's *The Psychoanalytic Situation* (New York: International Universities Press, 1961), an important book that is a favorite of many analysts but not widely known in the social sciences and humanities.

18. Ernest Jones, *The Life and Work of Sigmund Freud* (New York: Basic Books, 1957), 3:298.

19. Eissler, 47.

20. Jones, 3:287.

21. See Freud, "Lines of Advance in Psycho-Analytic Therapy," *Standard Edition,* 17:157–68.

22. Freud, *Standard Edition,* 20:249.

23. Ibid., 250.

24. Marianne Horney Eckardt, "Organizational Schisms in American Psychoanalysis," *American Psychoanalysis: Origins and Development,* ed. Jacques M. Quen and Eric T. Carlson (New York: Brunner/Mazel, 1978), 148–49.

25. See Robert Wallerstein, "One Psychoanalysis or Many?" *International Journal of Psychoanalysis* 69 (1988): 5–21, and "Psychoanalysis: The Common Ground," *International Journal of Psychoanalysis* 71 (1990): 3–20.

26. He protested the influence of a representative of a splinter organization, the American Academy of Psychoanalysis, on a program of the American Psychoanalytic Association. See Arcangelo R. T. D'Amore, "Historical Reflections on the Organizational History of Psychoanalysis in America," *American Psychoanalysis: Origins and Development,* 139.

27. Erik H. Erikson, "The Dream Specimen of Psychoanalysis," *A Way of Looking at Things,* 274, 277. The essay was first published in 1954.

28. Erik H. Erikson, "The Problem of Ego Identity," *Identity and the Life Cycle* (New York: Norton, 1980), 164. The essay was first published in 1956.

29. Ibid., 165.

30. See Erik H. Erikson, "Freud's 'The Origins of Psychoanalysis,'" *International Journal of Psychoanalysis* 36 (1955): 1–15.

31. Erik H. Erikson, "The First Psychoanalyst," *Insight and Responsibility* (New York: Norton, 1964), 41.

32. Ibid., 42.

33. Ibid., 43.

34. Freud, *Standard Edition,* 20:258.

35. See E. James Anthony, "The Contributions of Child Psychoanalysis to Psychoanalysis," *Psychoanalytic Study of the Child* 41 (1986): 61–87.

36. He does so, typically, with great generosity, perhaps in this case more than was warranted: "It is tempting to treat these superstitions as primitive obsessions, and to pity the people who did not know any better and who must have felt haunted. But we should not overlook the fact that within reason—that is, to the extent that the superstitions were not exploited by mass panic and neurotic anxiety—they were a form of collective mastery of the unknown. In a world full of dangers they may even have served as a source of security, for they make the unfamiliar familiar, and permit the individual to say to his fears and conflicts, 'I see you! I recognize you!' He can even tell others what he saw and recognized while remaining reasonably free, by a contract between like-minded, of the aspersion that he imagined things out of depravity or despair, or that he was the only one to be haunted. What else do we do today when we share our complexes, our coronaries, and our communists?" (*Young Man Luther,* 60–61).

37. "Our own ideology, as it must, forbids us ever to question and analyze the structure of what we hold to be true, since only thus can we maintain the fiction that we chose to believe what in fact we had no choice to believe, short of ostracism or insanity; while we are more than eager to find the logical flaws, and particularly the insincerity and captivity, in one who operates in another system. We may therefore fail to understand that the indoctrinated individual of another era or country may feel quite at peace and quite free and productive in his ideological captivity, while we, being stimulus-slaves, ensnared at all times by a million freely chosen impressions and opportunities, may somehow feel unfree" (*Young Man Luther,* 135).

38. While working on his biography, he collaborated with his son Kai, a sociologist, on an essay, "The Confirmation of the Delinquent," *Chicago Review* 10 (1957): 15–23.

39. For samples of the interpretive controversy, see Roger A. Johnson, ed., *Psychohistory and Religion: The Case of Young Man Luther* (Philadelphia: Fortress Press, 1977).

40. See Erik H. Erikson, *The Life Cycle Completed: A Review* (New York: Norton, 1982) and my essay "Aged Erikson: The Completion of the Life Cycle," *Journal of Aging Studies* 3 (1989): 253–62.

41. Erik H. Erikson, *Young Man Luther,* 20. Subsequent references appear in the text.

42. See Geoffrey Cocks and Travis L. Crosby, eds., *Psycho/History: Readings in the Method of Psychology, Psychoanalysis, and History* (New Haven, Conn.: Yale University Press, 1987); William McKinley Runyan, ed., *Psychology and Historical Interpretation* (New York: Oxford University Press, 1988); and the special issue of the *Journal of Personality* (March 1988) devoted to psychobiography and narrative.

43. Erik H. Erikson, "Reflections on Dr. Borg's Life Cycle," *Adulthood,* ed. Erik H. Erikson (New York: Norton, 1978), 30.

44. Erik H. Erikson, "On the Nature of Psycho-Historical Evidence," *Life History and the Historical Moment* (New York: Norton, 1975), 116. An early version of this long essay appeared in 1967 as part of Erikson's report on the progress on his biography of Gandhi. A useful introduction to the clinical theme of countertransference is the group of essays appearing in the *Journal of the American Psychoanalytic Association* 34 (1986), especially Robert L. Tyson, "Countertransference: Evolution in Theory and Practice," and Hans Loewald, "Transference-Countertransference." See also Eva Scheleper, "The Biographer's Transference: A Chapter in Psychobiographical Epistemology," *Biography* 13 (1990): 111–29.

45. Freud, "The Future Prospects of Psychoanalytic Therapy," *Standard Edition,* 11:144. For a useful statement of this theme in other psychologists, see George E. Atwood and Silvan S. Tomkins, "On the Subjectivity of Personality Theory," *Journal of the History of the Behavioral Sciences* 12 (1976): 166–77.

46. Erik H. Erikson, "'Identity Crisis' in Autobiographic Perspective," *Life History and the Historical Moment,* 40.

47. Recent studies include Edwin R. Wallace, IV, "Freud and Religion: A History and Reappraisal," *The Psychoanalytic Study of Society* 10 (1984): 113–61, and Peter Gay, *A Godless Jew: Freud, Atheism, and the Making of Psychoanalysis* (New Haven, Conn.: Yale University Press, 1987). Gay notes that "[t]he discovery of common ground between faith and psychoanalysis has been made again and again" (93). My point is that Erikson's case is of unusual interest because he was a figure so close to the origins or ideological core of psychoanalysis. For studies of Freud but mainly of other figures see Peter Homans, ed., *The Dialogue Between Theology and Religion* (Chicago, Ill.: University of Chicago Press, 1968).

48. Martin E. Marty, "Religion in America since Mid-century," *Daedalus* 111 (1982): 152.

49. Erikson, "'Identity Crisis' in Autobiographic Perspective," 30.

50. Erik H. Erikson, "Words for Paul Tillich," *A Way of Looking at Things,* 727.

51. According to Edwin Wallace, "[p]sychoanalysis is on most solid ground when it is investigating the *psychological* meaning of the religious beliefs of *any given practitioner*—i.e., the more or less idiosyncratic (because of childhood history and constitution) contribution of each religionist to what is otherwise a cultural affair" ("Freud and Religion," 154). This does and does not account for *Young Man Luther,* where Erikson makes general claims that Wallace believes can only come from many similar "clinically based" studies.

52. Cited in Gay, *A Godless Jew,* 46–47.

53. Erikson, "'Identity Crisis' in Autobiographic Perspective," 25.

54. See Richard Pells, *The Liberal Mind in a Conservative Age: American Intellectuals in the 1940s and 1950s* (New York: Harper and Row, 1985); and Russell Jacoby, *The Last Intellectuals: American Culture in the Age of Academe* (New York: Basic Books, 1987). I have treated this theme in the introduction ("Intellectuals, Scholars, Craftsmen") to my study of post–World War II writers, *Intellectual Craftsmen: Ways and Works in American Scholarship, 1935–1990* (New Brunswick, N.J.: Transaction, 1991).

■

William H. Epstein

(Post) Modern Lives
Abducting the Biographical Subject

I

In the opening chapter of Norman Mailer's controversial "novel biography" of Marilyn Monroe occurs a crucial, emblematic moment in
modern American biographical narrative.[1] This moment is significant
because it is simultaneously exemplary and *sui generis,* a reflexive gesture of metacritical self-awareness that plunges its biographer into a
gap, perhaps *the* gap, between traditional and emergent cultural formations. The moment to which I refer issues from Mailer's assumption
that Monroe's "factoidal," "schizophrenic," "ambitious," and "exceptional" life "opens the entire problem of biography" (18) and from
Mailer's anxiety that "not having known her was going to prove . . . a
recurrent wound in the writing" (19). This discursive wound, a metaphor with which (Mailer ought to know) he is recalling the Freudian
concept of penis envy and thus (in traditional psychoanalytic terms)
attributing his narrative's potential failure to a lack already written on
to the female body, is, as Mailer explains, "frustratingly" painful for
him because he missed an opportunity to meet his future biographical
subject when she lived a few miles away and was married to Arthur
Miller, his not-so-secret rival for literary fame. Mailer's reflexive biographical narrator remembers: "the call to visit . . . never came. The
playwright and the novelist had never been close. Nor could the novelist in conscience condemn the playwright for such avoidance of drama. The secret ambition, after all, had been to steal Marilyn" (19).
    Reinscribing Eve Sedgwick's and Luce Irigaray's emplotments
of the recurrent scene of patriarchal culture—a homosocial bonding

between men (even, or especially, if they are rivals) that triangulates and victimizes women as it eroticizes, commodifies, and exchanges their bodies[2]—Mailer's biographer figures the relationship between biographer and biographical subject as an *abduction,* as "the illegal taking away or detention of a young woman under a certain age (in Anglo-American law, it varies: usually 16 or 18) for the purposes of marriage or defilement, with or without her consent and without the consent of her parent or guardian" (*OED*). That Monroe was in her thirties at the time, a rich and famous woman of the world married to her third husband (and thus not, it would seem, an appropriate target for abduction), only emphasizes the cultural trope I am pursuing here. For Mailer treats her as if she were Miller's property, or at least his dependent, as if meeting and stealing her were situational possibilities determined by men—in this case, by "the playwright and the novelist," a phrase I am treating as referring not only to Miller and Mailer but also to writers in general, to professional identities associated with the cultural production and distribution of literary texts, identities invariably marked (both in Mailer's narrative and in traditional patriarchal society) as male. Mailer can contemplate abducting Monroe because he assumes that he and Miller, the novelist and the playwright instancing here the desires of "fifty million other men" (20), constitute the *only* economy of cultural relations through which Monroe can be valued. Having been frustrated in that opportunity "to steal Marilyn," Mailer now finds another (in this economy, there is always another): his biographical narrative becomes the scene of an abduction, a discursive practice in and through which the biographer can detain and defile his biographical subject.

Now, the point I want to make is that this is not only an extreme, marginal example of a controversial modern American biographer reflexively remystifying "the last of the myths to thrive in the long evening of the American dream" (16) but a recurring pattern that characterizes the traditional practice of biographical narrative in post-Renaissance Western culture. Two other senses of the word "abduction" reinforce my point: "the surgical procedure by which the recession of two parts of a broken bone causes the gaping of a wound," and "the logical syllogism, also known as apagoge, describing an argument which demonstrates the hidden and not signified proposition" (*OED*). Traditional biographical narrative habitually reenacts the scene of an abduction because, in order to discursively repair the biologically irreparable fracture (the alterity, the otherness, the discontinuity) between any two human individuals (reified generically as biographer and biographical subject), biography recesses the broken parts and causes the gaping of a wound. Moreover, as I have suggested, this wound is metaphorically associated with that which is repressed and excluded—woman in patriarchal culture, the racial subject in an imperialist society, the underclass in a capitalist economy, gays and lesbians in heterosexual culture. Hence, in its desire to heal the break between self and other by syllogistically arguing for a generic procedure that bonds biographer and biographical subject in a more or less "sympathetic relationship" (a traditional narrative argument in Anglo-American life-writing since at least Walton's *Life of Donne*), biography inadvertently demonstrates the hidden and not signified proposition. What I mean here is that the discursive practice of reading and writing the biographical subject—which I have elsewhere called the generic frame "recognizing the biographical subject"[3]—is a way of being and becoming to which special significance is attached, a closely monitored cultural process of inclusion and exclusion in which the Western world's dominant structures of political, social, economic, and cultural authority are deeply implicated. In this process, every inclusion signifies an exclusion, a hidden, recurrent wound in the writing enabling the syllogistic demonstration of a proposition that cannot otherwise be signified. This is how traditional biographical narrative leaps the gap between self and other, biographer and biographical subject.

In other words and among other things, biographical narrative characteristically reenacts a complex scene of generic abduction in which the dynamics of detention, defilement, recession, wounding, repression, and syllogistic reasoning simultaneously abduce (lead away from) and adduce (lead toward) the emergence of specific human individuals in cultural discourse. In the patriarchal, imperialist, capitalist, heterosexual societies of the post-Renaissance Western world, this recurrent generic scene has most frequently been reenacted (as it is in Mailer's narrative) between two men over the body of a woman, an excluded other, an abjected and abducted object of exchange whom they must defile and repress in order to repair the break between them and reinforce their homosocial bond.

Thus Walton's *Donne,* the mid-seventeenth-century narrative out of which flows the mainstream of English biography, is written over the body of Anne More, whom Donne more or less abducts from her father's house, "notwithstanding much watchfulness," and marries secretly "without the allowance of those friends, whose approbation always was, and ever will be necessary, to make even a vertuous [*sic*] love become lawful." After his wife is "detained from him" by her father's revenge, Donne can only "get possession of her by a long and restless suit in Law." Although her father is later reconciled to the union, this marriage will remain "the remarkable error of [Donne's] life," redeemed only by the couple's *"sympathy of souls,"* a visionary and miraculous affection that Walton, whose "unwearied industry to the attainment of what we desire" matches Donne's, has already appropriated for his own purposes. In Walton's narrative, this sympathetic relationship between husband and wife (depicted in the familiar poetic imagery of the twin compasses, made famous by Walton's printing of "A Valediction, forbidding to Mourn") is displaced by the mutual affections shared first by Donne's enclave of poetic divines and then by Donne and Walton. Walton preemptively abducts the imagery and then the relationship in his Introduction, where he metaphorizes the affinity of biographer and biographical subject as a lifelong friendship *between men* interrupted but not ended by death: *"though their bodies were divided, their affections were not."*[4]

In another performance of this recurrent scene, Johnson's *Life of Savage* is written over the body of Savage's mother, Anne, Countess of Macclesfield, a noblewoman who refuses to acknowledge the destitute and importunate poet as her bastard son. In Johnson's narrative, she is metaphorically wounded and repressed, driven from polite society by the violent force of Savage's autobiographical and Johnson's biographical language. This symbolic exclusion then enables not only her son to reassume his rightful place in society as an "injured nobleman" but also Johnson, the provincial bookseller's son and Grub-Street hackwriter with whom Savage had wandered London's desperate streets, to assume *his* as Savage's vindicator, patron, and forgiving father. Thus the Johnsonian biographer adopts the patriarchal role proleptically adumbrated in the *Life of Savage* by Richard Steele, the coauthor of the *Spectator* papers and one of Savage's early patrons: *"the inhumanity of* [Savage's] *Mother had given him a right to find every good Man his Father."*[5]

Let us examine one more example from traditional English biography. Boswell's *Life of Johnson* is written over the body of Hester Thrale Piozzi, Boswell's competitor, who harbored Johnson in her home, nursed his physical and emotional illnesses, and published *Anecdotes* depicting their intimate, platonic relationship. Boswell, whose contact with the London-based Johnson was limited by his Edinburgh law practice and Ayrshire family property, constantly depreciates Mrs. Thrale's honesty, precision, and motives. Devoted to establishing the credit and credibility of his own relationship with and narrative of Johnson, Boswell presents Mrs. Thrale as a would-be biographer who has lost all her credit. Jealous, embittered, childlike, inaccurate, uncomprehending, and *female,* she destroys her reputation and her friendship with Johnson when she romantically ends her wealthy widowhood by marrying an impoverished foreign musician.

Her revenge, according to Boswell, is her *Anecdotes,* which diminishes and demystifies Boswell's sovereign, paternal object of filial veneration. In order to reassert the primacy of his own relationship with Johnson and metaphorically present himself as Johnson's only legitimate heir, Boswell inscribes his narrative on and over the discredited, disowned body of Mrs. Thrale, the recurrent wound in his writing, and thus establishes the most familiar and most abducted bond between men in the history of biography.[6]

As I have suggested, the poetics and problematics of "recognizing the biographical subject" in modern American biography can also be reenacted in and through the trope of abduction. We see emerging now a "rainbow coalition" of literary and cultural critics who (re)present themselves as historically excluded others, as repressed, brutalized, and colonized victims of various intellectual projects associated with Western humanism, patriarchal society, and advanced industrial capitalism. I refer here to feminist studies, gay and lesbian studies, African-American studies, Chicano studies, and Native-American studies (among others), as well as, in general, to the work of those who perform textual study in ways that intersect cultural materialism with a "third-world" or "postcolonial" perspective. Two of the most interesting features of this emergent coalition are its critique of poststructuralist inquiry and its turn toward biography. The increasingly familiar argument runs something like this (I am summarizing here from a congeries of writers and texts): contemporary theory's decentering or deconstruction of such transcendental signifieds as anthropological humanism and individual human consciousness tends to deny the radical situatedness of the subject, whose desire to enter cultural consciousness as (among other things) a biographer or biographical subject is thus "denatured" by a white, first-world, elitist, masculinist enterprise which, in decontextualizing the subject, effaces the specificities of race, class, gender, etc.

Now, this is a powerful and attractive argument that is winning a lot of adherents and that, at first glance, would seem to aggrandize the professional practice of those of us who would join or support this coalition and who are also engaged in the formal study of the poetics of biographical reading and writing (what I have elsewhere called "biographical recognition").[7] But there is a danger here. Biographical recognition, particularly those of its practices associated with the cultural inscription and description of the biographical subject, is not an empty vessel waiting to be filled, a neutral discursive formation that can be appropriated without consequences. The cultural activities of reading and writing the biographical subject have *histories,* marked by (among other things) a tradition of being allied with dominant structures of cultural, political, social, and economic authority. Such a historical tradition would seem to offer little aid and comfort to marginalized biographers and biographical subjects trying to emerge into cultural consciousness through an oppositional agenda that explicitly seeks to undermine these dominant structures.

Biographical narrative may look like a relatively unguarded provincial backwater in the sprawling imperialist realm of Western cultural discourse, but it is not and never has been. Rather, as one of the Western world's "master-sign[s] and . . . generative model[s]"[8] of individual human existence, it has always been a way of being and becoming to which, as I remarked above, special significance is attached, a cultural process of inclusion and exclusion that continues to be closely monitored. The entrance of a biographical subject into written discourse is still a momentous occasion, an event that can, among other things, reaffirm cultural eminence, contextualize social action, alter literary opinion, deputize political influence, or instruct economic conduct—and this admissions procedure, which is always in crisis, is constantly (if not often consciously) surveilled in and through biographical recognition, which, in this respect, functions as the generic agency of the proprietary powers. Thus, during the Roman Imperial Age, when Plutarch, Suetonius, and Tacitus produced the biographical narratives to which subsequent Western life-writing inexorably returns, biography, according to Arnaldo Momigliano, was both "an instrument of Imperial propaganda" and "a vehicle for unorthodox political and philosophic ideas"—it could be "the natural [that is, officially sanctioned] form of telling the story of a Caesar" or "a capital offense under the tyranny of Domitian."[9]

Now, in modern Western culture, biographers do not, as a matter of course, lose their lives over the (re)presentation of historically excluded, radically situated biographical subjects. Not *literally*. Rather, they lose their (biographical subjects') lives *figuratively,* in and through the interpretive violence inflicted upon those lives by biographical recognition. For the threat of losing its official sanction and becoming a cultural outlaw motivates, indeed nearly determines, the generic frame "recognizing the biographical subject." In order to understand how this is so, I shall offer a brief and partial explanation, an abduction, if you will (or against your will—abduction works either way), in which my explanatory narrative detains, wounds, and demonstrates a hidden proposition of biographical recognition.

II

First we must consider the conventional recognition of the biographical subject. That which resists semiotic encoding (because it is in some sense or aspect unknown or unknowable) sponsors and prefigures what can enter discourse as a biographical subject. This crucial theme of generic recognition supposedly distinguishes the biographical subject from (among other things) the fictional subject, which we conventionally recognize as an individual human that exists only in and through discourse and is thus thoroughly encodable. Jay Gatsby pre-exists the narrative first published in 1925 only as type or theme in cultural or literary discourse and cannot post-exist it except as a character or topic in creative or critical discourse. The *trans-discursive* pattern that Jay Gatsby thus describes as he moves across discourse is never biographical; his "life" is always mock-biographical, "lived" entirely in cultural and literary discourse and read always and only as fiction or criticism. Marilyn Monroe, on the other hand, is an *extra-discursive* figure in cultural and literary history. Enjoying the same opportunities as Jay Gatsby to be portrayed, satirized, analyzed, and typologized in creative and critical discourse, she can also be recognized as an individual human whose existence prior to Mailer's 1973 biography cannot be completely or ultimately reduced to semiosis.[10]

Thus, by appealing to the materially unknown or unknowable, to a transcendental signified that is formally outside discourse but is knowable only in and through discourse, the generic frame "recognizing the biographical subject" takes the form of an abduction, that is, it becomes a demonstration which (to deploy the most general sense of the term "apagoge") "does not prove a thing directly but shows the absurdity or impossibility of denying it" (*OED*). As paradoxical as this situation may seem when formulated theoretically, it is, in practice, a powerful way of being and becoming in Western culture. Extra-discursivity was a privilege accorded to very few individuals before the Renaissance, and then only to the received saints, heroes, and leaders of hierarchical authority structures that controlled access to written discourse. By abducting the biographical subject as the discursive model through which individual human existence was to be expressed (and suppressed), hierarchical culture effectively controlled the distribution of extra-discursivity. Although the political and social economies of the post-Renaissance industrialized nation-states have tended to democratize this network of distribution, they have not relinquished their control of it: it is still micro-managed by the kind of hegemonic cultural practices that Antonio Gramsci and Michel Foucault attribute to such disciplinary institutions as the prisons, the schools, the family, the church, and, I would add, biographical recognition.[11]

"In various forms," Foucault has written, "this theme has played a constant role since the nineteenth century: to preserve, against all decentrings, the sovereignty of the subject, and the twin figures of anthropology and humanism."[12] The generic frame "recognizing the biographical subject" returns again and again to this theme. In one sense, what Foucault is saying (here and elsewhere in his work) is that "recognizing the subject" (be it biographical, political, or whatever) is always an activity of subjection, violence committed in the guise of interpretation. As Roland Barthes has observed, "meaning is a force: to name is to subject, and the more generic the nomination, the stronger the subjection."[13] Thus generic framing is always a powerful agent of violent interpretive subjection. What makes "recognizing the biographical subject" an especially forceful frame of biographical recognition is that, like the political subject, the biographical subject conspires in its submission to the ruler, whose sovereignty "centers" the subject in a discursive formation that is thus already underwritten as an arena of cultural recognition. By submitting to the sovereignty of anthropological humanism, "recognizing the biographical subject" appears to resist Marxist, Nietzschean, Foucauldian, Lacanian, Derridean, and other efforts to decenter the subject, and to itself maintain sovereignty over the generic emplotment of the extra-discursive human individual.

But let us consider for a moment the apagogic situation of a denied absurdity, a cultural outlaw, a generic impossibility: the plural, nonhuman, trans-discursive biographical subject, which seems to delineate a pattern of distribution that is unimaginable and unmanageable. Yet that is so only if we assume that the ontological premise from which the biographical subject is conventionally abducted provides adequate existential demonstration. As soon as we question its status as a guarantor of extra-discursivity, we invoke another generative model for "recognizing the biographical subject," one in which individual human existence must be explained rather than taken for granted, one in which the synergy of biographical recognition and anthropological humanism emerges as an abduction, as a deviation from collective cultural experience. In this context, there are only decentered biographical subjects, for, Pierre Bourdieu maintains, "the history of the individual is never anything other than a certain specification of the collective history of his group or class, . . . expressing the difference between trajectories and positions inside or outside the class."[14] As an expression of difference, the biographical subject has no metaphysical presence in the ordinary sense; rather, it occupies the epistemological gap between presence and absence, singular and plural, self and other. If, as Derrida asserts, *"there is no absolute origin of sense in general,"*[15] then there is no ontological foundation upon which to model the biographical subject. It is always off-center, an abduction syllogistically demonstrated by the denial of an impossibility that is not impossible after all.

Mikhail Bakhtin claims that this is essentially the situation of the classical Greek type of *"rhetorical* autobiography and biography" from which modern Western life-writing in large part emerges. "In ancient times the autobiographical and biographical self-consciousness of an individual and his life was first laid bare and shaped in the public square," which, in itself, "constituted the entire state apparatus, with all its official organs." Here "was the highest court, the whole of science, the whole of art"; here "the entire people participated in . . . the laying bare and examination of a citizen's whole life." "[I]n such a 'biographized' individual," Bakhtin argues, "there was not, nor could there be, anything intimate or private, secret or personal, anything relating solely to the individual himself. . . . Everything here, down to the last detail, is entirely public." It is "[o]nly later, in the Hellenistic and Roman era," that "the classical *public wholeness* of an individual" breaks down and is replaced by the private, generic subjects of various life-writing forms like biographical narrative.[16] Momigliano concurs: "biography became a precise notion and got an appropriate word only in the Hellenistic age. The word is *bios* . . . , not a word reserved for the life of an individual man . . . [but] also used for the life of a country."[17]

From this perspective, marked by its nostalgia for a lost communal humanism, the biographical subject, as we know it, is always already off-center, a discursive fragment elliptically dispersed into written culture by the disintegration of a thoroughly public world in which the individual was openly and inescapably present and plural. In this view, the generative scheme of recognizing (or, as we might say now, *mis*recognizing) the biographical subject that characterizes post-Renaissance English and American biography is a reenactment of the generic history of all Western life-writing: the abduction of an abduction—an absent, singular, discursive proposition introduced into cultural practice as if it were the open individual of classical Greece, "laid bare and shaped in the public square." It is in this sense that an abducted, decentered biographical subject is the impossible possibility that instrumentalizes the generic frame "recognizing the biographical subject" and becomes the generative model of individual human existence.

Attempts to appropriate the generic frame "recognizing the biographical subject" as if it were *not* a culturally motivated vehicle of discursive formation with its own (often hidden) agenda are as ancient as life-writing itself, and as unlikely to fix the limits of biographical recognition as Domitian's making it a capital offense to write the life of a disestablished biographical subject. Two biographical theorists, one from the eighteenth century, the other from the twentieth, briefly exemplify the keen desire to formulate and control this agenda. Roger North posits the concept of an "untainted" biography of private economy, which, "out of all roads towards preferment or gain," instrumentalizes a direct transaction between biographical subject and biographical readership. Nevertheless, North distrusts the impact of eighteenth-century England's emerging bourgeois consumer culture on the circulation of sanitized biographical truth: "the very lucre of selling a copy is a corrupt interest that taints an historical work, for the sale of the book must not be spoiled by the dampness of over-much truth, but rather be made vivacious and complete by overmuch lying."[18]

Two hundred years later, Harold Nicolson's notion of "'pure' biography" ("written with no other purpose than that of conveying to the reader an authentic portrait of the individual whose life is being narrated") offers another variation on this theme. "'Impure' biography," in which category Nicolson places Walton's *Lives* and other "masterpieces of English prose," harbors the "'extraneous purposes' by which the purity of biography is infected." Nicolson's "pure biography" is itself whole and entire, a sanitized organism threatened but never nourished by "the pests and parasites that gnaw the leaves of purity."[19] Both North and Nicolson entertain a utopian vision of biography as uncorrupted and uninfected, a "natural" locus of private transactions and intrinsic purposes within and yet isolated from cultural practice.

This desire to sanitize and isolate biography is itself a way of (mis)recognizing the economy of biographical recognition. The purifications of biographical theorists are a mere variation on the purges of imperial tyrants—instances of institutional or state terrorism that, in trying to legislate similitude and purity, expose the arbitrariness of any effort to proclaim the "naturalness" of generic framing. This is what Derrida calls "the law of genre," the desire, as North expresses it, "that the truth be unfolded just as in a legal testimony, whole, sole, and nothing else."[20]

Of course, as we have seen, theorists and tyrants have no exclusive purchase on (mis)recognition. The biographical subject is persistently and perpetually (mis)recognized; seldom approached as an abducted alterity in the decentered discourse of collective cultural experience, it is habitually treated as the sovereign model of individual human existence in a sanitized system of cultural exchange. As such, it presents itself as a discursive formation that can be easily and harmlessly appropriated. Yet this is, as it were, its protective covering, its way of seeming to blend "naturally" into its surroundings as it stalks its prey. Although it is the instrument by which cultural outlaws

("Domitian's enemies," among whom we might list the heroines of a new feminist discourse, the leaders of a decolonized third world, or the hipsters of a revolutionary counterculture) can emerge into social consciousness and thereby assert their difference, it is also the means through which they can be co-opted by a discursive formation that stresses the "original" sameness of all biographical subjects and thereby maintains itself as one of the ways that dominant structures of authority have traditionally reproduced anthropological humanism and (mis)recognized difference.

III

You may remember Mailer's definition of "factoids": "facts which have no existence before appearing in a magazine or newspaper, creations which are not so much lies as a product to manipulate emotion in the Silent Majority" (18). The problem of Monroe's life, as Mailer sees it, is that it was lived almost entirely in factoids—a consequence of her own extraordinary capacity to exist in the gaps between the discontinuous roles of her repressed pasts and constantly shifting futures. Monroe is "the whole and double soul of every human alive" (97), "a study in the search for identity" (22), "an undying will existing in conditions of hopeless entombment" (22). She is also, he constantly reminds us, insane—a "labyrinth of interlocking selves" driven by "the uncontrollable ambition to dominate one's own life, the life of others, or the life of communities not yet conceived, that simple rage to put one's signature upon existence" (22).

Something strange is going on here. Despite his announced desire to disrupt the conventions of biographical narrative by writing a "novel biography" that occupies "a warp in the matrix of lost space-time" (262), despite his demystification of modern psychiatry as "a maze of medical disciplines that seek to cure, stupefy, or *pulverize* madness" but have failed "in every effort to find a consistent method of cure for psychotics" (22–23), despite his depiction of Monroe as an "undying will" "buried alive" in orphanages, foster homes, failed marriages, Hollywood, and other institutions of American life dominated by the Silent Majority, despite his identifying with her as a creative intelligence alienated from the American mainstream ("Set a thief to catch a thief, and put an artist on an artist" [20]), Mailer is unable to grant Monroe's insanity (her "rage to put her signature upon existence") the status of a viable cultural project. It is as if her insanity is, to quote a Robert Graves poem, "dumb to say,"[21] an inarticulate condition of existence that can neither speak nor sign its name, and as if only his narrative can bring it to the threshold of discursive articulation and cultural consciousness. In this respect, at least, Mailer's work (from *The Naked and the Dead* and *An American Dream* through *Marilyn* and *The Executioner's Song*) is Foucauldian, a history of the discontinuous relations between madness and civilization that represents discursive formations like psychology, popular culture, sexuality, the law, the family, the military, politics, and biography (among others) as more or less irresistible cultural practices, hegemonic disciplines that determine, or overdetermine, our acceptance of (and even our resistance to) their distribution and reception.

Although Foucault's work is undoubtedly important in documenting the ways in which the proprietary powers have historically excluded others and controlled the quotidian lives of those historically included (I would make the same claim for Mailer's), it does not offer a protocol for resisting, undermining, or circumventing these disciplinary discourses. The plot of Foucault's work (and of Mailer's) is invariably tragic, an unavoidable fall from grace occasioned by a fatal flaw in human character and society. This is why Monroe's death cannot be suicide, a tactic which would be, Mailer speculates, a "reaction" to the suffocation of modern life that she has "kept" in reserve, a way for her to exercise "a total control over her life, which is perhaps to say that she chooses to be in control of her death" (244). Rather she must be "murdered, murdered again" (227), the victim of a crime of passion and politics concocted by the FBI or CIA to protect John and Bobby Kennedy, with whom, he claims, she had been sexually and romantically involved. Such an ending (and, as we shall see, it is not an ending at all) diminishes Monroe's capacity for control over her life and death, isolates her from other marginalized, oppositional utopians who would also imagine "the life of communities not yet conceived," alienates her from other culturally symbolic suicides by women (such as that of Virginia Woolf, whose lament that biography cannot account for an individual's many different selves Mailer quotes at the beginning of his narrative), and enmeshes Monroe once again in a paranoid network of powerful institutional forces that determine the manner of both her living and her dying.

In the inventive speculation of this murder plot, Mailer has contrived perhaps the most remarkable, most memorable, and most insidious factoid of Monroe's life and death. He has stolen from her the one thing that, he admits, she was keeping in reserve, has muted the statement she was making with her death, has molested from beyond the grave her much desired and exchanged body, which even now cannot rest in peace. Recently I read a cover story in a supermarket tabloid which factoidally reported that Monroe is not really dead, that she had been (what else?) "abducted" by the FBI to protect the Kennedys, drugged, brainwashed, and relocated to the Australian outback, where today she is married to a sheepfarmer and suffers fragmentary flashbacks.[22] This is a ludicrous and disgusting story, one of many similar examples of journalistic necrophilia for which Mailer's last chapter and (for the paperback edition) an appendix called "The Murder File" are the prototypes.

"It was the most unforgiveable act I ever committed as a writer," Mailer admits in "The Murder File," but not because, as he confesses, he was working against deadline and left "the research unfinished."[23] Mailer knows or ought to know, for he implies it throughout his experimental "novel biography," that the research can never be finished, that Monroe's factoidal existence is the essential condition of modern life, that (despite his reprinting of the coroner's report and other documents associated with the official inquest into Monroe's death) the traditional biographer's desire that "the truth be unfolded just as in a legal testimony, whole, sole, and nothing else" cannot be fulfilled. "The Murder File" belies everything else about the instability of facthood and the indeterminancy of selfhood with which Mailer endows the meaning of Monroe's life and death. Here, in "The Murder File," in the most conventionally responsible, most carefully researched section of his biographical narrative, Mailer finally abducts Monroe, detains and *de*files her in the "law of genre," in the suffocating, hierarchical network of discursive formations from which his oppositional narrative was supposed to rescue and reanimate her. Once again, and tragically, she is "buried alive."

The problem for the emergent "rainbow coalition" of oppositional biographers, for whom Mailer's *Marilyn* is a much abused antimodel, is how to avoid burying *their* subjects alive in the murder file of traditional biographical narrative. As I have been suggesting, the discursive practices of biographical recognition are powerful agencies of cultural coercion historically aligned with dominant structures of authority. They cannot be simply and harmlessly appropriated; they must be resisted, even if we cannot predict, control, or perhaps even recognize the changes our resistance might bring about. If an oppositional agenda is going to make a *difference* (and what else is it supposed to do?), if the emergence into cultural consciousness of those who have been repressed by their race, gender, class, sexuality, etc., is going to disrupt and (some day, somehow) help to change the social, economic, political, and cultural relations that have induced such repression, then the "disciplinary technology" into which the interpretive "violence of order is transmuted" must be disrupted.[24]

This is why I would like to see the (post)modern biography of the future *re*situate biographical recognition within Michel de Certeau's "tactical, antidisciplinary network of diversionary practice," which explicitly posits what Foucault cannot—a theory and protocol of social and political action, and also within Luce Irigaray's analysis of the "situation of specific oppression," which would be inscribed in "a critique of the political economy that could not, this time, dispense with the critique of the discourse in which it is carried out, and in particular of the metaphysical presupposition of that discourse."[25]

The de Certeauvian (post)modern biography would occupy no *proper* "place that can be delimited as its own and serve as the base from which relations with an exteriority [its biographical subjects, biographical recognition, cultural discourse] . . . can be managed." Rather than operating as if they deployed a *strategy*, a "specific type of knowledge . . . sustained and determined by the power to provide oneself with one's own place [inside or outside biographical recognition and cultural discourse]," (post)modern biographers would proceed as if they were improvising a *tactic*, "a calculated action determined by the absence of a proper locus," a transient yet specific maneuver that "must play on and with a terrain" which is both foreign and familiar. They would become, as it were, biographical and cultural guerillas, exercising "a mobility that must accept chance offerings of the moment, and seize on the wing the possibilities that offer themselves at any given moment." They would "vigilantly make use of the cracks that particular conjunctions open in the surveillance of the proprietary powers," improvising a tactical, *im*proper approach that "boldly juxtaposes diverse elements in order suddenly to produce a flash shedding a different light on the language of a place"—in this case, the "place" traditionally occupied by the generic practices of biographical recognition in modern American cultural discourse.[26]

Irigaray, who seeks to "*disrupt*" the traditional "discursive economy" of patriarchal culture, which maintains itself by trafficking in the bodies of women and by "*eradicat[ing] the difference between the sexes* in systems that are self-representative of a 'masculine subject,'" suggests how (post)modern biographers might begin to "redefine this language work [so] that [it] would leave space for the feminine [and other historically excluded and repressed biographical subjects]." Initially, she posits, there may be only one "path" to follow,

> the one historically assigned to the feminine [and, we should add, other repressed cultural identities]: that of *mimicry*. One must assume the feminine [African-American, gay, etc.] role deliberately. Which means already to convert a form of subordination into an affirmation, and thus to begin to thwart it. . . . To play with mimesis is thus . . . to try to recover the place of [one's] exploitation by discourse, without allowing [oneself] to be simply reduced to it. . . . It means to resubmit [oneself] . . . to ideas

about [oneself] . . . so as to make 'visible,' by an effect of playful repetition, what was supposed to remain invisible: the cover-up of a possible
operation of the feminine [the African-American, the gay, etc.] in
language.

Such "playful repetition," deliberately and reflexively assumed, can
induce the "jamming of the theoretical machinery itself, . . . suspending its pretension to the production of a truth and of a meaning that
are excessively univocal." Resisted and undermined by disruptive mimicry, the discursive *"economy of the Same,"* to which Irigaray traces
the "domination of the philosophical logos" of traditional Western
culture and in which (as we have seen) the generic frame "recognizing
the biographical subject" is deeply implicated, can no longer remain
indifferent to difference but must deal with and be changed by the
radical situatedness of the specific subject.[27]

   If the oppositional agenda of (post)modern biography is to *make*
a difference, then it will constitute itself and function *as* difference.
Improvising guerilla tactics that opportunistically take advantage of
momentary gaps in the discursive surveillance of the proprietary powers, this emergent cultural project will disruptively mimic the indifference of traditional biographical recognition—and thus *abduct* it,
lead it away from its historical alliance with dominant structures of
authority by recessing its parts and revealing the hidden, but now signified, recurrent wound in the writing. Perhaps then biography will
become what de Certeau claims it already is but can seldom be recognized as: "the *self-critique* of liberal, bourgeois society, based on
the primary unit that society created[:] the individual—the central
epistemological and historical figure of the modern Western world, the
foundation of capitalist economy and democratic politics." Perhaps
then, to paraphrase de Certeau once again, the generic frame "recognizing the biographical subject" will become "the stage upon which
the certitudes of its creators and beneficiaries . . . [will] finally come
undone."[28]

IV

I close with a personal anecdote, a reflexive gesture of metacritical
self-awareness that tactically seizes the opportunity to playfully repeat
my own specific situatedness and that makes visible (or at least sheds
some light on) my own involvement in both the (post)modern poetics
of biographical recognition and the discursive abduction of Marilyn
Monroe. Some years ago, when I was an assistant professor coming
up for promotion and tenure at a midwestern state university, I was
asked to give a twenty-five-minute talk on Mailer's *Marilyn* in an

outreach lecture series cosponsored by the English department, delivered to a town-and-gown audience, and later broadcast on the campus radio station. Giving a lecture in this weekly series, for which individual faculty members reviewed recently published books, was an almost required rite of passage for assistant professors, a way for voting senior faculty to evaluate a candidate's public persona, teaching ability, and intellectual mettle. Appropriately or inappropriately, this occasion often influenced votes and affected academic careers, and we were informally warned in advance that it could do so.

I had just finished writing a biography of an eighteenth-century British novelist, which had been published by a university press and was to be the major evidence of my scholarly qualifications for promotion and tenure. I was also known to be generally interested in the theory and practice of biographical narrative and to have read Mailer. Hence my lecture-series assignment. As the time for both the public lecture and my p-and-t decision approached, I worked intensely on the talk in sporadic bursts of nervous apprehension. Adopting the kind of reflexive, third-person narrator with which Mailer had been experimenting in this and his other non-fictional works, I developed a reading in which I (re)presented myself as a biographical theorist alternately repelled and attracted by Mailer's hubristic experimentation with both the theory and practice of biographical narrative and the dynamics of Marilyn Monroe's life and death. Hardly anything I wrote then survives in this essay, but it was my first pass at the subject.

I delivered the lecture with my usual mixture of serious brooding critic and amateur ham actor; the large, mixed audience seemed to respond well; and afterwards, at the faculty cocktail party, many of my senior colleagues assured me by various nods, gestures, and gnomic remarks that, as far as they were concerned, I had likely secured my place in the great lodge of the academic spirit. Finally, I felt, I could begin to relax; I was about to come in from the wilderness. This era of good feeling lasted about a week. Then I received a note in my campus mailbox from the most powerful full professor in the department, an Americanist who specialized in contemporary fiction and who called Mailer by his first name (I doubt he had ever met "Norman"; he just had, shall we say, a proprietary interest in him). This full professor notoriously judged candidates by *his* standards, which were rigorously and unshakably idiosyncratic, and he controlled the votes of about half the members of the department's promotion committee. His note simply stated that he had been out of town, had thereby missed both my talk and the radio broadcast, and could he have a copy of the lecture? I complied with his request and awaited my fate.

A week later, in a brief note paperclipped to the returned copy of my talk, I read my future. It was inscribed in a one-sentence comment: "I always suspected Norman had a yen for Marilyn." That was it. To some, perhaps, this may seem the most gnomic of academic remarks, but I knew what it meant. It meant that I would be tenured and promoted. At that moment, which now seems long ago and far away, I smiled back at the silent rows of mailboxes and walked, no doubt strutting a bit, down the corridor of my future. At this moment, when I am halfway down that hallway and marching to the beat of a different drummer, this professorial exchange communicates a more complex, less celebratory message. I realize now that the full professor was forging a homosocial bond with me, including me in his (and Norman's) sly leering. His note, written over Marilyn Monroe's dead body, inscribed a masculine gesture of solidarity that linked my desired object (an academic career) with "the last of the myths to thrive in the long evening of the American dream," a phrase that I now abduct from Mailer's narrative and resubmit to the scrutiny of a (post)modern oppositional agenda through which, I hope, the specific situatedness of gender, race, class, and sexuality can emerge into biographical recognition and cultural consciousness.

That is why, in a not inconsequential sense at all, I am still writing about biography and Marilyn Monroe, and why my professional practice is itself an abduction written over her body. I, too, have defiled Marilyn, detained her in my critical discourse, and found her to be a recurrent, hidden wound in the writing. Nor am I somehow isolated from contagion by this belated and belabored recession of the broken bones of my past and present. Mailer's reflexive gesture of metacritical self-awareness did not save him; why should mine immunize me? Rather, I still struggle, in sporadic bursts of nervous apprehension, to absolve the past and resolve the future. With no permanent strategies to deploy, no proper places to stand, I improvise tactics and "seize on the wing the possibilities that offer themselves at any given moment." Perhaps this is such a moment. It all depends, I suppose, on who is watching and reading.

Notes

1. Norman Mailer, *Marilyn* (New York: Grosset & Dunlap, 1973). This is the hardcover first edition, to which I shall refer parenthetically by page number throughout this essay; one reference to the later paperback edition, which contained additional materials in an appendix, will be cited in a note.

2. See Eve Kosofsky Sedgwick, *Between Men: English Literature and Male Homosocial Desire* (New York: Columbia University Press, 1985), and Luce Irigaray, *This Sex Which Is Not One,* trans. Catherine Porter with Carolyn Burke (1977; Ithaca, N.Y.: Cornell University Press, 1985).

3. William H. Epstein, *Recognizing Biography* (Philadelphia: University of Pennsylvania Press, 1987), 71–89; revisions of several passages from these pages appear below.

4. Izaak Walton, *The Lives of John Donne, Sir Henry Wotton, Richard Hooker, George Herbert, and Robert Sanderson,* World's Classics (London: Humphrey Milford and Oxford, 1927), 20, 28–29, 41, 60.

5. Samuel Johnson, *Life of Savage,* ed. Clarence Tracy (Oxford: Clarendon Press, 1971), 13, 20.

6. See James Boswell, *Life of Johnson,* ed. R. W. Chapman, corr. J. D. Fleeman, 3rd ed. (1904; 1953; London, Oxford, and New York: Oxford University Press, 1970), passim, but especially 51n1, 1327, 1329, 1333; also Epstein, *Recognizing Biography,* 90–137, especially 94 and 135.

7. Epstein, *Recognizing Biography,* passim, but especially 1–6.

8. Jacques Derrida, *Of Grammatology,* trans. Gayatri Chakravorty Spivak (1967; Baltimore, Md.: The Johns Hopkins University Press, 1976), 51.

9. Arnaldo Momigliano, *The Development of Greek Biography* (Cambridge, Mass.: Harvard University Press, 1971), 48, 96, 99–100.

10. Another way of saying this is to describe the biographical subject, *pace* Roland Barthes, as a supplemented sum of semes, that is, as a *"figure* (an impersonal network of symbols combined under the proper name)" to which "a precious remainder" has been added to produce a *"person* (a moral freedom endowed with motives and an overdetermination of meanings)." The problem with this approach, as Barthes acknowledges, is that it indulges "the vulgar bookkeeping of compositional characters," as if a narrative accounting of discursive traces can (mystically and mechanically) compose "something like *individuality."* See *S/Z,* trans. Richard Miller (1970; New York: Hill and Wang, 1974), 94, 191. The advantage of the term "extra-discursive" is that it characterizes individuality or personality as that which resists semiotic encoding, and thus draws attention to the radical discontinuity of the discursive and the non-discursive—a gap in biographical recognition that no modification of presence or intersection of discursive traces can bridge or fill. It should also be noted that my use of the term "trans-discursive" differs from that of Michel Foucault in "What Is an Author?", in *Textual Strategies: Perspectives in Post-Structuralist Criticism,* ed. Josué V. Harari (Ithaca, N.Y.: Cornell University Press), 153.

11. See, e.g., Antonio Gramsci, *Selections from the Prison Notebooks,* ed. Quintin Hoare and Geoffrey Nowell Smith (New York: International Publishers, 1971); *The Modern Prince and Other Writings* (New York: International Publishers, 1959); and *Selections from Political Writings (1910–1920),* ed. Quintin Hoare (New York: International Publishers, 1977); and Michel Foucault, *Madness and Civilization: A History of Insanity in the Age of Reason,* trans. Richard Howard (1961; New York: Vintage, 1973); *The Birth*

of the Clinic: An Archaeology of Medical Perception, trans. A. M. Sheridan
Smith (1963; New York: Vintage, 1975); *Discipline and Punish: The Birth of
the Prison,* trans. Alan Sheridan (1975; New York: Vintage, 1979); and "Af-
terword: The Subject and Power," in Hubert L. Dreyfus and Paul Rabinow,
Michel Foucault: Beyond Structuralism and Hermeneutics, 2nd ed. (1982;
Chicago: University of Chicago Press, 1983), 208–26.

12. Michel Foucault, *The Archaeology of Human Knowledge,* trans.
A. M. Sheridan Smith (1969; 1972; London: Tavistock, 1974), 12.

13. Barthes, *S/Z,* 129–30.

14. Pierre Bourdieu, *Outline of a Theory of Practice,* trans. Richard
Nice, Cambridge Studies in Social Anthropology 16, gen. ed. Jack Goody
(1972; Cambridge: Cambridge University Press, 1977), 86.

15. Derrida, *Of Grammatology,* 65.

16. M. M. Bakhtin, *The Dialogic Imagination,* ed. Michael Holquist,
trans. Caryl Emerson and Michael Holquist (Austin: University of Texas
Press, 1981), 131–32.

17. Momigliano, *The Development of Greek Biography,* 12–13.

18. Roger North, *General Preface & Life of Dr. John North,* ed. Peter
Millard (Toronto: University of Toronto Press, 1984), 79–80.

19. Harold Nicolson, "The Practice of Biography," *American Scholar,*
23 (Spring 1954): 153–61, excerpted in *Biography as an Art: Selected Criticism
1560–1960,* ed. James L. Clifford (New York: Oxford University Press, 1962),
197–205. I quote from 197–98, 202. See also Nicolson's *The Development of
English Biography* (1928; rpt. London: Hogarth, 1968), 9–13, where Nicolson
first differentiated "pure" and "impure" biography.

20. Jacques Derrida, "The Law of Genre," trans. Avital Ronell, *Glyph,*
7 (1980): 202–32; Roger North, *General Preface,* 70.

21. Robert Graves, "The Cool Web," in *New Collected Poems* (Garden
City, N.Y.: Doubleday, 1977), 27.

22. *Weekly World News,* late September-early October 1990. I wish I
could be more specific about this elusive source, which seems to lead a factoidal existence of its own. I originally read the article in a supermarket check-
out line (where else?). By the time I went back to purchase it for citation here,
the supermarket and all other local outlets had returned their unsold copies
to the distributor, who had shredded them. I then called the editorial offices
of *Weekly World News* in Lantana, Florida; the unidentified male who answered remembered the story but not the specific references to date, pages,
etc.; he also claimed that his office did not keep back issues (!), and referred
me to the Library of Congress. The only LOC location for *Weekly World News*
is the Los Angeles Public Library, which is supposed to save six months of
back issues. After a search of their holdings, librarian Patricia Clark informed
me that most of their back issues (including this one) of *Weekly World News*
are missing, presumed stolen, but she remembered seeing this cover story. Considering that copies of *Weekly World News* seem to be discarded, destroyed,
disowned, or disappeared as a matter of course, I doubt if a conventional
citation would be of much use anyway. I guess you will have to take my word
for it, which is, after all, how factoids get started.

23. Norman Mailer, *Marilyn,* Warner pb (1973; New York: Warner, 1975), 340.

24. Michel de Certeau, *The Practice of Everyday Life,* trans. Steven F. Rendall (1980; Berkeley and Los Angeles: University of California Press, 1984), xiv.

25. Luce Irigaray, *This Sex Which Is Not One,* 85.

26. Michel de Certeau, *The Practice of Everyday Life,* 36–38.

27. Irigaray, 74–79, 84–85.

28. Michel de Certeau, *Heterologies: Discourse on the Other,* trans. Brian Massumi, Theory and History of Literature 17 (Minneapolis: University of Minnesota Press, 1986), 15.

Index

Female biography, 5

Female self, 128

Female virtue, 26, 39

Feminine, the, 89; as universal in Woolf, 94

Feminism, 110, 113; and anti-biography, 126, 128; and biography, 5, 128; and biographical criticism, 86; and commitment to pluralism, 128; and different-voice theory, 127, 128; and literary tradition, 86

Feminist criticism, 111–12; and intertextuality, 4; Anglo-American, 88

Feminist critics and biographers, 4; and authentic self, 127

Feminist theory, 5, 125; and biographer, 127; and literary biography, 123

Ferguson, Joseph, 49

Fictional and non-fictional life-writing, 3

Fictional subject, 223

Fielding, Henry, 26; *Shamela,* 26

Fiorenza, Elisabeth Schussler, 190n

Fischer, Michael M. J., 184n

Flax, Jane, 127

Fliess, Wilhelm, 201

Formalism, 9, 13

Formal linguistics, 10

Fort/da, 159n

Foucault, Michel, 13, 86, 111, 113, 168, 190n, 191n, 228; and author function, 110; and death of the author, 86, 110; and genealogy of form, 181; and the scriptor, 111; and technology of selfhood, 184n; "What is an Author?," 112, 136; *The Archaeology of Knowledge,* 157; *Herculin Barbin,* 157; *The Use of Pleasure,* 157

Franklin, Benjamin, 170; as businessman, 178; *Autobiography,* 171

French Revolution, 4, 53, 54, 55, 56; and British counterrevolution, 58, 61, 63, 65, 69, 76; and illusion of politics as theatrical state, 56; and "men of theory," 59; and the practice of biography, 54; and revolutionary man and poetical character, 55; as spectacle, 53, 55; career of, 57; end of, and British discourse, 54–55

Freud, Anna, 195, 198, 202, 209

Freud, Sigmund, 80n, 159n, 185n, 193–210 *passim;* and child analysis, 202; and innovator's achievement, 210; and overdetermination, 193; and resentment of medical establishment, 197; and rhetorical gifts, 201, 205; and scientific inquiry vs. humanistic interests, 198, 207; on plot of education or vocation, 90; *Question of Lay Analysis,* 197, 198, 209

Fromm, Erich, 199, 204

Fruit, John Phelps, 149; and disindividualization of author, 152

Furet, François, 53, 54, 69

Fussell, Paul, Jr., 82n

Gandhi, Mohandas Karamchand, 197, 203

Gaskell, Elizabeth, 102

Gatsby, Jay, 223

Gay, Peter, 210n, 214n

Gender, 5, 40, 91, 111, 112, 113, 116, 117, 118, 137, 138, 139, 142

Generative schema of recognizing the biographical subject, 225

Generativity, 200, 201, 206; crisis of, 207

Generic emplotment of individual, 224

Generic frame "recognizing the biographical subject," 219, 221, 222, 224, 225, 231; as abduction, 233

Generic recognition, 223

Genius, 98, 110, 116, 117, 147

Gilligan, Carol, 127

Gillman, Susan, 182, 191n

Ginsberg, Allen, 176

Gitelson, Maxwell, 211n